America's

Educational

Crossroads

Continue Widening
the Achievement Gap
or
Make a Seismic Shift Forward
Into the 21st Century

A Collaborative High School Campus Model

JULIE COLES

America's Educational Crossroads:
Continue to Widen the Achievement Gap or
Make a Seismic Shift Forward Into the 21st Century
by Julie Coles

Copyright © 2022 Julie Coles

Developmental Editor:	Ebonye Gussine Wilkins, Inclusive Media Solutions LLC
Copyeditor:	Lynette M. Smith, All My Best
Book Cover and Interior Designer:	Elena Reznikova, DTPerfect
Publisher:	Imagine a More Promising Future Publishing ImagineAMorePromisingFuture.com

ISBN (hardcover): 978-1-954912-00-7
ISBN (paperback): 978-1-954912-01-4
ISBN (eBook): 978-1-954912-02-1
ISBN (audiobook): 978-1-954912-03-8

Library of Congress Control Number: 2021910174

Contact the author at
ImagineAMorePromisingFuture.com

Collaborative High School Campus Model video is available at
ImagineAMorePromisingFuture.com/video

Contents

IV. New Schools Alone Won't Close Achievement Gaps

V. Closing Academic Achievement Gaps

VI. How We Close Academic Achievement Gaps

VII. Focus on School Culture

VIII. The Prosperity of Inner-City Schools' Reliance on Safe Neighborhoods

IX. Policies Preventing Forward Progress

X. The Detrimental Impact of Politicizing Education

XI. Appendix

Foreword

IN THE FALL OF 2006, I BEGAN ONE OF THE GREAT JOURNEYS OF my life when I started teaching at an alternative high school in Boston, Massachusetts. Nestled in the city's Roxbury neighborhood, Greater Egleston High School had recently emerged as the stable anchor of an area long stigmatized, neglected, and overlooked. I joined the faculty as the new history teacher, and Julie Coles was our headmaster. Without exception, she was the most important professional mentor and leader I have ever worked with. In a historically challenged subsection of an already marginalized community, her little school began hacking away at a labyrinth of obstacles, transforming learning and lives in the process. During the 16 years under her leadership, the school built on success after success, implementing bold new curriculums, establishing post-secondary pathways as an accessible norm, and vastly improving on traditional metrics such as graduation rates, assessment scores, and college acceptance rates. In some years, more than 75% of the graduating seniors were admitted into colleges, and multiple classes boasted merit-based scholarship winners. But these impressive KPIs do not adequately convey the broader enduring impact of her leadership.

Julie's greatest impact was her ability to inspire students to embrace lifelong learning, develop pride in themselves, and hold themselves to high standards. I long ago lost track of the number of alumni who have expressed how seeing her take such a personal stake in their success motivated them to press ahead in their academic, professional, and personal journeys. Her vision and guidance transcended inspiration of the students—it had a massive impact on me as an educator, a working professional, and as a person. Julie taught me that real leadership is being willing to put your personal position on the line in order to do what is right for the people you serve. She operated with full knowledge that public education bureaucracies are replete with insidious politics, destructive egotism, poorly conceived management schemes, and the omnipresent threat of funding cuts—but the clarity, depth, and focus of her personal and professional commitment was unwaveringly in service to her students, regardless of a district bureaucracy that continuously presented greater obstacles from lesser minds. Perhaps most critically, students always knew that they unequivocally stood at the center of her priorities.

I have spent the past decade reflecting on how to apply examples from Julie's leadership to my own work and life. I was thrilled to write this foreword because this book will allow others to benefit from the insights, vision, and ambition that have benefited me, and which have always permeated her work in the world of learning. I was familiar with many of the concepts and ideas outlined within, through discussions over the years. But now, finally, a significant share of her vision is available in one place for others to engage, absorb and, hopefully, apply.

This is not always an easy book to read. Julie, as always, does not reticently bypass difficult topics, challenging conundrums, or towering barriers. She methodically, rationally, and persistently approaches them with an open and analytical mind. Most importantly, she does not allow obstacles or complexity to obscure her commitment to positive goals and outcomes. This book is an ambitious project that dares to tackle a complex topic, inclusive of its troubling dimensions. But the book ultimately parallels Julie's general approach to management and leadership: difficulty is not an excuse for abandoning important goals.

In this case, the important goal at the center of this project is the incisive reimagination of education in the United States, and a brutally honest recognition of its crisis-level status in American society. The chapters that follow do not simply diagnose problems—they also offer detailed, actionable solutions that are flexible enough to be adopted and implemented across boundaries of geography, demography, socioeconomic status, and localized conditions. Her solutions are emphatically *not* framed around how to extract marginal improvements from minimal resources. That approach is emblematic of the very status quo that is collapsing before our eyes. Julie's solutions are based on how to maximize achievement by using—without compromise—the best approaches, practices, resources, and tools that are available anywhere.

"Sounds great—but who pays for all this?"

This question is perhaps the most predictable challenge to the ideas in this book. Negligible fractions of our national spending could enable the realization of the ideas and approaches detailed by the author. But more relevant, and revealing, is the very existence of a fiscal question as the default retort in the first place. That a comprehensive set of detailed, thoughtful, and bold ideas with universal national impact is most likely to be countered with a rote budgetary refrain confirms the steady, corrosive devaluation of education that has been deeply embedded into the American consciousness. The reflexive armchair fiscal micromanagement that constrains learning for millions across the United States is comparatively absent from discussions on the sprawling outlays of our scattershot military adventures, subsidies to already profitable enterprises, or ongoing largesse to earmarked pet projects—all of which, despite vast monetary inputs, have generated questionable returns on investment (ROI) at best.

When carried out properly, teaching and learning produce undeniable returns on investment. If decades of data on income, health, lifespan, happiness, and familial stability are not adequately convincing of education's positive ROI, I would ask a skeptic to simply observe the habits and behaviors of as many wealthy people as possible. Without fail, every single one of these people will commit all the resources necessary to ensure that their own children attend high-quality schools from the earliest age possible. The wealthy are no different from others in the diversity of their personal preferences, styles, and tastes, but they are uniformly consistent in safeguarding their children's learning opportunities. For anyone who wonders if the rich know something that others do not, the answer is a resounding *Yes*. They very clearly understand the fundamental role of education in stabilizing and securing intergenerational wealth.

I wish to answer the predictable fiscal retort with an alternative question: *What happens if we* do not *pay for this?*

If equality of opportunity, social justice, individual gains, and intergenerational wealth do not serve as adequate incentives to attract and support momentum for renewing our national commitment to education, then I would ask readers to consider the longer-term implications for the basic standing of the United States as a world power. At stake is nothing less than our economic strength; our leadership in science, technology, medicine, and the arts; and our position as the leading power in the world. A national economy cannot thrive without a vibrant ecosystem of jobs, incomes, commerce, and socioeconomic mobility to feed it. Science, technology, and medicine cannot be sustained at the highest levels without the highest caliber of minds to drive progress in these fields. The arts cannot flourish without the inspiration to imagine wildly and create freely. A United States populated by regressive, diminished minds will be poorer, sicker, sadder, and less fulfilled. That is not a nation that can continue to lead the world.

Even from the harshest, most utilitarian, business-minded, ROI-fixated perspective, there is an undeniable value to education that demands our most fervent commitment—yes, of money, but also of time, energy, passion, and personal stake down to every individual citizen. For you as an individual reader, if you can walk your mind, heart, and gut to the same depth of commitment as Julie Coles, then the ambitious goals she outlines in this book are no longer insurmountable. As you read the chapters ahead, think not just of yourself and your next proximate generation, but of the health, success, and prominence of our entire society as a whole—and of the choices between action and inaction that are ours to make. For me, the choice is clear.

America's Educational Crossroads reveals many of the obstacles that have contributed to our current beleaguered public education system, particularly in poor communities. Thankfully, Julie, whose innovative thinking is on display throughout the book, articulates a series of well-thought-out, highly constructive, and unique ideas for how we can ensure equal access to quality education for all students in every zip code across America. More importantly, as is typical of the Julie Coles I have come to know, this book emphasizes the need to be bold, to aggressively pursue systemic changes, and to impart skills that every student will need to access opportunities in the present century. It is apparent that the overall mission of this book is to help students find purpose in their educational journeys and to enable future success.

This book provides an instructive road map, imagined through the lens of an inspirational thinker, prescribing unconventional remedies for an education system desperately in need of repair. Julie's years of teaching, leadership, and curricular design experience are evident in the expansive range of topics she covers, as well as the depth and breadth she devotes to each topic. Ultimately, *America's Educational Crossroads* will leave readers with a clear understanding of the scope of problems—and proposed solutions—needed to address the broad landscape of issues concerning our nation's public education system. For this reason, and many others, this book has given me a renewed, and informed, sense of optimism for the future of education in America.

—Anshul Jain

A Letter to the Reader

DEAR READER,

Welcome and thank you for taking an interest in my book. Before you begin reading, I wanted to pass along a friendly warning. At times scuba gear may be needed because many topics require a deep dive. But those moments will hopefully help you better grasp the depth and breadth of dysfunctional schools that negatively impact the lives of children. If my efforts to describe in great, sometimes exhaustive detail help readers better understand what is at stake if we don't address it, the scuba gear will have been well worth it.

On the surface, *America's Educational Crossroads* is about the unproductive education experience too many students receive while enrolled in poorly funded public schools across many communities in America. For most poor families, schools feel more like a place where they just send their children for school daycare. To the best of my ability, and based on my extensive career in education, I have tried to shed some much-needed light on systemic problems in our public education system and propose innovative and, hopefully, more effective measures to improve the quality of public education for all children in America. Investing in a new a public education system has the greatest potential for making schools an exciting place to be and where all children and youths can find purpose.

America's Educational Crossroads covers a range of topics that represent just a portion of the broad span of issues contributing to the current dysfunctional state of our public education system. But the hardships for poor minority students attending public schools are where the harshest and most consequential policies have had the longest-lasting impact on their quality of life in and beyond school. However, substandard learning conditions are no longer just occurring in communities stereotypically perceived and accepted as *underperforming* student populations. Recent teacher protests across many states reveal what was previously unknown, yet hiding in plain sight: America's public education system in many states is in crisis. In a nation that was once rivaled and held in high regard by other western nations, evidence has shown we have lost our long-standing reputation for achieving at the highest educational standards. The decline of our status globally is because education is no longer among our highest priorities. The protests in many states revealed the consequence of underfunded schools. Expecting poorly paid teachers to provide equitable and quality education under unimaginable draconian policies inside of deteriorating schools is very concerning.

Today, educational inequality is rapidly rising and spreading across all low-income and working-class communities. But inequality in education has always been a class problem in our country. Unfortunately that fact has been overshadowed by a long-standing national acceptance of subjugating America's lowest caste to substandard education in public schools.

There is no doubt that this timely issue now concerns the overall educational well-being of students across multiple cities, towns, and rural communities immersed in the same plight: being denied the right to attend adequately funded public schools and receive a quality education. This not an us-versus-them problem. It belongs to all of us.

We should build a more modern, equitable, and high-quality education system, complete with new schools, contemporary curriculums, expanded and more diverse methods of instruction, and including career and college readiness programs. Modern schools should also establish new and more humane policies to improve school cultures to better facilitate the learning experiences for all students.

Admittedly, the proposed recommendations for fixing what is broken will be in stark contrast to the policies and practices that have been the norm in public education. Those norms are at the root cause of what's wrong with how we educate our children today.

Among the root causes contributing to our broken education system is our inability to effectively raise academic expectations and performance standards. Blocking forward progress with raising expectations and academic performances are centuries-old racial, ethnic, social, and funding barriers. Those barriers are also contributing to our public education system's inability to keep pace with advances in industries that currently need well-educated candidates to join their labor force.

Recent employment trends make clear that vast numbers of high school graduates lacking the level of quality education aligned with the needs of various industries are ineligible to apply for those positions currently available. The glut of available, but ineligible, graduates is a byproduct of an education system rife with barriers. *America's Educational Crossroads* makes it clear we can no longer allow the continuation of widening academic achievement gaps because we now see evidence of how inadequate education constrains our students' ability to move forward and participate in a labor force that can free them from a life of poverty. But *closing achievement gaps* has been our public education system's biggest conundrum. Any chance of producing highly educated students prepared for labor markets that need well-educated workers will require our public education system to immediately shift its focus toward new and more efficacious methods of educating our school-age population.

America's Educational Crossroads introduces readers to ways to rebuild our public education system by linking the reservoir of exceptional educational resources of our current century to all public schools. Readers will also have an opportunity to view a video of *A Collaborative High School Campus Model,* a companion to the book, at *ImagineAMorePromisingFuture.com/video.* The video does not require scuba gear, but it will take readers on a visual journey through a network of state-of-the-art career and college development programs. What you will see is how I reimagined a way to make educational programs in high schools compatible with students' career and higher education aspirations, so upon graduation they could select a path that would lead to a destiny of their own choosing.

∾

I.
Providing
Historical Context

Dreams Still Deferred in the 21ˢᵗ Century

A FRICAN AMERICAN POET, WRITER, PHILOSOPHER AND SOCIAL
commentator, Langston Hughes, once asked, "What becomes
of a dream deferred?"

At the time, Hughes pondered over and then offered an eloquent analysis of the possible consequences of dreams deferred. He described the current conditions of an American society that had disregarded and ignored the potential aspirations of generations of Black American citizens. Over a span of decades, willful ignorance and continued educational, employment, and economic inequities left many more generations of minorities living in urban communities stagnating in the same conditions experienced by previous generations, who also happened to be their ancestors. All of the indicators that reflect how well citizens across the country are doing show overwhelming evidence that high numbers of Blacks who live in poor urban neighborhoods are still lagging way behind. Despite those indicators, current generations of students attending underperforming schools are the victims of a continuing education achievement gap in urban and rural public schools across America. While states continue to require mandatory annual assessments, we have quietly learned to ignore the results of those tests: decades of substandard education are why many adults are denied equal access to quality jobs with good incomes, affordable housing, adequate health care, and safe neighborhoods. Our criminal justice system disproportionately imprisons Blacks who are disproportionately uneducated or undereducated. We do not need annual assessments to confirm what we already know.

We need a new educational system to reverse the underperforming outcomes of those assessments. Ignoring the annual humiliation of predictably low performance has exacerbated the problem. The casual dismissal of all of the blatantly obvious indicators that show our public schools are continuing to fail our students should give everyone pause. But rather than finding the ongoing failure reprehensible, we simply behave as if those outcomes do not matter. Fortunately, parents, teachers, and other passionate educators who advocate for adequate funding and keeping schools open, are declaring that those outcomes absolutely do matter and are unacceptable. It is not the absence of caring about what many know is irrefutable proof of our widening education achievement gap. It may simply reflect one of two possible things worth positing. We must discontinue current policies from past eras that led to cultural norms of leaving Blacks and other minorities languishing in economic, social, psychological, emotional, and educational poverty. But the real quagmire has more to do with how we replace outdated, racially hurtful norms,

2

so we can prevent future generations from inheriting the emotional and psychological scarring and instead invest in trusting that there is a way forward. That will require an ability to reimagine the purpose and mission of one of our country's most relied-upon institutions: our public education system. If we can reimagine both the purpose and mission, we may be able to construct a more student-centered education framework—one that supports a belief in every student's ability to learn when given access to quality resources and instruction; and that will lead to their ability to achieve at the highest standards.

Hughes' plea for America to intervene and reverse the conditions of Blacks during the 1950s, '60s, and '70s resulted in an outpouring of accolades and admiration for his well-articulated observations and analysis; but sadly, nothing more. Even more disheartening is how the country that he described then, mirrors the current conditions in most of America's urban communities today. In today's America, an overwhelming number of Blacks, neither willingly nor voluntarily, languish in impoverished neighborhoods. Both then and now, America's education system has not done enough to elevate young people in these communities up and out of poverty. Hughes warned of the consequences of allowing a society to continue fostering perpetual disenfranchisement of poor citizens, but particularly Blacks who have had to suffer the most while receiving the least for centuries. In the 21st century, the number of citizens living in impoverished conditions is alarming and on the rise. Sadly, so is the level of apathy shown towards Blacks, Latinos, American Indians, other minorities, and people with disabilities forced to live in impoverished conditions. It is deplorable and consequential that we, as a nation and one of the richest countries in the world, allow the current level of indifference, shown to citizens unable to access resources that would transform their current plight, to continue and hinder their progress towards a better quality of life.

The Consequences of Deferring Dreams and Aspirations

ONE OF THE MOST TRAGIC CONSEQUENCES IS THE ESCALATING rate of crimes and human fatalities that occur on a daily basis in many of America's urban communities. Complicating matters further is the media's focus on the daily occurrence of violence in urban communities perpetrated by a minority of its youths, and a complete disregard for the majority of law-abiding citizens residing in those same communities whose good deeds get overlooked. These same law-abiding citizens want to live in safe communities where their children can freely engage with one another on their streets and beyond their immediate neighborhoods without encountering threats or becoming a victim of violence. They are not casual observers of the increase in crime rates and deaths in their communities; their children, teens, and young adults are among the statistical casualties of those crimes. Despite the efforts of many parents to raise their sons properly and steer them away from crime, the majority of innocent lives taken in their communities are at the hands of their sons. The increasing crime rates in the poorest neighborhoods of urban communities are one of the main reasons why America's prisons are overflowing.

Another alarming trend is the high rate of students attending funerals of family members, friends, and classmates. Some students have missed school on multiple occasions over the course of one school year because they attend multiple funerals. The aftermath of losing someone in such a violent, and often unprovoked, manner is so devastating. For many students, the devastation manifests in being constantly preoccupied with concerns for their own personal safety. They begin to think about areas in and around their neighborhoods that they should avoid; and in order to strategically stay out of harm's way, they alter their traveling routines by taking multiple buses that will take them around, and not directly through, certain neighborhoods to get to school. Travel time to and from school increases, which means that they have to readjust the time they have to leave home each morning Yet they know that altering their wake-up time and bus routes is not an absolute guarantee that their fate will not be at the mercy of some uncaring fellow citizen bent on harming anyone at any given moment on any given day. Imagine having to be in a place of constantly wondering if you will be the next victim of a random bullet or knife wound or brutal beat-down while minding your own business. Justifiably, the fear paralyzes many of our children, teenagers, and young adults to the point where many of them decide the streets are too unsafe to go anywhere, including school, which then contributes to the increased number of absences and drop-out rate.

Public schools in urban communities have inherited the added responsibility of contending with a range of issues related to the increased level of crimes and fatalities. Schools are contending with the tragic loss of their students and consoling other students trying to grapple with the sudden and unexpected death of their peers with whom they shared classes the previous day. For some students, they did not just lose a classmate: they lost a childhood friend with whom they went through elementary, middle, and high school. Imagine one day sitting in class with a lifelong friend, then a few days later, standing over a coffin staring in disbelief at their friend's now-lifeless body. Then imagine the heartache of flashing back to the last days, weeks, months, or years, remembering the time they spent with this person; so full of life as they traveled from class to class, shared conversations in the school cafeteria during lunches, giggled at each other's jokes, and shared running commentary about other classmates during recess. Lifelong friendships are special because people become linked to one another through a variety of experiences. They often travel through most of their young life in one another's shadow in the fluid and carefree way that best friends tend to do.

Many of us probably have experienced the joy of friendships that lasted from elementary through high school. Try to imagine if, one day, that special bond between you and a lifelong friend suddenly and without warning came to an abrupt end at the hands of another person carrying a gun or knife. Having to deal with the finality of the unexpected loss of a classmate due to violence has become a common occurrence for many in urban communities. Some students have experienced multiple losses over the span of their middle and high school years. Another manifestation of living in high-crime neighborhoods is an increased anxiety level that robs kids of a carefree childhood. Teenagers voice concerns about the need to avoid conflicts with their peers for fear of creating an enemy, one who then may conjure up some real or even imagined grievance that will lead to violence. Too often, these grievances escalate into an exchange of words that the potential enemy believes to be a publicly humiliating outcome witnessed by their peers, and the exchange lingers in the mind of that person. While both parties may walk away from the initial exchange seemingly unscathed, in the current climate where disputes are resolved through violence and with added peer pressure, the offended party may perceive the incident as not being over.

Back in the day, if someone had a grievance with another person, the individuals involved had the luxury of resolving the issue with an argument or engaging in a good old-fashioned fistfight. Regardless of the outcome, everyone involved walked away from the conflict, lived to see another day, and went on to live a full life into adulthood. Today, any amount of hostility could be synonymous with a fatal outcome. Whoever is perceived to be the victor of a verbal or physical altercation between young people can be doomed within the span of a day or even a year. You see, the mechanism for resolving conflicts in some communities is to respond to an offense, often fueled by rumors, with a resounding statement, an act of revenge that manifests in violent retaliation in which the victim will be unable to survive or will be rendered too physically impaired and helpless to fight back. Someone needs so desperately to be victorious at the expense of another human being, to the point where they don't even fear the consequence of being imprisoned for the rest of their natural life.

Our society will be to blame for placing many innocent teens and young adults at the mercy of a small number who can wreak havoc and unleash fear throughout entire neighborhoods. As a society, we must take immediate steps to intervene with sustainable resources to address gun control, provide mental health services, develop protocols for preventing people with anger issues or mental illness from having access to guns, and do whatever else we can to aggressively reverse the increasing violence in our communities across America. Otherwise, we will have neighborhoods at risk of teetering on the precipice of lawlessness.

The increased number of school absences is clearly connected to students dealing with the emotional aftermath of the tragic loss of their peers, and dealing with the preoccupation of living in constant fear of being killed. Attending funerals increases anxiety levels as many children become consumed with concerns for their personal safety. They have to contend with neighborhoods where random acts of violence continually put them in harm's way; they are consumed by the need to strategically plan travel routes that they hope will keep them from being at the mercy of a fellow human being committed to uncaring, reckless behavior. And yet, rather than inquire about why they were late or absent, we just count their tardiness or absence against them. Schools in urban communities have had to contend with the rising rate of truancy, but until the issue of safety is made a priority, truancy will remain a prevailing problem. We cannot expect a change in one without addressing the other.

From Angst to Revelations

LIKE MOST PEOPLE WHO TRULY CARE ABOUT THE DECLINE OF civility, over the past several years I have felt a growing frustration and outrage at, and at times have been truly overwhelmed by, the high rate of crime plaguing our urban communities. The daily barrage of incomprehensible crimes reported in the news has also left me with a sense of helplessness. But instead of giving in to my sense of outrage and helplessness, I kept revisiting the same question: "What can be done to reverse the behaviors that put the lives of so many urban youths in peril?" Eventually, I recognized the need to lower the dial on my sense of outrage and to instead think about viewing the crisis through a more constructive lens.

So, I began thinking about the need to focus on the one area that has the capacity to positively impact the outcome of the lives of all people in America: *our education system.* The constructive lens through which I began to form my perspective about our current education system, particularly in public schools in poor communities across the country, was to start by unmasking the truth about why we still have not closed achievement gaps and to propose some remedies to break the cycle of underperforming schools. The vehicle I decided to use to give voice and clarity to my perspectives was to write.

Initially, it was a challenge to prioritize what topics to take on because of the enormity of questions relative to who is really responsible for under-performing students' receiving substandard education. Throughout my career in education, I juggled dividing my time between fulfilling my administrative obligations and addressing ways to improve the quality of education for students.

On so many occasions, as a teacher, I found my efforts hampered by imposing bureaucratic rules and regulations that often had so little to do with improving the quality of classroom cultures, instruction, and learning. Then, as a school leader, I had to learn how to navigate through additional levels of chaotic bureaucracy, which often overshadowed my time and efforts to focus on education in ways that should have mattered most. Most school leaders do not relish or voluntarily choose to spend hours in their office electronically submitting what feels like a scattershot of information to various department heads at the district office. But as most people know, bureaucracies seem to have insatiable appetites, and too often for mundane information unrelated to what those of us who applied for the leadership role intended to achieve: ensuring students are well educated. Ultimately, my decision to write a book was made because I wanted an opportunity to focus solely on issues related to the root causes of the erosion of trust in public education, and to explore what we can do to rebuild that trust in an institution worth saving. In writing *America's Educational Crossroads: Continue Widening the Achievement Gap or Make a Seismic Shift Forward into the 21ˢᵗ Century*, I describe constructive measures and strategies to significantly improve public education while imagining what a 21ˢᵗ century state-of-the-art public high school, designed to help students achieve their college and career aspirations, could look like.

After completing the segments of the book describing my vision of a 21ˢᵗ Century Collaborative High School Campus with additional resources to support the academic, social, and emotional well-being of all students, I had a nagging curiosity about how I could transform my written description of the Collaborative High Schools into a visual illustration. Realizing my inability to let it go, the question of "What if?" quickly changed to "Why not?" I just needed an architect to help me transform my vision into reality. I was fortunate to meet a very gifted architect who collaborated with me to co-create the Collaborative High School Campus Model.

We were nearing completion of the Collaborative High Schools project when another unexpected thought occurred to me. I suddenly realized new schools alone won't close achievement gaps. So, the book I thought I had completed was in fact not nearly finished. While developing the high school campus model, I realized investing in new buildings, although a great start, simply does not get at the fundamental issues plaguing underperforming public schools: persistent academic achievement gaps, and disruptive school cultures that are a challenge to manage.

Naturally, I felt compelled to explore the perils of creating new schools without addressing substandard educational practices that contribute to inequities in education. Reversing inequities will require infusing quality educational resources, elevating training to improve competency in school management of leaders, and making closure of academic achievement gaps a priority. Not addressing those issues would only result in new schools' retrofitting outdated ineffective educational practices and unfair policies into a new structure: a recipe for disastrous outcomes that would predictably set up new schools for failure.

The overarching goal of the book is to highlight why we must and how we can replace our current public schools and education system. The book also highlights consequences of not building new state-of-the-art facilities, not installing highly advanced technology resources, not modernizing curriculums, not improving or diversifying methods of instruction, and not expanding social developmental programs that would contribute to safer schools. The highest academic standards can be attained in schools that emphasize attributes of respectful communities and ways students can be responsible contributors to their school community. Students can learn ways to safely navigate through social issues by being surrounded with humane policies that model how to respectfully engage with others to achieve peaceful and safe coexistence. *America's Educational Crossroads* also proposes a new system of assessing academic performance that never results in failing students. The new system allows teachers to see errors as revelations of potential learning gaps in need of additional or a different kind of instruction.

Another long-ignored but detrimental contributing factor to academic achievement gaps is how schools are constantly impacted by upheavals in surrounding inner-city neighborhoods. Many organizations are committed to the development of programs and other initiatives implemented in urban communities to address violence and the increasing number of fatalities. While their efforts are admirable, they have yet to show any evidence of sustainable results. Why? Because the efforts only suppress and do not end neighborhood crimes for the duration of time that the programs are funded. These organizations require a societal and sustainable system-wide fix in order to help the citizens who have to endure living in the unsafe neighborhoods that surround their schools. Successful schools inside of safe neighborhoods will serve as co-anchors promoting safety, which also enables current and future generations of children to thrive within and outside of neighborhood schools. A new education system inclusive of new schools in urban and rural communities could be an agent of change, initiated by early cycles of success and then, over time, rooted in habits of continued success, transforming hope from a dream to reality in communities that have had to go without the resources to make it possible.

Decades of Ineffective Reforms

LOSING ACHIEVEMENT GAPS WILL REQUIRE EDUCATORS TO look through a different lens, one that enables us to see through the eyes of the clientele we serve: the students. Ultimately, all students aspire to have jobs in a career of their choice. The majority of middle and high school students just don't see the meaning or purpose of sitting in classes taking courses that they perceive as having little to no connection to their future. Their perception of their education as being disconnected to their future aspirations may be one of the strongest contributing factors to the high number of students underperforming over the span of many decades. Despite recent reform efforts in education, the continued decline in high school graduation rates in urban communities across America indicates that it is time for education reforms that adapt to the aspirational desires of our students who live in the 21st century. These 21st century aspirations cannot be met inside of learning institutions aligned with outdated policies predating the Industrial Revolution. Every other American institution has surpassed practices that were established in former eras, knowing if they did not make transformational changes to keep up with our current, ever-evolving technological revolution, then they, like our public schools in poor communities, would be left behind.

Students see everything around them being overhauled and modernized to keep up with the ongoing technological and cultural demands of the 21st century, with the one glaring exception being our education system. Students know that installation of wireless systems and other technological upgrades throughout their old school buildings does not constitute modernizing the quality of education, and therefore these changes are simply not good enough. Our 21st century students need to attend modern state-of-the-art schools that stimulate and sustain genuine interest in learning through curriculums linked to the eventual fulfillment of their career aspirations.

Imagine what student performance results would be if high schools collaborated with colleges and businesses to develop curriculums that integrate learning academic content with college preparation skills, while equipping students for entry-level positions in careers of their choice. Collaborative High Schools puts the student's interests first. Collaborative High Schools partnering schools with colleges and businesses would benefit the students and respond to the common assertions of colleges and business leaders that students are not adequately prepared for college or the labor force.

The past several decades have been dedicated to finding and implementing education reforms that would close achievement gaps.

There has been some progress in many urban school districts, but overall results have not shown a significant or sustainable level of closure, and we are still faced with the challenge of finding solutions for how to effectively engage students in their education. We will continue to lose that battle if we do not summon the courage to listen and respond to our students who, when asked if they understand the importance of getting an education, often reply, "Why?" or "What's the point of going to school?" It is no wonder that our education system and recent reforms have had little success in closing or even narrowing academic achievement gaps, if our students cannot identify any meaningful reasons to attend school; no one can be truly surprised when they choose to drop out.

Rather than spending time focusing on decades of overwhelming data that reflect the persistent failure rates for high school graduation, particularly in low-income urban school districts across the country, let's consider a more student-centered education reform; reform that consists of several career-oriented high schools located together on one campus, similar to colleges and universities; and a three-way partnership with collegiate institutions and businesses that consists of a four-year curriculum plan developed by a team of teachers, college professors, and business instructors. The curriculum would integrate core high school subject areas with college readiness assignments such as thesis and research-based projects. Each career-oriented high school's curriculum planning team would identify and embed information related to its career into the math, science, history, English Language Arts, foreign languages, financial literacy, technology, general arts, and other standard academic requirements for earning a diploma. Injecting career-related content into and throughout the curriculum not only enhances the relevance of the curriculum with the student's area of career interest but enriches the overall high school curricula.

The focal point has to shift from the current and outdated methods of developing curriculums to a new model that combines the resources of schools, colleges, and businesses. Ultimately, many high school students want and need access to educational resources that enable them to earn a high school diploma; but a Collaborative High School Campus Model would bring greater weight to diplomas in the 21st century. The remedy for preventing students from dropping out of school is to provide students with a more holistic four-year educational experience completely immersed in resources that prepare them with the skills necessary to complete a college degree program and provide access to job-skills development programs.

The model would also reflect a bifurcated quality education that includes both highly educated students, whether or not they enroll in college, and highly skilled and career-ready students well prepared to enter the workforce. *America's Educational Crossroads and Collaborative High School Campus Model* provided me an opportunity to illustrate how to bring each student's educational potential to full fruition. Closing academic achievement gaps will be bolstered by the enthusiasm of students attending high schools created to support collaborative efforts that combine the professional expertise of high school staff, college professors, and business leaders—all dedicated to integrating lessons consisting of academic content, college preparation skills, and practical training for entry-level positions in careers of their choice.

Insidious Message Embedded in America's Educational DNA

E VEN THOUGH THE MYTH OF INFERIORITY BASED ON SKIN COLOR has been debunked, our public schools and other institutions have impeded the ability of millions of Black people to advance up the social and economic ladder of success. A generous interpretation of why that myth still persists might be, until recently, that a sizeable segment of our society has been either unable to recognize the harmful impacts caused by that false assertion or perhaps uninterested in removing racial barriers that impede forward progress.

America's educational DNA, evident in policies and the purposeful withholding of equitable access to quality educational resources for Black students, helped fuel the insidious and false belief that equates black and brown skin color with intellectual inferiority. It is evident when your real intellectual capacity has been starved of opportunities to learn, and instead you are fed the persistent message that being born into America's lowest caste entitles you to receive little to no education, it being assumed you were never capable of consuming content that required the ability to read and write, much less understand history, math, and science.

Look at the will and dedication scientists devoted to unraveling the mystery of our genetic DNA, where they discovered the relationship between chromosome structures in cells, which enabled them to unmask a code related to proteins and then alter the sequence of the genetic code to enhance our capacity to survive severe and potentially life-threatening viruses. If we were to apply the same degree of dedication to linking students previously denied access to quality education to quality instruction in quality educational facilities, it could reverse America's educational DNA, and students of all races and ethnicities could finally have an opportunity to achieve their real academic potential. America's educational DNA shaped policies designed to convince everyone, but especially Black American citizens, of being too intellectually inferior to be worthy of access to a quality education. These policies were highly effective in the educational marginalization and degradation of an entire race. It didn't stop there, though.

Those in power then created policies that made it lawful to treat black citizens as less than citizens, preventing them access to any human rights reserved and preserved for non-minorities; and these deplorable policies allowed Blacks to be openly scorned and degraded in public. Politicians, community planners, and civil engineers efficiently collaborated to develop and construct low-income housing in urban communities designed in many ways similar to prisons, restricting freedoms of poor Black and Hispanic residents penned inside.

Historically, black citizens have had to live at the most extreme and disproportionate end of our societal spectrum. Education and the criminal justice system are two examples of Blacks living in disproportionate numbers at the extreme end of the spectrum, where unfairness undergirds all policies. On the educational spectrum, Blacks had to exist without access and meaningful educational standards because of the classification of being deemed "have nots" and therefore unworthy. Yet when it came to monitoring behaviors thought to need the constant presence of overseers employed by America's criminal justice system, Blacks were disproportionately placed on the most extreme end of the oversight spectrum, where race became the justification for constant subjugation of humiliating oppressive tactics like racial profiling.

Disproportionality has followed Blacks into the 21st century. However, we seem to have recently realized that the abysmal high school dropout and incarceration rates of Blacks, which Langston long ago implored America to address, can no longer be permitted to continue. Most Americans are clearly in favor of bending the arc of America's Educational DNA towards all children's being given access to quality education. The changing of minds is a long overdue but welcome sign. We are now the social scientists charged with the task of breaking away from America's dysfunctional educational DNA code of restrictive and substandard education intended for certain populations. The challenge of dismantling or discontinuing centuries-old, racially unfair policies and practices that have had required decades to take hold, and in some cases time to perfect, needs fearless advocates and agents of change to help usher our education into the 21st century.

Recent changes in the late 20th century and early 21st century, currying favor with those working to entice families away from public education and into charter schools, are examples of the modern-day, racially unfair obstacles deployed to obstruct efforts to continue investing in public schools, and a sign that not everyone is ready to divest from the continual racial subordination of Black and other minority students. Like other formerly federally funded institutions, such as prisons, that were turned over to private corporations to manage, and coincidentally warehouse predominantly black and brown men and women, the privatization of public schools is also happening in predominantly minority and poor neighborhoods. Transitions from public schools to independent and charter schools enable public funding allocated per student to follow wherever students are enrolled. And, similar to prisons, the number of bodies incarcerated in prisons or students enrolled in schools of privately owned institutions achieves corporate entities' aspirations of profiting from the sale of black people in the 21st century, while accelerating the abdication of our federal government from its funding and regulatory oversight of public schools.

Regulations once committed to the promise of "No Child Left Behind" are being vanquished because the federal, state and local officials are fed up with the fiscal drain of funds provided to underperforming schools that perpetually provide substandard education to poor minorities. The aftermath of Hurricane Katrina provided a golden opportunity for an entire city to be handed over to private corporations as one of the recovery measures after the storm. Public schools that performed poorly prior to a natural disaster can be targeted, with minimal or no say from community members, for transference to charter-based corporations. All too often, corporate leaders discover how easy it is to find willing partnerships with politicians in favor of divesting and unburdening federal governments, at both state and local levels, of fiscal responsibility to our public education system.

Recent policies by the Secretary of Education appointed in 2016, for example, proposed updated education laws to lower funding for public schools and increase support for more charter schools. That decision was quite alarming and demonstrated the overall plan to dismantle public education. The recent proposal is rather precarious, but it is also proof of efforts to degrade further the one viable source left to potentially advance people out of poverty. Today's measure reflects a reversal of decades of efforts to reform education. In fact, it feels like a return to the normalization of disenfranchising people already living under the hardship of the worst economic conditions. Where do all children go each day to be educated, leaving parents so hopeful of their child's learning and eventually accessing the first rung on a hierarchical ladder of educational success? These children's parents, grandparents, and all their previous ancestors endured decades of being subjected to poor-quality public schools, driven by an educational system that shows such indifference to the disparity between the worst conditions of inner-city schools and all of the newer state-of-the-art schools built in surrounding suburbs and other affluent communities. This indifference makes evident who America deems worthy of access to the best educational resources.

If you are interested in refuting this assertion, please visit public schools in any of the many urban communities where American citizens reside in poor neighborhoods; there, in spite of the often-overlooked efforts of dedicated staff members, you will see poorly managed, under-resourced public schools operating under the most deplorable conditions. Evidence of the myth of Blacks being inferior to whites is visually present:

- In the unsanitary, unsafe, rodent-infested, dilapidated buildings we insultingly refer to as public schools;

- In the outdated curriculums and educational materials;

- In the expectation that students, teachers, and school staff simply ignore the broken water heaters in winter that cause them to sit in classrooms wearing layers of winter clothing;

- In the need to walk carefully in bathrooms with overflowing toilets that have not been attended to because of lack of funds in the district's facilities budget to fix them; and

- In the enduring of consecutive weeks of oppressive heat and humidity that permeate throughout settings we call classrooms, where students must pretend to learn under soaring temperatures and forecasts of even higher temperatures with little to no relief in sight, from the month of May until the end of the school year in mid-June.

Imagine being expected to learn in such suffocating or freezing conditions simply because of the color of your skin, which also forced your ancestors to live in similar conditions in designated neighborhoods. The claims of underfunded resources being the cause of the problem tell only half of the story. Often it is the complete absence of resources that belies the real intentions of neglect.

Can't get to those areas? Or perhaps you don't feel safe driving through the school's neighborhood? Yet we take little notice of subjecting kids to those same conditions that influence your decision to not travel through certain neighborhoods. If you decide not to go, please do an internet search. You can easily find posted images of deteriorating public schools in inner cities like Detroit. Those postings tend to produce a range of responses, including admonishing and re-victimizing those who already inherited the deplorable conditions by virtue of being born into poverty.

Victim blaming and shaming those subjected to redlining policies that dictated where they could and could not live is how Blacks in urban communities inherited the impoverished conditions in which they were forced to exist. An unsympathetic system condoned forced federal housing without access to resources to improve their surrounding conditions, perpetuating the cycle of many generations of babies' being born into poverty, subjected to substandard education, and unable to get good jobs. As a result, throughout their adult lives, they would never have the means to improve those conditions. And then they were burdened with accusations of being the *cause* of those conditions. This is just one example of indifference endured by Blacks in communities across America.

Another example of that indifference is visible in the images of urban public schools in those same communities. An internet search of Detroit public schools in January 2016 showed horrific images of unsafe deterioration of buildings with black mold in ceilings, soaked ceiling tiles, and insulation hanging in classrooms with mold on exposed pipes embedded in the ceiling that continually leaked. This was just the tip of the iceberg. Unsafe and unsanitary conditions forced the relocation of classrooms to spaces that didn't exist, so they doubled up classrooms or temporarily relocated to the gymnasium, where they joined other classes who also had to relocate due to similar conditions. This should alarm everyone. *Please don't look away.* If what you see terrifies and sickens you, shouldn't your very next thought be, "Why are we allowing any child, teacher, or staff member to live in such deplorable conditions?"

In that single moment, the images you see represent some of the most reprehensible policies of a nation that constructed racially biased social policies and laws that promoted and permitted the underfunding of public schools in inner cities to keep Blacks from advancing forward and to serve as a perpetual reminder that being born a different color was sufficient to disqualify and deem them of being unworthy of the liberties, civil rights, freedom, and access to the abundance of resources readily available to working class and privileged Americans fortunate not to have been born Black. And to ensure everyone, including Blacks, bought into the system so that it successfully led to a universal belief, on the part of not only Americans, both Black and white, but people in European and Asian countries, in the myth that Blacks and other people of color are intellectually inferior, the same system has continually rewarded those born in affluent zip codes by ensuring their ability to vote, which results in their having a say in policies, laws, and—the most coveted area of influence—decisions on how funds will be allocated. While that takes place in those communities, the exact opposite occurs in poor communities, where a high concentration of people of color or Native Americans reside.

Regardless of the fact that we are all living in the modern era of the 21st century, civil rights—and in particular ensuring all citizens in America participate in the political system, where the real power lies—are not available to everyone. It is those in power who have a real say in what and who receives funding and the amount to be allocated. People in power have the authority to fix many of societies' ills. But it's the ability of every citizen to vote that determines whether or not they can vote into office candidates who truly have their best interests at heart. But alas, those voting rights we thought were successfully fought for were apparently built on a foundation of corrosive sand; efforts to suppress voting rights never really went away in some communities where most residents are Black.

When we see attempts to rekindle reliable and sadly effective methods of trying to suppress and prevent minority populations from voting while simultaneously dusting off and dragging out malicious messages to stoke anger and fear as a means to motivate the shrinking population of those who were once in the majority to vote, it reopens old wounds many had hoped were healed. The formula is both familiar and highly predictable. There is a historical blueprint for how to successfully plant fear, nurture that fear with continual false allegations and assertions, and, over time, inflame those voters who share your ideology and are easily manipulated by century-old messages repeatedly echoed to flair-up America's most fragile wound: racism and fear of others who do not look like them. Fear of minorities, immigrants, and others who do not have the look of European whites is thriving in a few communities. But because their actions make national news, it would have the appearance of being widespread. Fortunately, the majority of white people in America are so outraged by efforts to suppress the voting rights of Blacks and other minority groups, that they are joining the national resistance against voter suppression.

That same level of passion and fervor is needed from all Americans united in our outrage by continual efforts to use racism to perpetually divide and prevent people of all ethnic backgrounds from having equal access to their rights as American citizens, in ending the racism that contributes to sending minorities who live in poor communities into public schools and an educational system that are in dire need of a major overhaul. If we work collectively to demand and then persist in insisting that all children, but especially those living in poor communities, have the right to attend new state-of-the-art schools that reflect the 21st century and to receive the highest level of relevant and engaging education aligned with the 21st century advancements enjoyed throughout the many other sectors of our society, we can finally open pathways for all students to potentially close academic achievement gaps and instill in each child, teenager, and young adult the idea that their college and career aspirations not only matter but are America's most important priority.

When—not if—we fulfill this commitment, we will finally see evidence of a nation's willingness to move forward in ensuring that all its kids who attend public schools—whether those kids were raised in inner cities, rural communities, or other economically challenged communities—are educationally prepared to attain a prosperous life in their future. Not only will we finally stop allowing any student based on race, ethnicity, or economic status to fall further behind in underfunded and underperforming public schools, but demanding new public schools in new facilities with significantly updated curriculums and instruction will signal America's willingness to embrace the belief that, when given equal access to quality education, all children will prevail. And when they demonstrate what they are and always have been truly capable of, we may arrive at a moment in a history where America took an important step forward in eradicating racial barriers that once, but no longer, supported false claims of inferiority of any human being.

Imagine the kind of nation we could ultimately become when we shed any and all barriers motivated by long-held misconceptions that only a select few were entitled to one of the most influential and life-changing resources so desperately needed the most by those residing and left languishing for decades in the most improvised and dehumanizing conditions, condoned by a society that knew full well the only means of advancing up and further away from poverty was then, is now, and always will be receiving a quality education in any public school.

Examining the current status of public schools sadly proves we haven't yet arrived at that rosy moment in history of having successfully removed barriers. In fact, the ever-widening academic achievement gap in inner-city schools across the country makes even more elusive any possibility of truly fixing an educational system that has been broken for so long. Clearly, schools and their communities would benefit from an education model that includes addressing social challenges in the school's surrounding community.

How Marginal Efforts Contribute to Marginalization

WELL-EDUCATED BLACKS ARE OFTEN PERCEIVED AS EXCEPTIONS to the rule of what is expected of the majority of Blacks during initial encounters with many non-minorities. The telltale signs are generally being "well spoken" and "articulate." Often times, while such remarks toward Blacks are intended as compliments, those of us who benefited from receiving a quality education tend to wince when hearing them. Why? Complimentary appraisals by non-minorities of how well-spoken well-educated Blacks are, reveal to us the potential of what can be achieved by a majority of black citizens in America if they were able to access the same level of educational resources made available to those of us who have ascended and reached higher echelons in society. When only a select few are allowed entry into quality education programs and then become examples of what Blacks in America are truly capable of achieving when educational barriers are removed, those well-intended compliments remind us how many more minorities could have had a chance to show their true potential if only they had been educated well enough throughout their elementary through high school years to be eligible to attend and complete a four-year college program. Then the majority of well-educated minorities would be well-spoken and highly articulate, making well-spoken Blacks in America the norm, rather than the few who received quality education programs the exception.

Many Black high school students have successfully applied to and were accepted into college, but being inadequately or marginally prepared academically proved to be insufficient for the demands required of college-level courses. Marginalized performances usually align with marginalized expectations during one's educational journey. But the continued marginalization of populations in our society is also the responsibility of members within that population. Teachers, school leaders, parents, mentors, and members of communities where students live have to expect and insist on better efforts from students. The successful persistence of underperforming and failure is also the responsibility of those who surround the students and of the students themselves. Yes, Blacks have endured centuries of racism and bigotry. Yes, it has had and continues to have a psychological, social, and emotional impact on how so many of our youths perceive their ability to achieve in school, often marginally at best. But as an African American author, I feel we Blacks, too, bear some of the responsibility of continuing the perception that we are less than capable of achieving. Whenever we experience failure, instead of our focusing on the need to apply ourselves, improve our work ethic, or perceive ourselves as possessing the will to eventually overcome obstacles, we rely on the ability to evoke either guilt or sympathy from others by blaming racism. In those moments when we Blacks want to blame bigotry and race, and insist that we be given a break because it isn't our fault but the fault of our society's systemic racial injustices, we become addicted to apathy, which in turn perpetuates the marginalization of our race. Racism is real, and it is reprehensible! Blacks and other people of color across America are subjected to reminders of racism across the spectrum of their daily lives. And oh, how it hurts to be a victim of racial intolerance; in our careers, or when we witness unarmed and innocent black men and women recklessly executed by police officers, and killings in churches and other places of sanctuary where so many worship and pray for better days for Blacks in America.

It's even insulting that, because of the color of skin someone is born with, they are perceived as something to be tolerated. People of color should not attend or participate in workshops or other gatherings that advocate *tolerance*. What is intolerable is the mere suggestion that black- and brown-skinned people must be tolerated, rather than accepted and respected regardless of the color of their skin. Having to contend with racism and bigotry is central to every facet of daily life for Blacks in America. For too many generations, the racist marginalization of a population in *our* country has stunted the growth of so many. Examples abound, showing how successful the marginalization process has been. But one of the most effective means of marginalizing a race has been the long-held myth that Blacks are intellectually inferior. And without a doubt, the continuation of this myth has effectively served as one of many carefully constructed barriers meant to impede the forward progress of Black Americans.

That is what makes achieving the goal of obtaining quality education and employment, and pursuing prosperity and happiness, within our lifetime, our responsibility too. But we did not design or create the barriers intended to stymie our ability to show what we are capable of achieving. Those among us accepted into institutions of higher learning and successfully earning a college degree understood the importance of needing to perform well; we wanted the doors we went through to not only remain open, but also to widen so that others could follow. But we have to prepare them better to prevent them from inheriting marginalized beliefs of what they are capable of achieving and marginalized habits that get in the way of their ability to perform at their highest potential.

It Won't Be Easy . . . But It Never Has Been

W E KNOW THE MYTH OF BLACKS BEING INFERIOR IS DEEPLY embedded into the social, emotional and psychological fabric of not only our society but the entire world. Black- and brown-skinned people from around the world are also living in class systems where social status is predetermined by skin color. Black- and brown-skinned people are living in various forms of apartheid designed to denigrate populations of people through a caste system where they are referred to as "other" and meant to serve as a reminder of being outcasts. Any society that purposefully separates, actively denigrates, and prevents full integration of all races—regardless of ethnicity, religion, gender, emotional-sexual preference, or any other attribute that a society views as abhorrent and therefore must be seen and treated by those in the majority as not just different, but deviant from the rest of society—reflects the most debase, inhuman, and perverse morals that dictate the unnatural norms of their oppressive society.

Centuries of protests, marches, lives given and lost advocating for civil rights, relentless appeals to get and then maintain and uphold new laws protecting the civil and human rights of all American citizens—all have yielded only tenuous victories. Affirmative Action, desegregation of schools, voting rights, and various other laws enacted to disallow the continuance of anti-racist policies have proven to be less reliable, despite assurances promised during ceremonial presidential signings followed by jubilant celebrations declaring victory. Rather than granting a permanent voting rights law, the Voting Rights Act enacted in 1965—prohibiting racial discrimination and ensuring all American citizens, including Blacks, the right to fully, and without exception, participate in all political elections—periodically requires presidential approval for extending the period of time the law remains in effect. But there have also been successful efforts, led by political leaders in southern states and aided by a Supreme Court decision in 2013, that resulted in weakening protections; declaring an important government oversight of proposed changes to the law by individual states to be outdated.

The 5–4 decision by the Supreme Court in 2013 was seen as a signal to states that they were no longer going to be held accountable for enacting voter suppression tactics. This not only weakened the original intention of the Voting Rights Act but triggered a series of actions, including new voter ID laws, purging voters from lists to prevent them from voting and a variety of other nefarious tactics mirroring practices of the Jim Crow era. Driven by a fear of the majority of black citizens' voting for Democrats, efforts have been made to undermine the Voting Rights Act, in order to deny a segment of America's citizenry from exercising their right to vote. This is a reminder of the hypocrisy that plagues a nation that promotes democracy for all yet remains linked to practices from past eras that cultivated and perpetuated racial divisions, and prevented access to democracy by all who have been repeatedly promised and assured of their right to partake in a democratic society. The continued perpetuation of something that has been so deeply and firmly rooted in American soil for hundreds of years, makes one wonder: are changes in education possible, or will the current climate of a country under siege by the few continue unabated? In spite of its feeling like an insurmountable challenge, racial tensions resurrected by those invested in a return to the past can be overcome, and eventually muted into a scar that will always exist but will gradually do less harm, if only we seize opportunities in the one reliable resource to all children, teens, and young adults across America: *our public education system that provides quality and equal access to everyone.*

Over time, and after a sustainable period of investing in new schools with modern curriculums, academic gaps can be dramatically narrowed. Successfully narrowing the pervasive academic gaps will lead to the potential narrowing of other gaps impacting generations of poor and minority students into and throughout their adult life. Education success alone cannot fix income inequality. But a quality education is essential to one's ability to gain entrance onto paths that provide access to college and good careers. Quality education remained beyond the reach of Blacks because of the ongoing subjugation of black citizens to a myriad range of racially biased barriers. But the barriers in education served as the initial obstacle preventing black citizens from gaining access to all of the resources in our democratic society created to benefit all Americans.

We are in the 21st century, and America has gotten good at cultivating messages about the need to improve race relations. But cultivating promising messages without eradicating the systemic racial barriers in education and employment renders those messages as disingenuous empty rhetoric.

On the one hand, everyone sees and truly wants to believe in the messages encouraging and welcoming participation onto the open field that will lead to achieving their dreams and aspirations. But just because there is a field that appears to be open and welcoming to everyone, doesn't mean it is always a level and fair arena, permitting everyone who enters to play by the same rules or standards. When a system is intentionally gerrymandered to benefit those who habitually outperform others socially and structurally, the victors are determined before a race begins. It is not a level playing field. Instead, it is designed to protect and perpetuate the dominance of one group, while supplanting barriers and other obstacles (like the continued erosion of equal voting rights) intended to place those less affluent or poor, as well as people of color, at a major disadvantage; it ensures hurdles are insurmountable enough to slow them down or prevent them from being successful. Those in charge of the rules of the field will always prevail. The outcomes are exactly what the system was designed to produce.

Every day we Blacks experience or have come to expect that we will not be afforded access to the American dream. It's as if we are constantly tested in every social arena. When applying for jobs, we anticipate walking on a minefield of hidden obstacles that we know exist. While candidates who submit an application and résumé that clearly indicates they meet the qualifications for the position, the submission of a photo as one of the required steps in the application process gives qualified candidates of color reason to pause. Couple that with an Internet search of highly successful companies steeped in traditions where brochures featuring glossy displayed profiles of past and current staff cause the applicant to pause a second time. The hierarchy of the company's flow chart proudly displays all who occupy the senior and mid-level executive positions, and there is not one person of color among them, though a few are featured at entry- and low-level tiered positions. In this instance, the black applicant is applying for a mid-level executive position.

The decision to move forward is framed in a question that is a common refrain within communities of color: "Do I feel like being a pioneer in a culture where black and brown candidates have never been allowed entry?" Those among us who have been the first, or pioneers, may have successfully broken the racial glass ceiling based on our qualifications, but in addition to carrying out responsibilities outlined in a job description, the unspoken additional burden of breaking through racial barriers supersedes all else. The candidate bears the burden of proof that they earned the right to be there based on the qualifications and previous achievements noted in their résumé that reflect an illustrious career boasting even more achievements earned at the highest standards than the candidate's closest white colleague, who, in spite of having the same level position, job description, and responsibilities, earns more money. That person's salary is equal to all of the other same-level colleagues who happen to be white, although several of you and them were hired at the same time. Income inequality, regardless of the same level of responsibilities, date hired, and stellar credentials, is a real problem—not just for minorities but also for women, differently abled people, and members of the LGBTQ community.

The absence of employees of color in any company's brochure is often a way to dissuade well-qualified brown and black candidates from even submitting an application. While politically correct and socially tactful messages of the 21st century are meant to bolster the perception that America is closing income, employment, education, and social gaps of racial inequality, qualified candidates of color see evidence that they still are not truly welcomed. That company brochure where a qualified candidate of color sees every position filled by not one person who looks like them is the modern-day version of racial barriers conveying that "Blacks need not apply."

But black- and brown-skinned pioneers who do ascend to positions in the upper ranks of a company often contend with covert resentment from those who already occupy positions at the top and beneath them. Those at the top who are white are dubious about the new hire's having been chosen not based on qualifications but because the company needed to improve its reputation of welcoming diversity. To do that, it had to reverse the practice of denying qualified applicants of color into the upper ranks. Black- and brown-skinned candidates hired at high-level positions in predominantly white organizations know they are a part of a grand experiment. Pioneers brought on to jumpstart a racial quota initiative that had been ignored or denied for decades can experience perilous challenges. Expectations to participate in a one-way cultural exchange, where most inquiries by white colleagues are often centered around the unspoken question, "So really, what makes you so special that you deserve a seat at our table?" Or, being subjected to conversations related to other Blacks they know as a means of letting you know they are cool because they know other Blacks. Those white colleagues fail to understand how their efforts to win your approval and view them as culturally and ethnically sensitive as a way to create an alliance or friendship, have the opposite effect. You, the new hire, are repelled by their obvious discomfort with people of color. If they have to reference others who only have skin color in common with you and nothing else, they fail to recognize it is not skin color that makes you who you are. In fact, that is the only point of reference that really marginalizes your individual identity, when they associate you and your potential attributes with what they assume about you, based on the one or few others they think they know—because you know they have likely marginalized those individuals too. Their behavior lets you know you are seen as a category of a population of people they regard as different.

Respectful conversations with white colleagues that focus on the exchanges of ideas, interests, hobbies, and other matters of personal importance between people genuinely interested in getting acquainted with one another are a rare occurrence. When conversations are initiated by white people and start with inquiries related to race, it's not only offensive but a missed opportunity for both parties to potentially establish a meaningful connection that truly invites exchanges about topics of personal importance to both people. Many initial encounters between Blacks and whites fill Blacks with apprehension because previous personal experiences have taught us we are rarely afforded the courtesy of being genuinely greeted first as a person rather than based on some preconceived and unfair assumptions about an entire race of people. But when we do encounter others who immediately and without hesitation extend a hand, making us feel genuinely welcome, we are receiving a signal that they and we will be receptive to judging one another by the content of our character, rather than being boxed into some preordained stereotypes, which then requires us to show evidence to the contrary in order to be taken seriously. Respectful communication between two people is more likely to grow when both sense they are in the presence of someone who, as a person and not based on their status, is their equal across the spectrum of humanity. In that context, anyone and everyone can initiate that first introduction, while making eye contact, that signals, "It's truly nice meeting you," and genuinely mean it.

Greetings of "Hello" and "Welcome" are embedded in the way children across the country are received at their public schools, from kindergarten through high school. Parents escorting their children into school buildings immediately develop a sense of how their child truly will feel welcome, which also connotes the level of education their child will receive from the moment they arrive at the school. Upon their arrival, the condition of the building and educational resources inside of classrooms conveys the level of quality education they can expect and the degree to which the city and district feel members living within a particular community are worthy of the level of quality education that awaits them. There is probably no worse greeting that people from poor communities can experience, when they enroll their child into what will be his or her "new" school, than the messages conveyed by the school's poor condition and obvious signs of deterioration. And if there is a plaque prominently displayed on the main door entrance boasting the building was built in 1924 . . . well, any school that old is usually equipped with technology, textbooks, and maybe even curriculums that also date back to the 1920s. What a way to say "Hello" or "Welcome."

America, how will we ever know and appreciate the true content of a poor child's character if we never see them deserving of receiving a modern education in modern facilities, with modern curriculums linked to advanced technological resources and updated instructional practices? Is it reasonable to expect that continuing to warehouse poor children and teens in old and poorly managed schools will ever enable them to achieve their true academic potential or build their self-esteem high enough to withstand life's challenges? One thing that certainly shows evidence of content of character is the level of resiliency among those who, despite the barriers they worked hard to overcome, have successfully graduated from high school and completed college. Resiliency shows up in other forms, but success in education is the benchmark most people perceive as having "made it."

Those who "made it" are examples of how schools can play a pivotal role in building the foundation that can lead to a better quality of life, especially among students fortunate enough to have attended high-quality and significantly upgraded schools in high-income neighborhoods. Not only did their education experiences allow them to achieve academic success, but they were immersed in a culture that promoted healthy and safe social interactions among their peers while receiving a quality education, which over time strengthened their self-confidence. Their 13 years in an educational environment that provided quality education while helping them learn how to cultivate healthy social interactions, were the building blocks that contributed to their feeling of self-worth and helped shape their character. But the initial sign that they and their parents intuitively saw as an indication that their educational, social, and emotional well-being was an absolute priority was the condition of the schools they entered. Over the past several years, many affluent communities advocated for and provided financial resources to modernize their public schools.

Children who come from families with fewer financial resources and therefore lesser political influence are no less deserving of equal access to a high-quality education. Let's reimagine our schools so we can imagine a new way of greeting children at the front door of every new public school in every zip code across one of the most prosperous countries in the world. *We simply have to see them as worthy.* I'm not asking us to make their pathway to successful futures easy. I'm simply asking to make it possible.

If we do not invest in providing access to high quality education in modern schools for everyone, many poor and working-class communities in cities, towns, and rural communities will be forced to continue sending their children, and future generations of kids, to underfunded and underperforming schools. Such woeful disregard in attending to the educational needs of every child, regardless of economic status, perpetuates the misperception that those who are born into the lowest economic status and/or a particular color pigmentation are less worthy. And those conditions may be indicative of old myths about poor people and minorities residing in impoverished neighborhoods that constrain the forward progress of the people from those communities. The modernization of public schools and our entire public education system is our only hope of jumpstarting the process of ending poverty. We simply have to agree that we are no longer willing to accept allowing children born in low-income neighborhoods to attend poorly managed, under-resourced public schools in unsafe and unsanitary old buildings. Nor will we continue to condone the continuation of decades of downsizing school budgets that force teachers to use outdated educational resources, including old and frayed textbooks held together by layers of masking tape and containing multiple student signatures inside the cover, confirming a succession of students who were assigned the same book 20 or more years ago.

It's easy, and we are not wrong, to blame systemic social policies and laws designed to restrict people of color from accessing economic prosperity. Despite centuries of disproving myths that assert Blacks and other people of color are intellectually inferior, we have not completely dismantled the institutions—such as our public education system that allows for the continuation of substandard education—that were erected in the past and still serve as a reminder of the perils of being born a different color in America; that their being so born is sufficient to disqualify and deem them unworthy of access to all of the opportunities afforded to the rest of America's citizens. And those misconceptions about intellectual inferiority were not contained within our American borders. That perspective had gained traction across the world, particularly in European and Asian countries where many non-black- and non-brown-skinned people universally participated in peddling the myth and then treated with disdain those countries predominantly populated with black and brown citizens, making racially disparaging remarks and mocking their leaders. But in many of the countries predominantly populated by people of color, those in power or members of the ruling class constructed similar segregation policies that mirrored the same restrictions or privileges in accordance with degree of color pigmentation. Those with white and lighter skin were afforded access to resources enabling upward mobility, while those of a darker hue of skin color were not only denied access but endured the double insult of having to live in designated neighborhoods and impoverished conditions.

But there's a saying, "As America goes, so goes the rest of the world." So, if we remove antiracial policies and other barriers that keep citizens living in poverty, might it influence other countries to follow our lead? In many countries, people of color—particularly those born with brown or darker pigmentation—experience degradation, segregation, and oppression based solely on the color of their skin. Educational, social, and economic oppression is a global problem. And many countries look to America to be the example, by leading by example, of addressing issues related to ending poverty. There is absolutely no doubt that ensuring equitable access to quality education for all will significantly reduce, and maybe even eventually eradicate, the number of American citizens and global citizens currently forced to live in impoverished conditions.

The Long-Term Consequences of Dropping Out

P AST AND CURRENT REPORTS ABOUT THE STATUS OF AMERICA'S urban public schools reflect ongoing efforts to reverse such all-too-common trends as increased dropout rates that decrease the number of students completing high school. While some urban public-school districts have shown a level of success, numerous reports and studies indicate declining success in too many of America's urban public schools. The correlation between the number of Black males who drop out of high school and the number who end up in prisons is cause for greater concern. When students drop out of school, the absence of a high school diploma and job skills creates social barriers that deny them access to college, jobs and other resources that educated students have access to. This results in a vacuum of fewer options, which then entices dropouts to roam the streets, where an entirely different set of rules and standards governs their lives. When young people leaving school less educated but deeply embittered, they are free to unleash their anger in the same neighborhoods they grew up in.

Dropping out of school is made too easy, and for a range of reasons. It may be due to a lack of interest in what is being taught, boredom, inability to understand or keep up with what might be, for some students, the quick pace of information being delivered during lessons. These sentiments are quite common and resonate among many youths in urban public schools. But another more troubling factor influencing their decision to leave school is the quality of interactions they have with teachers who simply do not care. Students are quite sensitive to comments, both positive and negative, made by teachers.

When students are subjected to sarcasm or overhear teachers making cruel comments about their peers, they are justifiably suspicious of excessive targeting by teachers who have behaved in a malicious manner that results in those teachers' earning a reputation as someone to be avoided because of their continued involvement in unethical and highly unprofessional behavior. The students become good at detecting which teachers are truly invested in teaching and in the well-being of every student and which ones seem bent on inflicting harm on students. Those latter teachers have to be immediately removed from the profession. The level of abuse many students experience at home or in their neighborhoods is intolerable. But teachers who are easily angered by students' conduct can become vindictive. If they arrive at school with a combative posture, usually it isn't just the students who are uncomfortable. Their colleagues, who also witness outrageous and unfair behavior by a teacher, can sometimes come in the direct line of that teacher's anger and also be subjected to verbal abuse.

Fortunately, there are many more compassionate and caring teachers whom students also recognize as having a positive influence on their decision to continue with their education. Students who develop a genuinely positive rapport with one or more staff members at their school is so important and very underrated.

Professional development must include ways to respect students instead of discourage them. When students endure public taunts from their teacher for being absent and then are ignored when they return to school, it stunts their educational growth. They feel embarrassed and wounded because they are being humiliated, and it is taking place in the presence of their peers. So, they adapt by developing a protective instinct: they leave school. Actually, the ease of dropping out indicates they have learned one thing for certain: why should they bother staying in school if they know they will continue to fail? Sadly, current generations have witnessed the high levels of indifference about education among their predecessors and, like them, casually decide to just stop attending school. And that level of casual indifference towards education leads them out of school doors and onto neighborhood streets, giving them a lot of time and no direction from reliable adults to steer them towards constructive alternatives. They are left unsupervised, uneducated, unskilled, and unmotivated to achieve any aspirations except the one that requires no training: getting involved in criminal activities.

The increase of urban crime in America has to be addressed at the school level. If youths continue to leave school and resort to life on the streets, urban communities have no chance of reducing violence. It's really that simple. So, if we want to address crime and substantially reduce violence in urban communities, we need a new kind of education reform.

Uneducated youths who cannot find employment are susceptible to the trappings of having nothing to do and a lot of idle time, and these young people with nothing to do typically end up on the streets and in trouble. With almost 70% of America's prison population consisting of black- and brown-skinned males, there is a high probability that urban males who drop out of middle and high school are falling into the schools-to-prison pipeline that is causing our overpopulated prison system. It has become routine that America has a new and constantly growing class of incarcerated citizens.

But what if we had the means to reverse the trend? American public schools in urban communities need to help black- and brown-skinned males to access careers and colleges instead of prisons. This is possible by creating Collaborative High Schools that focus on preparing students for college and fostering career readiness. Collaborative High Schools are career and college-prep high schools partnering with colleges and businesses, responsible for providing an all-inclusive education that integrates instruction in academics, career readiness, and college readiness skills for students interested in earning a two- or four-year degree or entering careers after high school.

II.
Making the Case
for Overhauling the
Public Schools System

Education Is Still the Most Viable Pathway to Success

FOR THE MAJORITY OF YOUNG PEOPLE WHO ASPIRE TO OBTAIN jobs in careers that will place them on pathways of upward social and economic mobility, education is still the only viable option. Few, if any, other resources can change the trajectory of their lives. Even the community-based resources are struggling to provide sustainable support to families who live at or below poverty level. The ever-shrinking funding sources of the many community-based organizations trying to help are no match for the broad span of needs of families in low-income areas.

One area of concern is providing health and counseling services for the increasing number of families with undiagnosed mental and physical illnesses, obesity, and a range of other health-related issues that contribute to already existing economic challenges that families must contend with. Families who seek resources to help them address health-related issues are encountering fewer organizations or agencies to turn to for help. Consequently, schools are burdened with the responsibility of trying to educate students who arrive each day unable to focus or function in a classroom setting, due to undiagnosed and untreated mental, emotional, or physical illnesses that are often chronic conditions.

In particular, teachers are inundated with the task of counseling, rearing, training, mothering, feeding, and caring for the welfare of students who, through no fault of their own, arrive at school with baggage that becomes the central focus of the interaction between teacher and student. Yet recent professional performance evaluations of teachers are predicated on the assumption that teachers and school leaders are at fault for students' being unable to academically achieve due to a host of non-school-related issues.

One way to avoid unfairly judging and blaming teachers for the poor learning performance of their students is to bring social and medical services into schools so we can remove those issues from the classrooms and enable teachers to focus solely on teaching. Education is no longer a process where students enter school prepared to learn, and public education is at the mercy of a society currently governed by policies that decrease funding for resources that could serve to stabilize and strengthen families. The decrease in funds results in the steady rise of teachers' having to address non-school-related issues that cross the threshold of their classroom door each school day. Schools once had the luxury of referring students and families to external agencies and organizations equipped to adequately address the needs of family members. Not anymore.

For many teachers, the challenge of juggling the demands of planning lessons and providing quality instruction to a very broad range of different-leveled learners with diverse learning styles is enormous. Over a span of many years, general education classes have had special education students with Individualized Education Plans, 504 Education Plans, or ESL (English as a Second Language) Plans. (See "What Is ESL" at *ESLDirectory. com* and also "IEP vs. 504 Plans: What's the Difference?" at *Understood. org/articles/en/the-difference-between-ieps-and-504-plans.*) In well-resourced communities, overall, schools were able to successfully accommodate the needs of their special-needs student populations. Changes in laws mandated that public schools include a broader range of special-needs students with different and far more extensive needs. This naturally required more intensive resources, but many public schools in urban and poor communities were unprepared to fully accommodate the level of these students' needs.

Visitors to almost any public-school classroom may be surprised by the increased class size and makeup of the student population, which may include a broader spectrum of students with Individualized Education Plans, 504 Education Plans, and ESL Plans. Expansion of the inclusion laws, requiring regular-education settings to enroll more students from across the spectrum of special needs, without including the resources needed to ensure those students' success in these settings, led to disastrous results. Although the resources needed were specified in writing, districts often had difficulty in hiring qualified staff, purchasing assistive-technology resources, and/or obtaining adequate funding (and having time to plan) transportation. Prior to the new inclusion mandate, it was evident in urban public-school districts that available education resources were insufficient to effectively meet the needs of the diverse student population consisting of both current general education students and those with IEP's, 504 Education Plans, and ESL Plans. It is easy to imagine what became of those general-education classes that were forced to include student populations with much higher levels of needed resources. Add the challenge of students' arriving to school burdened with a crisis or other serious issue that schools lack the resources to effectively address, and the results are turmoil and valuable time being diverted away from instruction and learning. Depending on the magnitude of each incident, classrooms—and sometimes an entire school—can be impacted to the point of not accomplishing anything that remotely resembles an education. Instead, schools enter a state of academic paralysis where instruction and learning do not occur, and problematic situations potentially become worse due to the lack of adequate resources required to address them.

Even for the best and truly invested teachers, it can take a few years to research, construct, and implement a comprehensive system that creates a classroom where the majority of students make incremental and measurable progress. Now, classrooms are the new catchall for the ills of society—and many wonder what causes the constant flux of new teachers entering and exiting the profession at higher rates each year. In spite of these monumental challenges, teachers miraculously manage to find a way, and schools are still the best pathway out of poverty. However, poverty is no longer limited to students and families from impoverished communities; an overburdened education system overwhelmed with the broadest range of responsibilities in history is creating impoverished schools.

Other factors contribute to the mounting frustration of exceptional teachers, and an abundance of exceptional teachers whose skills get overlooked when their performance is tied to the lack of progress of students whose state of mind and behaviors are not conducive to receiving instruction. Failure and dropout rates will persist until we equip schools with the necessary resources to adequately address the needs of our students. Then there are factors related to cultural divisions between teachers and their students. Teachers who come from affluent suburban communities, where they grew up benefiting from an abundance of educational and other resources, arrive at schools in poor communities that have a host of cultural customs, perspectives, and priorities that are different from anything they have ever experienced. Despite their well-intended and high aspirations for their students, many of these teachers lack the preparation required to acclimate to, and then work for, a population completely foreign to them, and this stymies their ability to make meaningful connections with their students. Recruiting higher numbers of minorities raised in urban communities for teaching positions proves difficult because underperforming schools are not producing graduates who would eventually qualify to become teachers in the first place.

The new trends in education, such as longer school days and an extended school year, work in schools that already function well or at the highest standards. But for many underperforming urban schools, these trends may just extend the time students receive poor or average instruction. One cannot help but wonder if expanding the school year is society's attempt to keep students in school and off the streets.

Another recent trend is the infusion of large sums of money into underperforming schools. However, generous amounts of funding gradually disappear over the span of a few years. When these funding sources begin to vanish, underperforming schools that are showing significant improvement may not be able to sustain their improved performance levels once the funds have dried up. If we concentrate funding sources into the construction of new state-of-the-art 21st century schools with adequate and sustainable resources to address the broad range of students' needs, school districts can fairly judge teacher performances based on their teaching ability, without the inordinate burden of addressing issues related to a student's mental, emotional, or physical well-being.

Equal Access to Quality Education for Everyone

I F WE ARE TRULY COMMITTED TO GOING BEYOND THE DECADES OF rhetorical promises to address and ultimately close academic achievement gaps in our public schools, we can no longer pretend that words alone are the way to keep that promise. Instead, as the first step in attaining equal access to quality education for everyone, we need a monumental and financial commitment to fund preschools for all children, and new public elementary, middle, and high schools in urban and rural communities across America. Ensuring equal access to quality education for all students, regardless of where they live, has to start with preschool education and new schools with adequate funding to support significant upgrades in curriculum and instruction. In fact, the urgency to move forward with the modernization of public schools, curriculums, and instruction is even greater in towns, cities, and rural communities populated by America's citizens living in poverty. Access to quality schools with well-funded staffing and other valuable educational resources is not an issue in affluent communities; but lack of access to quality schools and education is a systemic problem for generations of American citizens of all races, colors, and ethnic backgrounds who reside in poor communities.

People living in poor communities across America, and in fact globally, have been denied access to achieving their educational and career aspirations for decades because of their inability to access quality educational institutions. In the United States, severe public-education budget cuts across states and cities are not because of lack of available funding resources. Interest in investing in quality education in public schools, particularly in poor communities, has steadily declined and is an indication that public education in urban and other economically struggling communities is no longer a priority. If the decline continues, it's fair to assume that in future years more public schools will be closed. Public schools that remain open will likely continue to see a decline in funding of their school budgets and a decline in a school's most valuable resource of quality, highly dedicated and underpaid teachers who have to improvise and make do with limited and eventually outdated instructional materials.

Ending the Perpetual Cycle of Impoverished Education

THE ONLY WAY TO ADDRESS THE NEGATIVE IMPACT OF THE years of educational neglect endured by urban populations in many of America's public schools is to identify academic deficits to eliminate learning gaps. If the latest data is true, that 7,000 students drop out of high school each day and 1.3 million drop out each year, one factor contributing to these outrageous dropout rates is underskilled readers and writers in urban schools. In defense of many high schools, they inherit underskilled students. In defense of all students in urban communities, it is also not the students' fault. Somewhere along their educational journey, expectations began to decline, as did the level of instruction that mirrored the changes in expectations. Instead of recognizing the negative impact of lowering the quality of instruction and expectations, students who continued to perform at substandard levels were branded as "underperformers." If a student is labeled as "underperforming," which is synonymous with failure, they are likely at risk of always being perceived as incapable of learning, which is so detrimental to their self-esteem. But if students are instead perceived as not *currently* achieving their real potential, it leaves open the possibility of achieving a higher rate of academic success if provided access to effective alternative methods of instruction and learning strategies. Teaching students learning strategies is absolutely necessary, and yet it is one of the most frequently overlooked tools in the professional development of teachers.

Many students have mastered the appearance of learning, but in fact they have no way of comprehending the volume of information shared because they were never taught how to learn. At all grade levels, teaching students content at the same time as strategies for how to learn will deepen their engagement in lessons and ensure better comprehension of content being taught. Continuing the practice of blaming students for underperforming, without their being taught skills for how to learn or providing access to alternative methods of instruction, is one of the most consequential flaws in our education system. Labeling students as "underperformers" devalues how students see themselves, regardless of level of effort they make. If students are not adequately educated, why are we not focusing on the underperforming educational institutions they attend? It's time to stop suggesting that students are responsible for underperforming. On the contrary, it is the underperforming schools and school districts that perpetuate the systemic normalization of providing substandard instruction influenced by low level of expectations fueled, or at the very least exacerbated, by years of inadequate resources.

Is it fair to hold individual schools solely accountable for languishing under the status of underperforming, when often times public schools in urban communities are unable to improve the quality of education due to the systemic inequitable distribution of funding resources in communities that are continually given a low priority status in the annual town and city budgets? School leaders and teachers in underperforming schools are also victims of economic and racially biased decisions beyond their control. But we can no longer tolerate or accept the status quo in our public schools. Why? Because we continue to lose generations of highly capable students. More importantly, if recent data is true, that 85% of low-income kids in America are not reading at proficient levels by fourth grade, then we are obligated to embark on a mission to educate our students well and with integrity. In spite of, or maybe more accurately because of, the enormous education gaps that have not shown significant or sustainable improvement despite decades of multiple reforms in education, it is obvious that Collaborative High Schools will have to own and take full responsibility for remediation of reading and writing skills in order to close the gaps of academic deficiency for all content areas, as well as taking on the necessary and much overlooked need for emotional rehabilitation.

When people endure years of underperforming, they eventually begin to embrace the erroneous belief that they are incapable of learning. Reversing that mindset will require taking measures that will enable students to reconnect with their belief that they were once truly capable of accomplishing anything, in and out of school, and that they can do so again. To do that, we will need to provide effective remedial instruction and net positive learning results in the short span of time during high school. We must establish a pattern of success, which will improve their self-esteem and restore their belief in their ability to achieve anything they put their mind to.

In many cases, the gap starts in the elementary school years and then gradually widens as they progress through grade levels. Over the span of years, students experience a state of arrested skill development. As they increasingly experience failing grades, the accompanying negative messages make students internalize a self-assessment of inability. Their lack of self-confidence increases accordingly, and eventually it can result in a diagnosis of disability. Along this vein, the high rate of Blacks, especially males, referred for special education services by middle-school age is astounding and cannot be ignored. We must ask ourselves when these referrals start, and question the systemic increase in the number of minority students referred for special education services over several decades. For many years, researchers have identified grades three and four as pivotal. The third grade is especially important because it is "the year students go from learning to read to reading to learn."[1]

Partnerships with Community Resources

W E ARE FAMILIAR WITH THE PHRASE, "IT TAKES A VILLAGE TO raise a child," but often we do not comprehend the broad scope of reliable long-term resources needed to raise a child, especially those raised in poor neighborhoods. Without wraparound services that link a network of community-based resources to schools in support of students who are struggling in school due to extenuating circumstances outside of school, any expectation for closing achievement gaps, increasing graduation rates, and reducing the dropout rates is moot. Simply put, we have spent decades trying to isolate and fix the academic performance of students in schools while disregarding the need to expand our lens of academic support to include wraparound resources needed to effectively address all things that impact a student's ability or inability to perform well in school. While academic remediation and educational self-esteem rehabilitation will be needed to close the achievement gap, there will also be a need for wraparound services to assist students with life matters that often impede a typical young adult's ability to maintain their focus on school.

In communities that have typical, but no less important, issues common to our average teens and young adults, these trials and tribulations are multiplied tenfold in poor communities. In poor communities, the resources are scarce or inadequate and never sufficient to meet the complex demands of kids who are raised in some of the worst conditions most other Americans could never imagine or survive in. The ability to achieve in school while burdened with one serious issue is enough of a challenge. Unfortunately, kids raised in low-income communities are often charged with the responsibility of raising themselves, and a high number of them bear the added burden of raising a child. For those who do attend high school, they bring with them a multitude of issues. When academic performance is measured to determine levels of ability without considering the overall context of what students are burdened with while trying to earn a high school diploma, the data outcomes are solely a measurement of how well one can perform in the midst of many competing and demanding challenges that interfere with true academic ability.

The typical challenges that most teens face are likely to be exacerbated when ill-equipped students from impoverished communities must contend with a poor education, lowered teacher expectations, and more life challenges outside of school. When students grow up in underperforming public schools in at-risk communities with few or overextended resources, the challenges are even greater. All too often, high schools act like emergency-care triage centers, dealing with several crisis-related issues that students have to contend with. Some of these issues would be minimal or nonexistent, had they been dealt with in their early stages; instead, those issues have festered and grown to an acute level because they were not appropriately addressed. Students who enter high school with one or more chronic issues face more difficulty when they arrive burdened with the added misfortune of being among those experiencing a poor education that has resulted in arrested skill development, lowered teacher expectations, and challenges outside of school. Most of these students are typically even less emotionally, psychologically, and socially equipped with the skills necessary to successfully navigate any crisis, and their state of mind may make matters even worse.

Poor communities have always needed, and will continue to need, wraparound services that include sustainable partnerships between schools and community agencies specializing in a broad range of support related to physical, emotional, and mental health issues. No one should be surprised by the state of life in our urban communities when the normalization of fear over the past several decades is considered. This has resulted in the expectation of attending the funerals of family members, friends, or loved ones whose precious young lives are taken violently at the hands of another human being too easily influenced by others to perform a reckless and irreversible act upon a fellow human being. Public schools are operating in unsafe communities and burying their citizens on a regular basis. The ones doing the killing belong to all of us, and they once attended school themselves. Our urban communities need to have a mechanism for reversing the violent trend of normalizing death at an early age. Collaborative High Schools that appeal to the aspiration of all kids, teens, and young adults to have a high-paying job will attract them back into school, keep those currently attending school enrolled, and reverse the dropout rate.

Well-funded and sustainable wraparound services will be necessary to support those with short-term and long-term needs during the elementary school, middle school, high school, and college years of education, because these problems do not disappear upon arrival at college. In some cases, students may need ongoing support during college in order to remain enrolled in and successfully complete college. Even while students demonstrate the ability to handle coursework and achieve academic success, the fragility caused by previous experiences in many of their lives arrives with them to and through college. Most of these students have not learned how to peacefully coexist with unresolved emotional baggage, and they take old problems with them into the next phase of their lives. When the only way they have learned to respond to any perceived conflict, real or imagined, is "fight or flight," students often need to be taught about the range of options available to respond to different situations.

Many of the challenges our urban youths live with daily and need support in overcoming are related to the normalization of fear and dysfunction in their communities. Examples include avoiding violence while walking through their own neighborhoods and having to uphold the street rule of "no snitching" to police when it comes to violent killings, for fear of reprisal, even when they often know the identity of the person or people responsible for the death of their family member or loved one. At home, students face difficult living situations such as being a parent of a child while attending high school. At school, they do not want to be labeled as smart because being seen as bright is viewed as taboo and not cool at all. These are just a few of the challenges our urban youths need support to overcome. In the face of these circumstances, it is unreasonable for educators to expect to get good academic results on tests or class assignments when students arrive at high school. Coming to the point of helping students to coexist with accepting death in their communities on a regular basis is one hurdle that I hope we never achieve. I find it to be utterly unacceptable because it will communicate to them that not only do we not have the resources to adequately respond, but as a society we are no longer interested in remaining invested in trying to find a resolution.

The Myth of "Healthy Economies Lifting All Boats"

MANY SCHOOL DISTRICT LEADERS AND SCHOOL COMMITTEES do not place quality instruction at the top of the list of their priorities when allocating financial resources to school budgets. When budgets shrink after the dismantling of various programs with proven records of being beneficial to students, professional development resources begin to disappear.

When economic times were good, even with the availability of funds, financial abundance didn't always translate into an abundance of qualified professionals responsible for the professional development of school leaders and teachers. They were generally found among people who knew people who knew other people—you get the gist of how it has worked for decades. And this policy of hiring people you know, as opposed to truly qualified people with expertise in professional development, has contributed to the stagnation of growth among teachers who really are passionate about teaching and are sincerely interested in expanding their repertoire of instructional methods to advance many more students up the academic achievement ladder. They feel let down by the pace of how quickly the district abandons decisions from one year to the next in pursuit of the next flavor of the month, rather than committing to practices that actually netted degrees of success, as verified by data.

Then there is the reliance on the degree of comfort by each teacher's individual level of passion, or in many cases, preference, for using professional development provided to enhance instruction and learning. Some teachers choose not to invest the time or energy to improve their level of familiarity, and that then decreases their level of engagement. If no consistent means of observation by school administrators is used to insist the teacher make a more sincere effort, teachers are left with deciding how much effort they think they ought to apply. Those same teachers, who routinely implore their students to "try harder," should apply those same expectations to themselves. Similar to students who do "try harder" and achieve higher rates of success, teachers who learn new methods of instruction or other professional development skills might actually see results and feel motivated enough by those results to want to continue making a more sincere effort.

Truthfully, degrees of ownership of a particular instructional method, use of new textbooks in support of the district's contract with a new educational vendor promising professional development and on-site guidance, are up to each individual teacher when no one is looking. Another problem. Scheduled and occasional unannounced visits to classrooms to observe teachers are not adequate. But what about school leaders who are not experienced teachers, who know little or nothing about instruction, never mind the content taught? In fact, many aren't even aware of the distinction between teaching content and knowing how to provide instruction. As one of those educators familiar with instruction but less familiar with every content taught in high school, I requested in-person support from highly knowledgeable, content-based professionals to co-evaluate teachers responsible for instruction of specific subjects; I knew I needed the presence of someone very familiar with the content area and subject to help me determine degree of competency in a more holistic way. My evaluation of determining instructional competency was a two-tier process. How well teachers knew the content area they were hired to teach required a different level of assessment from how well lessons were planned, whether students were engaged in learning, and the degree of effectiveness of instructional methods used. Ultimately, both depth and breadth of content knowledge were interwoven with overall quality of instruction, but true respect for teachers capable of doing both well meant they deserved acknowledgment for their expertise in both areas.

Most importantly, school leaders are meant to lead. This means we must occasionally lead by example and acknowledge areas about which we possess less knowledge; and, like our teachers and students, we must have the freedom to raise our hands and request additional support when needed. When a content expert has assisted with the co-evaluating process, teachers who know their craft and earn high performance-level evaluations are generally pleased with the presence of a content specialist who could give them genuine feedback, including a detailed description of how well they performed, followed by recommendations, that I alone, as a humanities educator, could not adequately provide a STEM instructor. Like anyone, teachers are worthy of qualitative assessments from colleagues who are true experts in the subjects they teach. Their feedback is highly informative and far more gratifying. The two-tier approach to the observation phase, with the teacher's approval, can be done with a seasoned, highly respected, and impartial colleague possessing years of expertise in the subject area, but strictly for the purpose of gathering information and not empowered with any degree of authority in determining the overall outcome of their colleague's evaluation performance. Another tier could be added in determining a teacher's performance: students are often reliable assessors of their teacher's ability to teach effectively.

The Gravitational Pull of Exceptional Teachers

Disclaimer: While the scenario depicted is not directly attributed to any actual teachers, nor is the lesson about a rock a real scenario, there are teachers who exude enormous enthusiasm while teaching. What makes them so exceptional is their ability to create a gravitational pull that draws and sustains students' interest in learning. I've known a few. This is a tribute to those sincerely dedicated to teaching and deserving of their rock star status . . . yes, pun intended. The following is a fictitious scenario of two different kinds of teachers capable of cultivating different educational experiences for students. It's also a tale not only of how two different force fields influence the way students learn, but also of the challenges inherent in the collegial coexistence of entirely different teaching styles.

THE BEST CLASSROOMS ARE NOT MANAGED BY AUTHORITATIVE, overbearing, punitive-minded adults who seem to have no real appetite for teaching kids. Heck, some of them don't even like kids. It's true.

Instead, the best classrooms are managed by teachers who plan interesting and highly engaging lessons. Give a highly skilled and passionate teacher a simple rock and ask them to create and teach an engaging lesson related to the structure and other features of that rock, and they will likely succeed. Often times, when defining quality teaching, we place greater emphasis on a teacher's knowledge of content. While knowledge is very important, generally the most successful teachers are also gifted with an ability to engage and sustain the attention of students in lessons by conveying enthusiasm for the opportunity to teach students about the topic. Engaging all students in learning is essential.

It also requires the willingness to explore or create diverse methods of instruction to make learning something students can actively experience through direct interaction, rather than as passive listeners. Imagine having the ability to capture and hold onto the attention of every student and make them love learning without their even realizing they are learning. Students know, respect, and look forward to learning from teachers who they know love teaching. Basically, unabashed passion for the opportunity to teach students, combined with authentic interactions with students, are among the hallmarks of good teachers who know about the importance of building a rapport with students to support a positive learning culture in their classroom.

Let's return to the teacher assigned to teach a lesson about a rock. What's immediately evident is not what she is teaching, but her engaging demeanor, enthusiasm, and how she structured the lesson.

She sees herself as the facilitator who invites student curiosity, by allowing them to use their imagination to discover the variety of elements. Efforts to have students working in groups to have thoughtful interactions are guided by prepared questions distributed to each group. It's also a great sign of learning how to prepare for every phase of a lesson. Preparation combined with her enthusiasm and level of passion for teaching makes learning in her class so contagious that the level of energy generated by every student fully engaged with discovering every facet of that rock— including its origins, properties, various ways of using it, and a range of other previously unknown information—is the reason students can barely hear the bell signaling the end of the class. On the surface, the topic of exploring the dimensions and properties of a rock sounds like it would likely put most people to sleep. But in the class taught by this teacher, when the bell rings students are audibly and visibly disappointed that the class has come to an end. The lesson was done so masterfully it generates a buzz that travels with the students fortunate enough to have experienced "this fantabulous lesson about a single freakin' rock" to their next class. (Author took the liberty of imagining that comment being said by students.)

Let's resume the story. So, the students proceed to their next class, where the teacher impatiently awaits their arrival. He is annoyed that they are late because the bell rang several minutes ago. The moment students arrive at the door, even before crossing the threshold between the hallway and the room's entrance, they pick up on his vibe. It's a vibe that is usually communicated in a familiar demeanor that conveys, "My job is to teach, and your job is to enter the room quietly, sit down, take out your books and notebooks, grab a pen or pencil, look up at the board, and do the 'Do Now.' No talking!"

But prior to students' entering the room, he heard the commotion of their laughter as they were coming around the corner and knew from whence it came. You see, he's fed up with the noise and exuberance that frequently emanates from the class around the corner and down the hall. In fact, there are moments when lessons erupt into laughter and good-natured cajoling among the students and his colleague, and that actually infuriates him even more. At the end of the day, when all teachers submit their attendance for each class to the main office, he can't resist looking at the class attendance of the teacher he inherits the ruckus bunch from on Mondays and Wednesdays. *But he hears the ruckus even on days he isn't scheduled to receive his colleague's students.* While examining the attendance submitted by his colleague, he notices the disparity: despite being assigned the same number of students as his colleague, the volume of students *always* in attendance in her class drops by a third or more by the time students arrive to his class. On this particular day, only half of those same students made it to his class. Naturally, that sets off his feelings of resentment. But fueling his ongoing discontent was the absence of any action taken by the school leader when he reported the disparity in student numbers between the two classes several weeks ago. Unbeknownst to him, action was taken by the school leader. Instead of starting discussions admonishing students for their absence, the leader thought it best to inquire about the reasons why they were "no shows."

Students seemed eager to share their reasons for frequently showing up late or deciding to skip the class. Their perceptions ranged from the teacher's obsession with consequences to his preoccupation with rule infractions, which seemed to matter more than anything else, and that no learning was taking place due to the little time the teacher devoted to teaching. But the one common complaint repeated by students was enduring the teacher's rants when the "no shows" eventually return to class on subsequent days. The rants were cruel and degrading. The teacher also had a tendency to invent subtle or, depending on the kind of day he was having, not-so-subtle ways of letting them know he was in charge and had absolutely *zero!* tolerance for their absences from class, but especially in the case of those who intentionally skipped his class after attending their previous class.

School leaders who are genuinely concerned about the well-being of students and their right to an education are left with two choices in situations such as this: either ignore the situation and hope it eventually blows over, as is too often the default response, or proceed with documenting incidents and meet with the teacher to convey concerns about what students report, followed with a plan of actionable steps they need to take to improve their performance. The outcome of the second choice has to be anticipated, and the meeting cannot be concluded without making expectations clear that retaliatory actions against students not only will not be tolerated but will be perceived as a direct violation of the entire agreement. Retaining their job is often the greatest motivating factor in altering professional behaviors. However, while strongly preferred, that is not always the outcome. In fact, requests to the district for dismissal from teaching and other staff positions, despite well-documented reasons why, are rarely expedited.

Students are impacted by teachers who impede their ability to learn. When students accurately assess a teacher who has no passion for teaching and who lacks compassion, over time, the students' efforts begin to mirror the level of apathy and indifference authoritative and compassionless teachers show them. Ironically, when uncaring, less-than-qualified teachers fail to do their job, their status as a union member protects and rewards them by overriding the school leader's documented reports showing evidence for why they declined to offer the teacher a contract for the following year. Yet when students behave with the same level of indifference about learning from someone who is less than interested in providing quality instruction (and who sometimes provides absolutely no instruction), they too are rewarded: they earn failing grades from the authoritative, non-compassionate adult imbued with the power to decide the fate of students he or she does not like. If you know anything about science, you know that chemistry between teachers and students truly matters. Of particular concern is the level of potential abuse that can be created by authoritative and uncaring adults responsible for the educational care and well-being of students. Volatile chemistry between student and teacher, from which many students are unable to escape, is one of the harshest and most unfair dynamic some students are sometimes subjected to.

Oh . . . and one more thing. Adding insult to injury, let's remember that often the teacher who fails a student at the end of the school year is likely to inherit that same student the following year because, as is so often the case, a failed student is often "rewarded" with another year of purgatory with the same teacher. It's just one of the mandatory statutes that hold students, who may have legitimate grievances against authoritative and insensitive teachers, responsible for the inequitable rights afforded to teachers. The consequences of requiring the student to repeat the same course for another year and with the same teacher are detrimental. The fate of any student being assigned to the same teacher who failed them the previous year can be preordained, unless the student can convince his or her parents to transfer them to a new school prior to the start of the new school year. In high school, volatile chemistry between students and teachers is what leads students to seek out doors with "Exit" signs and then never return to school. Students who succeed in transferring from one school to another are not guaranteed they will not encounter other uncaring and authoritative teachers in their new school. If students are assigned to another teacher with a persona similar to that of the teacher who led to their departure from another school, it can simply be too much for some students to endure . . . again; particularly students who tend to be fragile. While rarely spoken about, factors influencing dropout rates at the high school level should include the examination of what influences a student's erosion of trust. Decades of recurring bad chemistry experienced by students is factored into their decision to drop out. To continue to ignore the dynamics of volatile student-teacher relationships that cause students to just quit because they see no way of being able to resolve what they know is an unfair situation, elevates the statistic pile and growing number of children we failed on the promise to never leave them behind.

While many students may outwardly appear unconcerned with receiving failing grades, each *F* builds like a callus, adding another layer of feigned indifference. Some students develop the ability to mask what they may really feel: disappointment, embarrassment, and humiliation. Students perceived as unable to meet academic standards, regardless of the possibility that if provided additional and or alternative methods of instruction they could have achieved academic success, are forced to repeat the same grade the following year. The continued accumulation of failing grades not only makes any possibility of students' reversing the trend of constant failure feel insurmountable, but students are pushed towards the decision to abandon their education.

For those who manage to make it into high school, if some form of additional academic support to address learning deficiencies is not provided during their freshman year, it will result in the continuation of failing and the plummeting of their educational aspirations. As the cycle of failure begins to be repeated by the time students turn 16, they can and often do decide to stop attending school. The decision to drop out is an easier and more viable option than having to withstand further humiliation. For other students who remain, determined to finish high school despite the academic challenges they continue to experience, the revelation about the consequences of earning failing grades on their official transcripts is unexpected and rather shocking news.

Unfortunately, in many urban public schools, students are unaware of the grade-point average (GPA) grading system, the numerical value of every grade earned, and how the overall accumulation of all grades earned throughout their four years in high school can determine eligibility for college acceptance. Instead of being informed about the importance of earning good grades in high school during their middle school years, many students are unaware until their junior year in high school. Consider: if they arrived at high school fully aware of the significance of earning good grades for the purpose of building and maintaining a high GPA, it could serve as a motivation for them to aspire to do their very best.

If the current grading system remains in place, in spite of many reasons why it should not, middle schools have an obligation to inform every eighth-grade student about the GPA system. Students have a right to know about a point system where every *F* is the equivalent to earning zero points, and when added with *A*'s and *B*s worth 4 and 3 points, respectively, each *F* worth zero points will significantly decrease the overall grade-point average on their official transcript. On so many levels, failing grades have a gravitational pull that not only negatively impacts the positive value of passing grades but can also result in long-term consequences. Such consequences can severely limit or remove access to pathways to college and/or career opportunities that lead to entry-level incomes, as well as eligibility for job promotions with pay raises that will eventually lift poor people out of poverty.

How Level of Education Influences Future Income Earnings

IN OUR COUNTRY, BEING BORN INTO POVERTY SHOULD NOT CONDEMN a person to a permanent status of poverty. But if we maintain the current status quo of continually providing 20th century education that, despite numerous well-intended reform efforts, continues to result in non-sustainable or insignificant improvements, more generations of students will be left behind. Many of the proposed reforms have been ineffectual because they were designed to retroactively fit into an education structure that currently exists, resulting in either a Band-Aid fix or the surgical removal of something, a few things, or many things that were identified as areas in need of improving yet netted no meaningful gains.

What we have inherited is the continuation of rhetorical promises ensuring all students will receive a quality education. But words and empty promises have left generations of poorly educated students in a state of stagnation that is directly attributable to educational neglect over a span of years in which they were eligible for and entitled to a quality education but did not receive it. Then, predictably, the lack of a quality education prevented any chance of poorly educated students from advancing up the social and economic ladder of success. Instead. it stunted the true potential of their educational growth that then condemned them to low-skilled jobs earning incomes at or below poverty level or being excluded from a labor force that requires a high school diploma. The pervasive widening of America's education achievement gap is reflected in the increasing level of income inequality among adults, who are also American citizens residing in one of the richest countries in the world, so that many of them live in abject poverty. Until we shift away from outdated and ineffective educational practices that are ignored by school district leaders and city officials who allocate funding for schools, future income disparities will persist for students who currently reside in poor neighborhoods and attend underperforming schools.

III.
Collaborative High Schools for College and Career Readiness

All Roads Leading to Prosperity

WHETHER IN THE CITY OR THE SUBURBS, HIGH SCHOOL students are entitled to quality education that equips with them with the skills necessary to access pathways to prosperity in college and careers. Access to pathways of prosperity for most youths residing in low-income and low-resource communities must begin with providing all students with quality education in state-of-the-art modern schools that are designed to motivate and support the achievement of student college and career aspirations. If we are to put all students on a path to prosperity in the 21st century, it will take reconstructing the way we think about education, and a commitment to constructing 21st century public schools. People in the US who have bachelor's degrees earn more in median lifetime earnings than those who don't; men earn about $900,000 more, and women earn about $630,000 more.[2]

One possibility of providing a modernized education system in public schools in urban and rural communities across America is the development of Collaborative High Schools. The Collaborative High School Campus Model is an education platform that integrates the development of career skills and college readiness with content-based instruction. Unlike the current education model, the curriculums, course content, and instruction are integral to, *not separate from*, each individual student's career aspirations.

The focus of the Collaborative High School Campus Model is to foster collaboration between career instructors, college professors, and high school teachers working together to plan a high-competency-based job-skills training program concurrent with academic standards-based curriculums. The job-training programs must include hands-on experiential career instruction resulting in students' attaining entry-level skills and a certificate or license for use after high school graduation. The college-readiness program of the Collaborative High School Campus Model develops skills that will result in students' building independent learning habits, gaining time-management skills, prioritizing assignments embedded in a course syllabus format, and developing competency in writing, reading, research, analysis, and other college-related skills for successful completion of a college-degree program.

Another significant difference from the current traditional high school model is giving students options in their senior year. Those who choose to attend college should be permitted to enroll in college-level courses and complete the equivalent of their freshman year during their senior year. Students choosing not to attend college but interested in pursuing a career after high school should be permitted to acquire employment as a paid apprentice for their senior year. Some students may choose to attend college part time and pursue a paid apprenticeship position. Collaborative High Schools will be a contemporary, progressive and flexible educational model dedicated to students who enter their freshman year with a lot of guidance and support but by their senior year will emerge as young adults ready to take on the responsibility of making their own choices and having successfully completed a year of college and/or become ready for full-time employment at or beyond entry-level employment in a career of their choosing.

One of the cornerstones of 21st century state-of-the-art Collaborative High Schools will be to improve the quality of education by overhauling the outdated instructional delivery system and replacing it with more rigorous and current education curriculums with content linked to specific areas of career interest. Linking content to careers will deepen interest in courses and make curriculums more relevant. Collaborative High Schools designed to prepare students for success in college, and the eventual careers they are truly interested in pursuing after high school or college, will result in well-educated students who will be better prepared to take advantage of numerous opportunities. One portion of a longitudinal study found that career and technical education students reported higher levels of involvement in career planning.[3] Highly skilled and well-educated high school graduates will be on a path of upward educational mobility, which will then lead to upward economic and social mobility. These students are also less likely to be at the mercy of life on the streets, where they are placed in harm's way and ultimately left to make potentially catastrophic choices. Having a quality education will also significantly decrease the rate of incarceration among urban youths.

Outside urban areas where people of color reside, people living beyond the borders of this violence have the luxury of watching those in the throes of absolute inconsolable bereavement on their television or other media outlet, and then casually moving on to something else. These well-resourced, stable, and safe communities allow the illusion of distance between the lives they live and those living in poverty, pain, and grief—all predictable byproducts of living in dysfunctional and poorly resourced communities. Compared to people living in less-than-ideal conditions, the availability of high-quality resources serves as the only contrasting difference for the way they deeply and lovingly care for their children. Access to good schools, healthcare, and high-paying jobs enable them to provide a higher quality of life for their children from birth to adulthood.

If we really want to take measures to end this cycle of burying our children while they are still children, or burying young adults in the prime of what could have been a promising life, it is time to do many things differently. Education always has been and still is one way to make a significant positive impact on the lives of those who could potentially pick up a gun or knife and use it against potential victims. We can and must intervene on behalf of current and future generations of black males killing or being killed. The needless high rate of violence and loss of life, combined with the ever-increasing numbers of uneducated or poorly educated youths in many poor urban and rural communities, can be radically changed by addressing one of the main contributors to decades of perpetual poverty in those communities across America: our public schools.

There is no doubt that providing our urban youths with better public education opportunities will allow them to access a higher quality education that prepares them for success in college and careers. Access to the highest quality of education will also reverse the current trend of subjecting people living in our poorest communities from having to permanently remain victims of America's lowest living standards. Every American citizen has to feel the urgency of the current crisis we are in. We also have to collectively demand an immediate change that will shift the cycle away from allowing our poorest citizens and their children to continue spiraling towards a morally reprehensible abyss, where few to no opportunities exist. Significant changes in our public education system can truly alter the course for our urban youths. Collaborative High Schools will immediately alter every individual student's life, as well as our society overall.

If we continue to do nothing, do people really believe the dysfunction in urban communities will be contained? Do they think that these people will remain discontent within the parameters of their government-enforced enclaves, still known today, in the 21st century, as ghettos or the projects? The current zones that contain our country's most disregarded, disenfranchised, imprisoned, and severely neglected populations who are subjected to the lowest educational standards, poorest quality of health care, and lowest income brackets, contain untapped potential that is grossly overlooked and undervalued but includes enormous talent. These people are educationally capable and have waited long enough for meaningful and serious educational resources that will put them on a real path to success. How much longer do we think our young urban brothers and sisters will accept centuries-old denigration from a society that denies real access to a level playing field where they too can live up to their real potential? Current generations and their future offspring want to contribute to the economic and education growth of our collective society and demonstrate how capable they are through employment that will positively impact every American's life.

When our urban youths are engaged in their education and career training, their focus on achieving their aspirations keeps them in classrooms and off the streets. Redirecting their focus on academic achievement will also level the proverbial playing field across America because urban schools will produce well-educated Americans who, regardless of which neighborhood or socio-economic income status they were born into, will truly be able to gain access to a college-degree program or transition into a career-training institution or job after high school.

Ensuring social upward mobility and keeping our streets safe are just two of the many benefits that Collaborative High Schools will contribute to effectively addressing. Collaborative High Schools will focus on improving the quality of education and result in measurable outcomes such as attainment of higher grade-point averages (GPAs) among students across all of America's urban communities. This will render as moot those past but seriously considered discussions within the NCAA about the possibility of lowering GPA eligibility standards for student athletes. Rather than lowering academic standards in high school under the auspices of helping urban youths attend college, we can save our nation from the steady erosion of academic competency among our poor communities. All that proposed policy would have achieved is to increase the potential for a higher number of black student athletes with lower GPAs, and lesser abilities to read and write well enough to access college-level content. Predictably, their inability to understand and learn content taught would inevitably put them at greater risk for dropping out of college or being unable to qualify for a college degree despite completing four glorious years of success in their collegiate sport.

We must stop thinking only of enlarging the popularity of sports and endowments at colleges and universities and consider the consequences of student athletes with low GPAs being even less qualified to earn a meaningful career if they are not among the few drafted into a professional league after college. Student athletes who completed four years of college and managed to earn a national championship for their school, but departed without earning a degree, are left floundering. If they do not succeed in being recruited onto professional teams, they are humiliated to discover that their high school diploma and a national championship does not open doors to the opportunities promised by athletic directors, coaches, and college scouts when they were recruited. It's a challenge to read the technically written clauses among the flurry of documents stating in fine print that "no guarantees" can be promised of the incentives coaches and recruiters boasted about during those wild and frenzied days of recruitment.

Despite students' being barely able to read at middle school level, their athletic skills were their ticket into a four-year college program. But the wake-up call came on the day they left the campus without the privilege of marching in cap and gown and hearing their name inviting them to walk across the stage and receive their college degree. The reading skills they lacked when they arrived in college were never improved upon and likely contributed to their exit from college without a college degree. But those coaches and athletic directors who showered them with praise and "attaboys" while patting them on the back and who they fondly thought of as father figures knew about your low-level reading skills when they recruited you. They also knew and relied on your inability to read the clauses written in small print. And they were made aware of your academic status because they, too, received a copy of your transcripts at the end of each semester.

Coaches and the universities they represent have been eager to remove the low-standard education guardrails preventing them from exploiting poorly educated students for the purpose of entertaining alumni and enriching their schools. Sadly, considering lowering the GPA requirements was a blatant nefarious act of predatory behavior by colleges and universities who had no problem dumbing-down academic standards solely for the financial gain of their institutions. If colleges and universities are truly committed to recruiting students, who are also athletes, they should place greater emphasis on the *scholars* when rewarding students with scholarships while raising their entrance standards from the current 2.5 GPA to 3.5, *after* we overhaul our public schools in urban communities. Increasing the GPA prior to changes in the educational system would place those who are already at a disadvantage at even greater disadvantage because their schools offer education that just barely enables students to meet the current 2.5 GPA standard. Increasing the standard without improving the quality of education will make the current uneven playing field even more uneven. Placing more rigorous academic expectations among the criteria required of student athletes may improve performance and graduation success rates because schools will be more selective in admissions when choosing students for athletic scholarships.[4] Upgrades to our public education standards and instructional practices would ensure all students are well prepared to earn higher GPAs and succeed as scholars and athletes at the college level. And they will be eligible to walk across the stage and receive their degree.

It is also apparent that the economic recovery from the 2007–2009 recession has benefited many but not all of America's citizens. Prosperity seems to have eluded public schools across many inner cities, while those who live in communities where residents earn significantly higher incomes are the beneficiaries of education upgrades in curriculums, classroom resources, and newly constructed schools designed to adapt and integrate technological resources to support the mission of ensuring that every student receives the highest quality of education in the 21st century. And they continue to prosper. Those same resources, combined with the singular mission of providing the highest level of quality education, are exactly what public schools in many urban and rural communities need. Public school districts in affluent communities are succeeding because, in addition to having more wealth to invest in education, members of those communities have also been strong and unyielding advocates of education, making it one of their highest priorities. The disparities in levels of income between poor communities and communities populated with high-income earners is evident in the level of financial investment in education that citizens are able, or unable, to contribute to funding their schools. However, there are more equitable solutions available to level the educational economic divide. Unfortunately, because school districts in America are largely funded by property taxes, they offer lower-quality education in lower-income areas. Conversely, other nations provide equal per-student funding from tax revenue to all schools.[5]

Having strong community advocates unequivocally committed to achieving and maintaining high quality educational standards for their children, from pre-kindergarten through high school, is a universal aspiration among all communities. Allocation of tax revenues to build new schools equipped with state-of-the-art technology and other upgrades in education is a means to maintaining their most highly valued and systemic goal: their determination to keep pace with innovative changes in the 21st century to ensure their children are well educated and qualified for employment in industries requiring intellectually adept and emotionally intelligent employees who are capable of learning quickly and working collaboratively with others. Persistently pursuing educational achievement, for the purpose of obtaining future employment prosperity for any student, is admirable. Reconciling decades of economic disparities between students fortunate enough to be born and raised in financially well-off communities and others born into poverty is America's biggest challenge. Replacing run-down and dilapidated public schools with new modern schools fully equipped with 21st century technology in impoverished and middle-income communities will signal that we, as one nation, agree that the educational and career aspirations of every child matter, regardless of where they live. The most promising gateway to future prosperity for all students is to offer quality education inside of new schools built in every zip code across the country.

Why Our Students Need College- and Career-Readiness High Schools

EXTENSIVE RESEARCH CONSISTENTLY SHOWS DECADES OF overwhelming data that reflect the persistent failure rates for high school graduation in low-income urban school districts across the country. In recent years, there has also been an increase in the number of college freshmen enrolled in developmental-level math, reading, and writing courses due to the lack of skills required in freshman-level courses. The developmental courses are not worth any credits, but they do add the cost of an additional year of college. When students who have not been adequately prepared for college enroll in college, they are often forced to take remedial classes to catch up with content they should have learned in high school. These courses often do not count towards the degree, but the student still has to pay for them. Often, students who are enrolled in remediation cannot graduate on time, and they have lower rates of completion overall.[6] The additional year of tuition becomes a deterrent and disincentive for the few who want to but cannot afford to continue college. The high dropout rate of minority students in college-degree programs is abysmal. These students eventually join the growing numbers of unskilled adults who are unable to access 21st century jobs. Collaborative High Schools would break the cycle of inadequately prepared high school students who aspire to obtain access to college degrees and successful careers.

Collaborative High Schools would be career-oriented high schools partnering with colleges and businesses. The multi-partnership would consist of a four-year curriculum plan developed by the team of school leaders, teachers, college professors, career instructors, and representatives of school councils or governance boards. The curriculums would integrate the core high school subject areas with college-readiness assignments such as thesis- and research-based projects. Each career-oriented high school's curriculum planning team would identify and embed information related to the career into the math, science, history, humanities, arts, foreign languages, financial literacy, and technology courses required for earning a diploma.

Embedding career-related content into academic subjects would make lessons relevant and would capture and maintain the interest of students. Colleges would assign professors and businesses would assign career instructors and mentors to each high school. Professors would assist high school faculty in designing course syllabi that mirror the format and expectations of college courses. Class instruction could blend high school and college teaching practices. Career instruction would have performance- and competency-based curriculum standards to enable students to learn and perform hands-on tasks associated with the businesses. All career instruction should be in state-of-the-art, technologically designed spaces that accurately model workspaces found in career worksites similar to where students will eventually become employed. The industrial classrooms should mirror labs or workstations and be fully equipped with all of the necessary tools, manuals, and technology resources related to the specific career that each high school is designed for.

All 21st century, state-of-the-art, career-based Collaborative High Schools should also bring the collaborative team research-and-development model commonly used in most workplaces into the academic and industrial classrooms. If the contemporary workspace operates in a manner that encourages the exchange and development of ideas through collaboration, high schools should design models of project-based instruction where the students focus greater emphasis on learning through a more hands-on approach, while teachers and industry instructors take on the role of learning and collaboration facilitators. The ability to work collaboratively with colleagues at work exposes high school students to various models of working with others in a cooperative process. More importantly, building the habit of learning independently and in collaboration with others is the best way to prepare students for the broad range of working conditions they will encounter in their not-so-distant futures.

Another benefit of using collaborative-based team research-and-development projects at the high school level is the value of students' learning how to work through challenging issues. Whether the issues arise through determining the best approach to completing a project or resolving differences among one another, team members will learn through self-discovery and trial and error how to tackle challenges with the help of teacher as facilitator, not problem solver. Collaborative learning builds character while introducing students to the social constructs of how to be nurturing and encouraging of one another. Students will develop an understanding of the complexities of how to listen to a range of ideas, regardless of agreement or disagreement, and then figure out a fair and equitable process for keeping or eliminating recommendations or developing humane ways for respectfully rejecting contributions without its having the appearance of personally rejecting the individual. These same principles could have an impact, hopefully positive, on the way students resolve conflicts outside of the school setting; and over time, they will learn about the importance of having compassion for one another, recognize the importance of placing greater emphasis on team, and learn the benefit of investing in decisions that are in the best interests of their team.

Collaborative High Schools should also have school cultures that nurture team building and openly invite creative thinking and learning through discovery. The process of working collaboratively to create, design, and problem-solve in a cooperative manner to achieve collective outcomes, through contributions of team members responsible for completing projects, is a common practice in many industries. Unlike adults, students will need to experience through trial and error in order to determine what kind of process may be needed to effectively achieve the group's goals. Students need opportunities to learn the art of negotiation. The ability to include other people's perspectives and contributions may come through a process of testing the validity of everyone's ideas based on a set of neutral and fair standards agreed upon by the group. The process of including or eliminating ideas, hypotheses, or assertions can be determined by the results instead of by how students feel about their peers. Students must be allotted sufficient time to experience and then learn how to take risks in a group setting. Given that all students enter most group activities possessing different degrees of comfort zones when it comes to taking risks in public, the challenge of expanding comfort zones is achievable through exercises that build trust. But trust relies on everyone's being committed to respectful rules of engagement, where everyone feels encouraged to contribute; and whether or not their contributions are accepted, they feel their ideas were not simply dismissed through malice but welcomed and carefully considered as part of an inclusive and fair process. Business instructors and teachers can plan visits to various industries where high school students can observe, in real time, various methods companies use to facilitate team building. Seniors in pursuit of apprenticeships will benefit when company experts in team-based project-development exercises model ways students can acquire team-building skills throughout high school. Their training experience will strengthen their competency and confidence while applying for apprenticeships at real worksites. Prospective companies will appreciate their investment and support of hiring students from schools that invested the time and training to ensure they were well prepared to make a seamless transition into group-based projects at their organizations.

College preparation throughout the first three years of high school will offer great advantage to students by supporting a smooth transition from high school to college. Throughout high school, reading assignments should place a greater emphasis on teaching students how to read for depth to improve deeper understanding of all content while they learn analytical and critical thinking skills. High school students need to build the habit of fact checking, supporting facts with evidence, accurately citing sources, quoting references, and learning the difference between opinions and facts; and they need to become capable of producing a cohesive and well-written thesis. All classes should require students to present and defend their arguments in public speaking forums. Students should be able to demonstrate that they are knowledgeable, well-informed, and broadly familiar with the multiple perspectives pertaining to a topic. They should learn how to articulate clearly, in written and spoken form, what they have learned.

The focal point has to shift from today's outdated curriculums to a new model that addresses how earning an education is perceived, and that looks through the eyes of the clientele we serve: the students. This new model will be a collaborative partnership representing the combined resources of schools, colleges and universities, and businesses dedicated to providing the highest quality of comprehensive career- and college-readiness instruction. Ultimately, many high school students want and need access to educational resources that enable them to earn a high school diploma, prepare them with the skills necessary for completion of a college degree program, and provide access to job-skills development programs.

In today's classrooms across many urban school districts, the majority of middle and high school students just don't see the meaning or purpose of sitting in classes taking courses that they perceive as having little to no connection to their future. In spite of recent reform efforts in education, the high number of students underperforming over the span of many decades, as well as the continued decline in high school graduation rates in urban communities across America, serves as an indication that if we really want to improve academic performance, we need to shift our habit of developing pedagogical practices based on traditional educational thinking to asking two key questions: what do students aspire to achieve, and how do we develop education that directly links their aspirations to what they are experiencing in their day-to-day education?

One way to generate and sustain genuine interest in learning is to link learning to the career aspirations of students. Imagine schools' enabling students to deepen their investment in their education by accessing curriculum that integrates career content and topics with all content areas. Students choosing careers in medicine want to understand the relevance to their career choice of content learned in academic courses. Finding purpose in education can be strengthened through revealing the direct or indirect relationship of subjects to their potential careers. Highly educated Collaborative High School graduates would reverse the concerns and apprehensions of college and business institutions reluctant to welcome students from urban schools. Districts with 21st century college and career readiness programs would let those institutions know their concerns were heard; that they are being responsive to the common assertions of colleges and business leaders, that students are not adequately prepared for college or the labor force.

Many states have thousands of vocational high schools that have classroom settings equipped with industrial materials and aligned with curriculums designed to facilitate the acquisition of skills related to various trades or industries. Vocational schools are often popular because they focus on preparation for entry into the labor force, which is also experiencing the impact of a shortage of employment resources in the current economy.

Collaborative High Schools would be a hybrid of classroom settings combined with 21st century career-oriented vocational instruction. The primary purpose of Collaborative High Schools is to provide students access to adequate preparation for 21st century jobs.

There are several components to developing a cohesive Collaborative High School. The first is deciding what area of industry each school will represent. The second is having a physical structure designed for academic courses and workshops, laboratories, or industry spaces to accommodate industry-related instruction. It is vital that students are exposed to school-based learning labs to acquire the real-life skills applicable to their career of interest. All schools must also deliver quality education that meets the highest academic standards.

Recent developments in education, such as credit-recovery initiatives and statewide standards, are important steps in improving the quality of education. Many urban school districts have invested in alternative instructional platform options, such as online courses, to help students recover academic credit. Efforts are also being made to provide more student-centered methods of instruction to increase engagement in learning, such as blended learning for personalized instruction. However, urban public education needs more than the comprehensive overhaul of curriculum standards mandated by states, particularly in states using Common Core Standards. Research has shown that, in spite of the introduction of Common Core, achievement rates have not improved for students who are economically disadvantaged.[7]

It is the continued evidence of data provided in numerous researches that elevates the need for the newly proposed initiatives in state-of-the-art public schools in all urban communities across the country. The need to literally build new schools and programs from the ground up is because past decades devoted to reforming education were mostly stymied by an expectation that they could actually fix what ailed an already outdated and ineffective education system. Many reforms served as temporary Band-Aids, holding the system in place for a few years. There may have been a period of success for reforms and other new initiatives that were retrofitted on top of outdated structures representing an equally outdated educational system designed for a totally different era, but the continued existence of a failing system made reforms unsustainable. In fact, the recent education improvement initiatives over the past couple of decades have done little to keep high school students from dropping out.

Despite the best intentions, our inability to reverse dropout rates and keep students in schools could be an indication that it may be time to seek input from the primary clientele being served by schools: the students. We can start by asking our college students to help identify the deficits in their middle and high school education that may have contributed to their not being adequately prepared for college. We can also survey high school graduates who entered the workforce to share their entry-level work experiences. Presumably we will learn that high schools could have done a better job preparing them for their transition into the workforce. If we want to attract students to attend and remain in school, we must address the most crucial issue that has continually impeded our nation's ability to move forward and provide meaningful education: the overhaul of our schools. No amount of building renovations or continuation of retrofitting new curriculum models without upgrades to pedagogical practices will lead to more educational prosperity for students. Reversing the dropout trend is absolutely necessary and possible. There is a particular scene in a 1999 film, *Field of Dreams*, where the main character repeatedly hears a voice whispering, "If you build it, they will come." That line resonates in many ways with the potential of more promising outcomes that will result from investing in overhauling schools and our public education system.

We must summon the courage and financial resources necessary to finally take the most meaningful step in education reform that has eluded our common sensibilities for too long. It's time to overhaul our entire educational infrastructure, starting with the construction of new, state-of-the-art 21st century schools designed to support the development of academic scholarship, skills for careers, and meaningful preparation for college success. Collaborative High Schools on a campus setting in urban communities will help motivate students to want to attend and complete high school. The network of career schools and resources featured in the video, *A Collaborative High School Campus Model*, will appeal to families and students across the country. The model is intended to elevate education across districts where generations have been denied access to quality education. Modernizing all of our public schools is the one chance for us to prove our collective belief that all children possess the capacity to learn. Backing up what we believe to be true has to be shown by viewing all children as worthy of a new public education system with new schools designed to help them achieve their educational and career aspirations. Remember, "If we build it, they will come"—and succeed!

The video is available on the author's website at
ImagineAMorePromisingFuture.com/video

Imperatives of a 21st Century Education

PRAGMATICALLY SPEAKING, IF WE DO NOT REMOVE OUTDATED educational barriers, it will be a missed opportunity to move forward and away from substandard education. That matters because, regardless of a student's objectives after high school, it is imperative that their education prepares them for the rigorous demands of university or professional life. Businesses in the 21st century need a different labor force compared to what used to pass as even "marginally qualified" for employment in past centuries. Modern industries have surpassed outdated labor models, making our public education system—still using centuries-old models in old school buildings—a relic of our past. So here we are at a consequential crossroads where, ultimately, all students will need to be prepared for employment. Our public schools can no longer remain in a default position of bearing no responsibility for unprepared, yet potentially capable and available laborers leaving high school with no ability to participate in our growing labor industry. It could not be more evident that students today, who opt to pursue a career path directly after high school, need to be equipped with the job skills required to compete for employment opportunities.

The current education model presents a number of barriers that prevent adequate preparation for students to successfully compete for and enter the labor force of the current century. In addition to the need for employment skills, there is also a high demand for highly educated candidates. The quality of education in our public education system is so far behind that of other countries that many tech companies in need of highly educated workers recruit highly educated immigrants from countries that exemplify a commitment and willingness to invest in high education standards. Today's public high schools are in dire need of an overhaul if we ever want to give students a chance to participate in one of the most progressive and creative-driven labor forces in a historic time of welcoming people who are not just well educated but also highly imaginative. To rectify this issue, high school education must shift its curriculums and focus to the needs of the 21st century. If we do nothing to modernize our public education system, low-performing public schools will remain stagnant and may eventually be in danger of becoming extinct.

But like most revolutions, proposing a complete overhaul of our public education system, to many people, may seem potentially disastrous. Eliminating the current status quo under which public schools operate to install a modern education system is the revolution so many have been patiently waiting for. And therein lies part of the problem. The willingness to continue patiently waiting is no longer an acceptable response to mounting evidence that the overwhelming majority of students underperforming in our public schools are stuck in an education system that was created in a different era and shows no sign of having evolved to keep pace with the current educational and employment needs of today. People living in poor and many working-class communities unfairly exist in the throes of a widening chasm of quality education they receive compared to their counterparts living in upscale or higher-income communities. Narrowing the quality gap in education among those living in poor and working-class communities can be achieved across all public schools. We simply have to recognize the benefits of embracing a 21st century public education system that may hold the greatest potential for achieving a promise made over and over again: providing all children attending public schools, from pre-kindergarten through high school, access to a quality education. But unlike the current system, the newly designed schools have to have high academic standards embedded in high interest-based curriculums delivered through a broad range of instructional methods designed to be inclusive of the variety of student learning profiles. Lessons should be designed placing greater emphasis on student-centered learning through active engagement and exploration, to give students opportunities to experience education and not just sit and absorb what they are told.

For children raised in economically prosperous communities, the promise of providing quality education has been met and kept. But children from economically disadvantaged communities or working-class communities living on the precipice of poverty, if not at or below it, have so many obstacles to overcome. While equitable access to quality education will not cure all ills, access to quality education will dramatically increase the likelihood of academic success for children routinely left behind in underperforming schools. Elimination of barriers can end the systemic inequitable allocation of financial, staffing, and instructional resources. The yearly practice of reducing much-needed education resources has a ripple effect, impacting performance outcomes in other areas than can be used to determine whether or not schools remain open.

One particular area that influences decisions about potential school closure is statewide exams, even though exam performances are a reflection of student output of information linked to input of what may or may not have been taught—and obviously not learned. High-income and well-resourced communities that designate education among their highest priorities have had decades of success, which is evident in high scoring averages achieved by their student population on statewide standardized assessments. This is absolutely commendable. But is it fair to compare those results with the results of kids whose performances are significantly impacted by the perpetual cycle of educational barriers? Another area impacted by the ripple effect of education barriers and the annual reduction of school budgets is the plight of average-level performing students. They, like the rest of their peers performing at high or low levels, may possess an inordinate amount of ability to achieve at even higher levels if provided quality educational resources. But for so many students, regardless of their current levels of performance, the potential to have a real opportunity to obtain higher levels of academic achievement will never be realized if they reside in communities where educational barriers are the norm.

The plight of students across the entire public education spectrum attending underperforming schools ought to be of concern to everyone, but especially our academically challenged or differently abled and fragile learners with and without Individualized Educational Plans (IEPs). Also, we rarely, if ever, put a spotlight on one of the most overlooked population of students who do achieve academic success in class but who routinely are perceived as underperforming solely based on the results of a test . . . where the outcome differs from their exceptional daily performances in class. Many people are unaware of this population of students who are adversely impacted by tests. While taking the test, for some students it's the built-up pressure of expectations that is uppermost on their minds, not the items on the test. For other students, testing just seems to trigger an aversion anticipating the test or the moment they enter a testing site. Despite levels of anxieties for whatever reasons, insisting and sometimes forcibly making all students endure testing situations with little interest in at least making an effort to identify what is causing their level of apprehension or, for some, all-out fear, will no doubt result in scoring outcomes that are highly susceptible and inaccurate.

And still we have yet to design a broader array of assessments tailored to the needs of various individuals who should not be forced into another one-size-fits-all situation that not only has them forced to take tests that inaccurately reflect their real potential, but is detrimental to their emotional, psychological, and sometimes physical well-being. Students who exhibit none of those conditions but arrive at school on exam day, and often many other days, in a state of obvious stress related to home or neighborhood issues or ongoing conflicts with peers at school that make them feel unsafe, are also being forced to take the high-stakes exams under the worst conditions. How in the world can we ever expect to trust the accuracy of test results by kids subjected to any number of conflicting circumstances? The way to end identity shaming caused by failing grades and poor performances on any exam or standardized assessment is to change the failing system that keeps failing students.

The challenge of overhauling our public education system was inspired by thoughts about creating a system capable of helping every student gain entrance onto the proverbial *level playing field* that welcomes any and all who are qualified, with access to future employment and income prosperity. The constant wondering led to the reimagining of how to replace our public education system at the high school level. True access and entry onto all level playing fields is absolutely within our reach, except the focus must shift away from relying on whether or not the playing field is truly level and will guarantee fair access to everyone. We know it is not and will not be level. So called "level playing fields" were constructed under conditions designed to restrict access to a chosen population only. The only remedy for ensuring inclusivity of all students is to focus on amping-up the education performance levels of all kids. But the students will need a more progressive and modern education system designed to help them achieve high academic standards.

A progressive and modern education system at the high school level has to invest in preparing students for careers and college equally. But more importantly, as represented in the Collaborative High School Campus Model, it is an education system unafraid to embrace student choice. For students to be empowered to decide whether they want to pursue employment immediately after completing high school or attend college, they will need a modern education system that provides access to diverse educational pathways designed to help them achieve their aspirations. Enter any high school classroom today and you will find that many students, perhaps most, admit they are bored with school but enjoy socializing with friends. Then ask them if they know what they want to do after high school. Most students have been convinced they should and therefore will apply to college. But many of those students do not really want to attend college. Realizing the short list of options, including getting a job or signing up for military service, many students choose applying to college as a default preference, but not their true preference. While not openly communicated, students are very aware of unspoken expectations for all juniors and seniors to not appear to be in limbo or indecisive about their post-high-school plans. They are under so much social and emotional pressure from teachers, family members, community mentors, and especially their peers who exude so much confidence in knowing, with certainty, their future plans.

What's so unfortunate is that, even among those who are decisive, there is a sense of having to select a path based on the limited availability of options as well as what others expect of them, but not what they really may want to do. Even worse, many leave high school unsure of what to do next because they were never exposed to the multitude of options that exist but were never made known to them during high school; nor are they given an opportunity to select and then prepare to access a different option from applying to college. Consequently, they sign up for military service or just get whatever job is available. Many high school students are unaware of so many employment opportunities linked to different careers that may be of genuine interest to them. That is because they don't attend schools that reveal this information or provide career training programs during high school that would allow them to be ready to take advantage of those post-high-school employment opportunities.

Instead, many students attending high school in the 21st century are unsure about what they want to or will do upon completion of high school. They willingly abide by what is expected of them, 180 days each year. They attend school because they know it's where they ought to be, but for too many, it is not where they want to be. That is why students need a new way of experiencing education. The first step in building student enthusiasm and interest in attending school is to offer education programs promoting a range of career choices and development of skills related to careers throughout high school.

The second step is placing into students' hands the decision-making process about what college-preparation or career-training program to pursue. Putting students in charge of deciding, as a central core of their purpose for obtaining a quality education, will spike interest in attending school. Comprehensive career and college-based education programs providing skills-development experiences that enable students to incrementally progress towards achieving, by the end of their high school years, such aspirations as successful enrollment into college or obtaining employment in an entry level position in a career they chose, is so essential to the new way students can and should experience their education. If we link those two areas into a student's high school education experience, it will help them define a purpose for attending school, which then makes learning far more meaningful and beneficial. In fact, giving students the responsibility of making their own education decisions may ignite interest in learning and motivate students to aspire to achieve at even higher performance levels.

If you doubt this as certain, now may be a great time to pause and watch the video, A Collaborative High School Campus Model. *The video features a 21ˢᵗ century education model illustrating how schools can align career and college readiness programs with student aspirations. Visit* ImagineAMorePromisingFuture.com/video

Embedding students in highly advanced 21ˢᵗ century vocational and college-readiness high schools is the surest way students can acquire real skills for their eventual careers. Models like state-of-the-art career and college-readiness Collaborative High Schools are worth considering, and here's why. State-of-the-art, 21ˢᵗ century Collaborative High Schools are modern facilities with contemporary curriculums and instruction that reflect the current skills required for students to be prepared to access 21ˢᵗ century jobs. Triangulation of high schools working in collaboration with colleges and business industries would result in an opportunity to strengthen education at the high school level. For example, a School of Robotics and Engineering, working in partnership with the Massachusetts Institute of Technology's Robotics Program and a robotics and engineering company, could combine the valued resources of all partners to develop and operate the school's program.

Curriculum planning could focus on designing a curriculum that utilizes the knowledge of an industry expert, college professor, and high school teacher to infuse information about robotics and engineering into all required content areas. Students become invested in learning by having their courses and projects connected to their future careers and areas of interest they select. The current disconnect between students and the curriculum taught is one factor contributing to the achievement gap. Much greater interest in attending school will be generated by merging school subjects such as science, math, English language arts, financial literacy, technology, and history with the wealth of information about a specific area related to any 21ˢᵗ century industry that students may want to pursue for their career.

Basically, we would be joining the best practices of college and labor with high schools to ensure all students are participating in college readiness courses and career-based learning in a holistic and comprehensive learning culture that emphasizes performance at the highest standards of academic excellence, while acquiring competency in career-based skills. That is the only way we will successfully help students renew their investment in their education. It is also the way we arrive at educational equity in a systemically inequitable society that does not allow every citizen what is now a privilege for the affluent members of our society. The right of a high-quality education ought to be afforded to all members of our society. It will be a new America where everyone will be prepared to participate in the mainstream of prosperity.

How Students Experience Education in Collaborative High Schools

E DUCATIONAL SUCCESS NEEDS STUDENTS TO BE ASPIRATIONAL. But to be aspirational requires their ability to be surrounded by the abundance of encouragement and educational resources in grades K–12 that equips them with skills necessary to confidently see themselves as capable and ready to participate in a broad spectrum of high school and college readiness classes, including honors classes. Immersing students in pedagogical norms of college during their four years in high school will allow them time to master college-level skills while bolstering their self-confidence. An additional benefit of students possessing college readiness experiences is the potential reduction, if not complete elimination, of feelings of ambivalence, uncertainty, or apprehension that college-bound, but inadequately prepared, high school students from urban public schools across America struggle with.

Students become well prepared when they develop and normalize habits of listening, learning, reading, studying, researching, writing well-developed essays and research papers, performing tasks that develop critical thinking, and reasoning and analyzing various sources of information that represent both similar and different perspectives. This will result in the transformation of students who traditionally learn by regurgitating what they are told to intellectual scholars capable of filtering information through multiple and rigorously challenging processes.

Truthfully, much learning of the content falls to the wayside because greater emphasis has to be placed on multiple learning curves. Learning content while being introduced to the foreignness of an unfamiliar culture such as college life, makes transition into college more complicated. Lack of adequate familiarity of content taught in college courses, coinciding with how to interpret the college professor's class expectations, can be overwhelming for first-year college students. If skills related to time management or prioritization of a multitude of assignments were never addressed during high school, students unfamiliar with the college terrain are set up to fail. The Collaborative High School Campus Model mitigates those inadequacies by using every high school year to teach students these skills. Instead of arriving at campus as a novice, investing time they don't really have, to try to learn how to micromanage a multitude of what feels like insurmountable challenges, Collaborative High School graduates experience freshman year differently. How gratifying it will feel arriving on campus well prepared to survive college culture.

Recent attempts to shift the focus onto the importance of improving one's high school grade-point average and making sure students and their families become informed about and then complete the application processes for colleges, scholarships, and financial aid are vital, but they do not address the real issues of preparedness for college. What value do those steps serve if students successfully perform those tasks but continue to arrive on college campuses unable to read broadly and deeply from a variety of sources, synthesize what they have read, present a well-articulated written or oral analysis of a particular point of view, and properly cite or quote sources in support of their perspective without plagiarizing or neglecting to accurately attribute comments to an original source?

Imagine students from urban public schools being armed with a real sense of readiness and arriving on college campuses not just adequately but fully ready for college because their high school instruction embedded college practices that enabled them to develop competencies and skills related to college. These experiences will not only serve to enlighten them about what awaits them at college but also enable them to view something that once seemed inaccessible as very achievable. The only way to change the current mindset of America's urban-school teens, who typically think attending college is beyond the realm of possibility due to the perception that only so-called "smart" kids apply to college, is to expose them to real college-oriented experiences that will significantly reduce and may even completely eliminate feelings of inadequacy. We have to shift the focus away from the current method of ineffectual educational practices that fuel misconceptions about who should and should not consider college, to practices that include pedagogy and standards similar to those of colleges and universities, which require rigorous instruction preceded by learning how to learn across all content areas and at each grade level. When we do that, we not only debunk those current misconceptions and demystify the unknowns about college, but we can also change the minds of so many urban students who thought college was an elusive thing that they had no right to aspire to.

Students need access to comprehensive college-skill-development opportunities throughout high school to ensure that they are truly ready to successfully take on the range of responsibilities of college. Instead, the majority of public high schools are responding to the urgency to enroll more students into college by becoming factories churning out students capable of giving the appearance of being ready for college based on their ability to complete the process of applying to college, but not truly skilled in getting through college.

In addition to ensuring successful transitions into college and entry-level career positions, state-of-the-art Collaborative High Schools can also serve as an anchor of stability and improve safety in urban communities. After decades of escalating violence in urban communities across America, many have proclaimed intentions of taking measures to reduce violence. Unfortunately, even the best intentions were not always successful. One way to significantly reduce violence is to keep school-age students in school and encourage students between the ages of 16 and 20 to return to school. Reducing the number of students out of school will substantially decrease the number of students loitering on streets. Fewer students roaming neighborhoods during school hours will decrease the number of students engaging in illegal activities, but students do not want to return to the same education system that, for one or a variety of reasons, influenced their decision to drop out of school in the first place. They and their peers currently attending public schools want a good reason and sense of meaningful purpose for attending school. The creation of career-based Collaborative High Schools, with state-of-the-art learning centers designed to provide college readiness skills and career development instruction in urban communities, will motivate students and renew their interest in participating in their education.

Companies and businesses want highly educated and highly skilled candidates to fill the increased number of positions being created in the technological research and development industries. The gap is incredibly huge between the availability of jobs in many areas related to science and technology and citizens equipped with the high level of skills needed to apply for those positions. However, the need to have career-based schools that focus on a broader range of areas, including government, health care, the arts, communication, the trades, media, education, and other areas is equally important because these industries need well-educated and highly skilled workers. The US Bureau of Labor Statistics has information that students can access online to find out what employment projections for different industries will be. This can help students choose careers in fields that have long-term options.[8]

Career-based Collaborative High Schools would strongly support efforts to reduce crime in urban communities, but the model would also greatly benefit students in rural communities and suburban communities across our United States because, in truth, all students possess the same aspirations: becoming well educated and attending college or career training institutes in their high schools that will lead to employment in careers of their choosing.

The link between how students experience their education and their families, who take no pleasure in begging, cajoling, threatening, or promising gifts to incentivize their children and teens to get out of bed and go to school, is also in need of an overhaul. All new and highly upgraded elementary, middle, and high schools would break the long cycle of unenthusiasm so many generations of students and families have endured. Did you know most parents across the entire cultural spectrum in our country see the fulfillment of their children's aspirations as a fulfillment of their own personal aspirations? Parents simply want to experience the pride of seeing their children succeed after all of the time and support they invested in helping them attain success.

The attainment of academic success is even more remarkable when children and teens resiliently perform well, despite challenging circumstances. Those children learn how to coexist with sometimes unimaginable and turbulent circumstances beyond their control. The opportunity to attend school in a network of modern facilities with access to problem-specific counseling resources for any and all challenges, ranging from crises to common issues of daily life concerns, will facilitate a sense of security and comfort as students receive support in overcoming those challenges. Providing a network of counseling resources will help relieve some of the stress students have when they arrive at school and allow them to focus on learning. Perhaps just being able to eagerly anticipate going to school, for some students, provides an opportunity to be enthusiastic about engaging in something that is within their control, and that they can truly enjoy. So many families see education as vital because they know it is the one, and for many the only, available pathway they can hang their hopes on. New and modern schools will annually increase the number of student graduates and family members who fill high school auditoriums across the country, crying tears of joy as they witness something monumental achieved by their sons and daughters. For some, the depth of gratitude runs even deeper because they may have seen obstacles overcome by their sons and daughters who are now proudly earning their diploma in a new and more prosperous education system.

A healthy and prosperous society will benefit from well-educated students prepared for a successful transition into adulthood. At least that is the assumption. But to become a responsible citizen willing to make valuable contributions in all facets of our society, students need a broader and socially oriented educational experience that helps them develop into socially aspirational achievers. The tendency to base contributions to a vibrant and healthy society solely on the basis of academic achievement is simply not enough. A much-overlooked and undervalued attribute among many citizens is understanding that thriving and vibrant communities are the result of the time, effort, and good will that community advocates regularly contribute to their communities.

Ways to help students understand the importance of "giving" and being socially responsible include emphasizing their working collaboratively during lessons, being positive contributors to their school culture through respectful interactions with peers and adults, and taking opportunities to volunteer a few hours each week to support community organizations dedicated to responding to the needs of others. Those communities also recognize the importance of celebrating the results of contributions made by members of their communities. Academics is one area in which community organizations annually show their appreciation for their youths who achieve the highest standards. Providing academic scholarships and other rewards related to academic achievement is a form of letting students know that their academic success is valued by the community because education is a priority in those communities, and it reflects well on the entire community. Any form of student academic and athletic achievement is seen as a positive contribution to the community's reputation. But the most successful and vibrant communities recruit and engage youth participation in community-based organizations devoted to achieving the goals linked to maintaining the community's well-being. Not only do those communities recognize the benefits of engaging their youths in local organizations while attending middle and high school, but they are also cultivating their young citizens to become the next generation of social custodians of their communities.

Modern High Schools as Multipurpose Career Training Programs

INVESTMENT IN MODERN HIGH SCHOOLS WITH CAREER TRAINING programs presents a great opportunity for multiple uses. During the day, students can develop job skills in careers they choose to pursue, and they are ready for employment when they decide to begin their careers. Many will choose to delay starting their career, in order to pursue continuing their education at the college level. But so many others, those who want to pursue employment options and not attend college after high school, will be career ready.

Another benefit of modern schools with career training facilities is the potential of offering evening and weekend programs to train unemployed youths and retrain adults currently employed in jobs at companies that many economists predict will no longer exist in the near future. The Collaborative High School Campus Model is an ideal setting for corporations interested in partnering with communities in need of employment opportunities. Industries could develop programs tailored specifically to the skills needed for their workforce in low-income communities, where a great number of people are available and interested in learning skills that will result in immediate employment upon successful completion of the training program.

Career training programs in modern high school facilities could entice potential investors from various industries to relocate into communities usually overlooked. Communities could use the school's facilities to appeal to industries that often admit that investing capital to facilitate economic growth is tied to achieving one of the most sought-after resources for industries considering relocation or expansion opportunities in other regions: finding skilled employees. In this case they can start up with training programs that, over time, can evolve into providing a constant flow of available workers who annually enroll into their needs-based training programs. But in addition to the companies that already exist, the numerous successes in the fields of science and engineering will likely generate start-up companies in the near future. Investments in newly constructed modern high schools designed to accommodate the current and future wave of technology and other consumer service industries may attract the interest of companies in search of communities from which they could potentially derive mutual benefits.

The potential for profitable outcomes, for businesses and communities working in unison to grow industries by training future employees from within those communities, highlights an example of compatible economic growth that benefits both communities and businesses. It will also stimulate the closing of employment and economic gaps. Closing employment gaps between newly emerging high-tech and other currently successful industries and the people in dire need of employment opportunities, is an example of urban renewal that results not in the displacement of residents, but in a fulfillment of their desire to remain and earn a high-enough income to purchase a home within the community they always regarded as their home. Mutual prosperity that benefits both communities and businesses represent an area of growth initiated by a willingness on the part of companies to take a chance by tapping into a traditional formula of supply and demand. But shifting priorities to meet the demands of the new technology revolution, one that is replacing a deeply entrenched and once highly profitable industry that created the industrial revolution, relies on the same premise of supply and demand. Except in this instance, it may finally benefit the communities always left behind.

Collaborative High School Campus Model

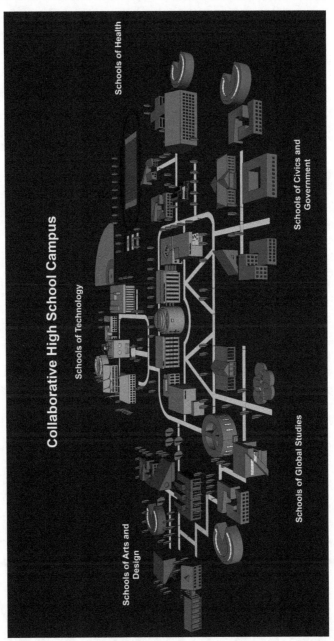

Julie Coles—*Creator & Co-Designer* | Juho Lee—*Illustrator & Co-Designer*

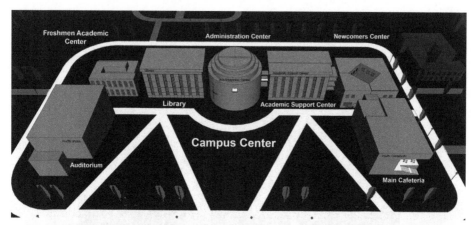

Campus Center

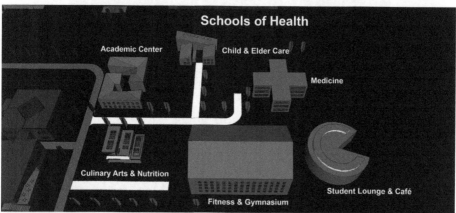

Schools of Health

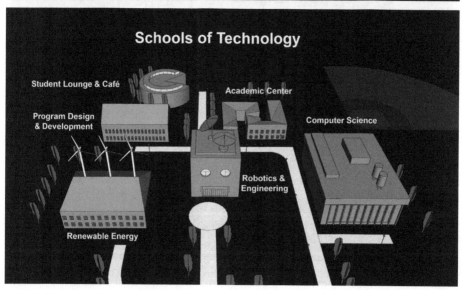

Schools of Technology

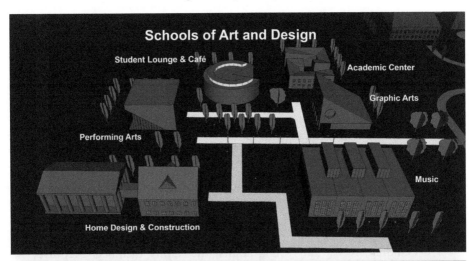

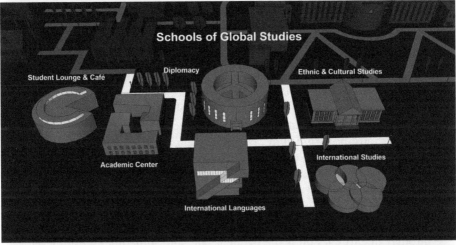

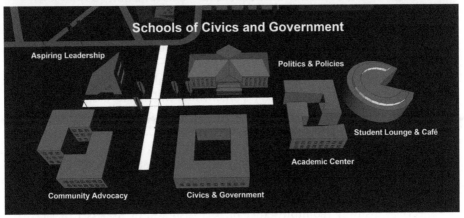

Shared Resources

T HE COLLABORATIVE HIGH SCHOOL CAMPUS MODEL PROVIDES a unique array of resources not typically included in most high schools. But the uniqueness is not the span of resources; it is the relevance of resources suited to meet the broad spectrum of critical needs in poor and under-resourced communities. No 21ˢᵗ century school with significant improvements to every facet of curriculums, instruction, and other educational resources can function at its greatest potential without providing academic support and counseling resources aligned with the needs of the students.

Children, teens, and young adults, the family members they live with, and their neighbors experience emotional, physical, and mental health issues that require proper care and routine access to a variety of health and counseling resources. When these needs are not met, they become the responsibility of schools. The moment some children enter school, their inability to focus on learning is evident. Other students show less visible signs of distress. But whether evident or not, for many students a school day can begin in a state of obvious or quiet turmoil due to non-school-related circumstances. A range of health and counseling resources must be included in 21ˢᵗ century schools, to respond to the myriad needs related to every student's well-being. It is necessary to anticipate the most common areas of need and provide the staffing and facilities to help students discreetly address whatever level of concern or crisis they are contending with, without interruption to class instruction.

Indeed, one of the most common reasons teachers are unable to get through an entire lesson is the frequent rate, and sometimes serious level, of interruptions that require the teacher's immediate attention. When instruction is interrupted, learning is disrupted. If a great deal of teachers' instructional time is consumed to address issues related to a student's well-being or disruptive behaviors, over time it results in a significant reduction of teaching and learning. The accumulation of time teachers devote to managing behavioral and other issues will impact every student's ability to maintain their focus on learning if the only predictable thing they learn is to expect some event, beyond the teacher's control, to pause their lesson, which diminishes their learning time.

Teachers cannot effectively provide quality instruction if they are dividing their instructional time to take on other responsibilities. They are not trained to act as a parent, counselor, therapist, bullying-intervention specialist, hallway monitor, settler of peer disputes, or disperser of facts versus myths found on the garden variety of social media platforms or other *sometimes* unreliable sources of information.

In addition to including both standard and non-traditional resources that ought to be a part of every 21ˢᵗ century school, schools should include a variety of learning spaces, such as study centers, function rooms to accommodate collaborative-based research-and-development projects, and conference spaces to help cultivate a culture of learning in diverse spaces that will appeal to young adults. These diverse learning environments will convey to students that classrooms and neighboring industrial labs and workshops are not the only venues where learning takes place.

Schoolwide Resources

- Library
- Newcomers Center
- Technology Support Center
- Gymnasium
- Cafeteria
- Auditorium
- Physical Fitness Center
- Day Care Center
- Comprehensive Health & Counseling Services

Commonalities among the 5 Collaborative Career Networks

- Network of Four Career Programs: Industrial Work Space & Classrooms
- Academic Center: General Education Classes & College Prep Academy
- Student Lounge & Café, Conference Rooms, Study Space, and Collaborative Work Space

Main Campus

Administrative and Health Services Building

- Welcome Lounge
- School Leadership Office

Counseling and Health Services

- Neighborhood Health Clinic
- Crisis Intervention Support
- Teen Parent Counseling
- Legal Advice Office

Student and Family Resources

- Day Care Center
- Student Government Council

Academic Resources

- Academic Tutoring Clinic
- Special Education Support Services
- English Language Learners Support Services
- Homework Support Center
- Academic Advocacy & Mentoring Center

College and Career Services

- College Counseling and Resource Center
- Career Placement Center

Technology Services

- Technology Responsibility Center
- Technology Support Center
- Computer Loan Services

Reduction in Incarceration Rates

THE RECENT INCREASE OF PRISONS TO ACCOMMODATE THE continually increasing numbers of poor minorities from urban communities is a trend that reinforces the disturbing downward trajectory fueled by a systemic cycle of continued failure. This is demonstrated by inequalities in school discipline. It is shown that minority students are disciplined more harshly in school, and there is a correlation between discipline in school and likelihood of adulthood arrest.[9] The increase in the number of prisons is also indicative of the failure of efforts to reform education in any meaningful way for a population that always seems to be at the mercy of the long-held belief of a self-fulfilling prophecy, that the majority of those born into poverty will remain at the same level of low economic and social status, regardless of the number of years spent trying to educate them. That premise is founded on the false assumption that education cannot add value to the lives of socially and economically disadvantaged citizens. Our outdated public-school systems in urban communities seem resigned to an acceptance of this false premise, and thus significantly contribute to sustaining this self-fulfilling prophecy and turning out high numbers of dropouts and low numbers of graduates prepared for college or careers.

The development of modern prisons appears to be willingly embraced across many regions of America. In fact, there is such an ever-increasing demand for more prison facilities that builders cannot keep pace with demand. Several states in the country spend more money on prisoners than on college students.[10] Most states spend more money per inmate than they do to educate elementary and secondary school students.[11] It's time for America to match the level of enthusiasm for building prisons and incarcerating increasing numbers of poor and minority citizens with an enthusiasm for building state-of-the-art elementary, middle, and high schools with 21st century curriculums and instruction designed to provide education of the highest quality, and reduce the rate of youths flowing into the prison system.

Our society seems to be indifferent to the plight of our poorest, but our ongoing efforts to reform education strongly indicate that many Americans remain resolved to find solutions to reverse the trend of systematic and systemic disenfranchisement of those born into poverty through no fault of their own. With access to real qualitative resources, we have the ability to influence our own educational, social, and economic destiny. It's time to build better schools that provide better education, allowing all to meet the highest academic standards while developing career-related skills, so everyone is on a truly level playing field, regardless of the station of life in which their lives began.

In fact, let's take the 21st century education model into our prisons and provide the same quality of college- and career-readiness preparation for all nonviolent prisoners incarcerated under the three-strikes rule that exponentially contributes to the overflowing prison population. It is proven that education in prison is effective in reducing recidivism and providing better employment outcomes to offenders.[12] After all, most of our citizens imprisoned for nonviolent crimes will one day reenter society; and access to the Collaborative High School education model will not only be valuable time spent while in prison, but result in a more meaningful method of rehabilitation. They will reenter our society well educated and highly skilled for 21st century jobs.

Teach Responsibility by Making Students Responsible

HIGH SCHOOL STUDENTS WOULD BENEFIT FROM SELECTING content courses that interest them instead of being assigned classes of absolutely no interest to them. States typically require a specified number of courses in each content area for students to graduate. The required number of courses within each content area could still be achieved if students were allowed the freedom of choosing courses from a diverse menu of courses for all content areas. History courses could include Political Science, Government, Criminal Justice, Constitutional Law, World History, US History, Global Economics, and others. In addition to those courses, Collaborative High Schools, such as the School of Innovative Renewable Energy, School of Robotics & Engineering, and the School of Government, would also offer history courses related to their area of specialty.

Freshmen who attend a model such as the proposed Collaborative High School Campus would benefit from having the freedom to take career-exploration electives of their choosing. Two-week orientations in each career program would enable every student the opportunity to explore the broad inventory of career programs available on campus. After a year of sampling courses from all or selected programs, students will be better informed about what specialty each career program offers and be prepared to select the career program in which they wish to pursue their education. Similar to some colleges and universities, the Collaborative High Schools model would not assign freshmen to a cohort of prerequisite freshman-level courses. With the supportive guidance of adults, students could review catalogs of academic courses and career programs distributed to students and their families prior to the start of the school year. Students would be free to select their own courses and make up their own schedules. Then, as most second-year college students do at the college level, after their first year of attending career orientation programs, high school students can declare a career major by their sophomore or junior year.

Granting high school students the option of self-selecting courses is an important college readiness skill that should be developed in high school. The gaps in cultural norms between high schools and colleges are so broad that high school students often have to spend their initial weeks, if not months, orienting themselves to many new facets upon arriving to a college campus. For many students, it is similar to being parachuted, unprepared, into a totally foreign country, armed only with a translation book upon landing. Although the book is intended to be helpful, the lack of preparedness or time to orient oneself about the customs while being unable to speak the language can be quite frustrating. Instead of waiting until students arrive at college to become acclimated to the college culture and norms, high schools should embed college practices into the high school culture. Students' experiences can be broadened in 21st century Collaborative High Schools to include direct access to college and career environment norms by replicating protocols and practices commonly found in those settings, thus significantly reducing the foreignness to what students will encounter upon their arrival to college and work sites.

Demystify College, Then Allow Students to Decide

COLLEGE READINESS SHOULD INCLUDE EXPOSURE TO SPECIFIC skills necessary to perform well in college classrooms and beyond. Students must also learn how to emulate college etiquette and become familiar with social protocols that are expected of college students on college campus and in the classroom setting. Such exercises will heighten competence and thus enable those students who choose to attend college, to arrive on campus equipped with a high degree of confidence in knowing what to expect, which will result in students' embracing college instead of feeling insecure.

But before we discuss familiarizing students with college life, let's stop the false assumption that all students want to attend college. It is that particular narrative that drives teachers and guidance counselors to implore students to consider applying to college. Then the endless stream of media messaging, where students are inundated with commercials meant to encourage college attendance, makes many students feel guilty about not wanting what others want for them. It can be overwhelming. As a school leader, I used to tell students that the option of attending college would always be available if they wanted to change their mind and apply in the future. You could almost sense a valve being turned and releasing the pressure they felt. Unfortunately, conversations about ways to exit from the college path are not the norm. Instead, the decades of being entrenched in some universal agreement that all students should attend college places enormous pressure on the high school students who sense that they are not adequately prepared. One reason many students in urban public schools do not want to take a leap of faith and succumb to the well-intended societal pressure that encourages them to go to college is insecurity, driven primarily by a fear of the unknown. Intuitively, students may not know specifically what they need to know to succeed in college; they just know they do not possess the requisite skills to succeed in college. They also might be too willing to believe they are not ready, and they are right.

Among the hundreds of thousands who do take that leap of faith under the false impression that they are ready, some are ready, but most are not. For most students who feel ready, apply, and are accepted, their sense of readiness is almost immediately challenged once they attend their first few classes, are handed syllabi for their courses, and feel completely clueless and overwhelmed by those foreign documents. Confidence and enthusiasm can quickly be replaced with uncertainty and a sense of despair, all of which could have been avoided if they had the opportunity to be exposed to and prepared for college while in high school.

The solution for alleviating insecurity about applying to college is to acclimate students to college while in high school, from freshmen through senior year. The current pathway of introducing students to college, primarily through discussions and visits to a college campus for informational tours, is not enough. High school students need multiple opportunities to access a college campus through more extensive and meaningful college-life experiences, in order to inform them about what to expect, as well as broaden their understanding of what makes college life very different from their current life.

Multiple visits to a college campus have to be highly informative, memorable, and impactful. These visits should be planned for the purpose of introducing college life while decreasing the fear of the unknown. High school students need experiences that include repeated opportunities to access college classes, familiarize themselves with student support services, have conversations with college students and faculty, and be assigned college-student mentors. These experiences will demystify the unknowns about what students can expect. Without any meaningful information or substantive experiences, so many high school students, especially minority students from urban and low-income communities, absolutely refuse to even consider applying to college. Having no idea about what awaits them often produces anxiety and fear. Why not reveal what awaits them by allowing them to experience college life through direct experiences that go way beyond a single campus tour?

High school students might appreciate discovering college life during high school before applying, when the stakes of immediacy are not a factor. Talking to students about why they should apply to college is important, but often times the topic of college can elicit an air of uncertainty and ambivalence from the student. Sure, they smile because they are genuinely flattered to be considered academically capable of going to college, but college is beyond the scope of their life experiences, and completely unfamiliar to them. It is also typically viewed as a place where really smart high school students are expected to go to because they are academically suited to achieve. You see, many Blacks have been inundated with a multitude of messages throughout their entire existence that they are not academically suitable, and therefore not adequately prepared, for a college environment. It is as if a whole new public relations campaign must be invented to change this message. Stereotype threat is a psychological term that explains the phenomenon in which negative stereotypes about groups affect performance of group members on tests. For example, when we think about women's lower performance on math tests, it could be partially because they are aware of the stereotype that women are bad at math.[13]

We must infuse new, positive messages to break the cycle of perpetually under-educating generations of highly capable learners and achievers. Number one: it is time to consider what is needed in order to inspire, in all of America's youths, excitement, enthusiasm, and anticipation for getting an education. If children experience joy in the pursuit of learning, they will be motivated to attend school.

Recognizing that not all students want to go to college makes it incumbent on public schools to also include pathways to career-training programs. All students should participate in low-key campus orientations to learn about degree programs and the range of resources. Visits to classes can be useful in informing all students about what learning looks like at the next level. College-immersion programs do have the capacity to change the minds of students who may initially be adamant about having no interest in attending college. The creation of career-based Collaborative High Schools that partner high schools with colleges and businesses will enable students who want to attend college, access to college readiness skills throughout their four years in high school. And whether or not students plan to attend college before pursuing their career, everyone will need employment after their college degree programs. Therefore, all students will greatly benefit from schools that prepare them for their eventual careers.

Students who prefer to enter the work force directly after high school need to know about off ramps available to those who have no interest in applying to college. One exception to the student preference rule is requiring all students to participate in a financial literacy session about potential incomes of high school graduates, compared to students with bachelor's and master's degrees. Career program orientations would also share information about potential incomes associated with every industry. In fact, one of the most persuasive incentives for changing the mindset of high school students who never considered college is learning about the potential earning power and salaries of a college degree graduate versus a high school graduate. Collaborative High Schools would give students who think they are not interested in higher education the option of participating in one or more college-readiness courses. Often, when students are exposed to resources and successful college-readiness programs, they begin to see themselves as being capable of attending college. Overcoming their apprehensions by exposing them to various academic, social, and financial-aid counseling sessions is a great way to peel away the unknowns without intimidating students.

Revealing the unknowns can be achieved with college campus visits that permit students to discover campus life through fun exploration. Team scavenger hunts are appealing because students enjoy the freedom of independently roaming around campuses. Providing students with campus maps and a detailed list of various departments they must find and collect artifacts from, verifying they did in fact complete their mission, is a great orientation strategy. Having to find and spend some time to learn about student support services and departments—including financial aid, academic support centers, health counseling services, academic deans, dorm resident assistance, minority peer counselors, and sports arenas—is particularly eye-opening. Real acclimation happens through opportunities to repeatedly visit colleges to expand students' knowledge and familiarity about college life while expanding their comfort level. Opportunities to participate in meetings with college students to discuss real-life situations about the realities of what to expect, based on the college student's experiences, is particularly helpful in preparing high school graduates for their transition into college. Devoting time to become fully acclimated to college prior to arriving for their freshman year is a self-esteem-building experience. Students arrive on campus equipped with the skills and habits of a scholar groomed to expect success because they are also acquainted with college life and have a sense of what to expect.

In addition to identifying specific areas and related skill sets, it is necessary to repeatedly expose students to college-oriented tasks so they can develop college-like habits for studying, performing well in class, and submitting quality-level assignments that meet the highest academic standards. Using the four years of high school to prepare students for college is imperative, particularly for students who come from economically disadvantaged living conditions. Many urban schools have a significant number of educationally disadvantaged students inadequately prepared to attend college, but it's time to reveal a long-kept secret: many suburban and middle-class students are also inadequately prepared for college.

Beyond low-income communities in urban areas, many students are currently burdened with high expectations and desperately want to perform well once they arrive at college; but the lack of exposure to the prerequisite skills needed to perform academic tasks at the college level places students at great risk for dropping out. Initial efforts to appear well-prepared and exude self-confidence belie conflicting emotions under the surface, and new freshmen constantly question whether they are prepared and to what extent they are unprepared. It only takes the first few conversations among their peers to discover that they are unfamiliar with the topics of conversation, and that they have arrived without possessing an arsenal of what appear to be the most basic college-level credentials, from knowledge about various topics to the ability to articulate what area or concentration they want to major in.

Meanwhile, their peers from more affluent backgrounds sound and appear as though they have whatever it is these students personally lack to succeed in college, also known as *college cultural cache*. College culture cache includes the ability to be at ease with one's peers because, like them, you are knowledgeable about a variety of issues and thus feel included in the group's discussions, topics such as famous writers and authors that less-prepared freshmen may never have heard of. It's those moments of being present in those groups but unable to contribute to discussions because none of the conversation is familiar to you that bring about a silent awkwardness. From freshman-year students' initial encounters of feeling like an outsider to finding themselves only able to discuss current trends and affairs, they quickly discover that college operates on an entirely different lingo from the school and community they came from. Once they begin to sense that they may be out of their element, their tendency to doubt whether they have what it takes to perform at the college level begins to erode their self-confidence, and eventually their self-esteem.

In addition to the experiences and resources, students need a continual diet of college-based skills integrated into the high school curriculum and pedagogy. This allows for students to be exposed to college readiness skills through experiences that realistically represent what they can expect when they arrive at college. It's time to reform our education system, not re-constitute what we already have in place. It is one of the reasons we have not made meaningful and sustainable gains in so many public schools, especially in economically challenged regions.

Imagine how different the initial college experience would feel if a student attended a high school that focused on acclimating students to college culture. Prior knowledge about all aspects connected with college life, in combination with a quality high school education, will empower students with an abundance of college culture cache and increase their capacity to successfully and confidently navigate their way through college. We constantly hear the well-intended messages about needing to better prepare high school students for college in order to increase the number of students successfully completing a two- or four-year college degree program. Until we equip our students for college in a way that provides meaningful access to college-simulated experiences and resources, these well-intended messages will remain empty rhetoric.

If we want to discontinue the cycle of poverty, we need to take steps to reverse the abysmal trend of failure and to provide a truly level playing field for all high school students. Of course, I would be remiss if I didn't also advocate for changes in middle and elementary schools, if for no other reason than to improve the performance level of students entering high school from grammar school. If freshman-year students arrive performing well below grade level, then teachers must focus an inordinate amount of instructional time remediating students. Many of those students feel a sense of hopelessness because they see how their academically prepared peers are enthusiastically embraced by teachers and encouraged to partici-pate in lessons. So, if we are going to talk about leveling the playing field, that process has to start in kindergarten and continue through college for every student. A study at Duke University found promising results that treating all students as gifted from their first years in school led to a decrease in the achievement gap. Basically, the quality of education and higher expectations does affect the performance of students. This can be good justification for the argument that we need to improve the education that we are providing.[14]

Society's Pivotal Role in Transforming Education

IN TRADITIONAL PUBLIC HIGH SCHOOL CLASSROOMS, STUDENTS learn content in core subjects. But learning content in core subjects for the sake of performing well on tests ignores an essential need to link what is taught in classrooms to the career aspirations of students and their daily life. Without linking what is taught in classrooms to career aspirations and relevance to their life, students become detached from their education. So many become uninterested in the day-to-day educational process because they experience it as a necessity for achieving passing grades that reward their ability to repeat back what was taught.

In a desire to increase student engagement in learning, many citizens from communities of color, whose children represented the increasing majority of students in public schools in urban communities across the country, advocated for minority representation in textbooks and other educational resources. Whether inspired by or forced to respond to the growing volume of people demanding their public education system demand the education-textbook industry to include people of color, eventually the pressure resulted in the redesigning of textbooks more reflective of America's cultural diversity, particularly including Blacks.

Initially it took an immense amount of pressure from advocates representing communities of color to make the public aware of why the lack of minority representation in textbooks needed to be addressed. But it was their ability to describe how including images of people of color in textbooks across all content areas could significantly benefit students of color to see images of people who look like them in educational resources that are their primary source of information. The advocates expanded their base of support by educating the broader society, which then led to sweeping changes in the revision of textbooks. The ability to transform our education system from one that represented a single portion of America's population to a broader spectrum of previously non-represented ethnic and racial populations is a milestone achieved by a society of citizens who saw the need to start removing racially unfair barriers in public schools.

We should applaud and encourage continued progress made by the textbook industry trying to keep pace with a continually expanding diverse population of students from ethnic and racial backgrounds. However, the contemporary needs of our advancing society cannot be addressed in revised textbooks. Adding images of people from different cultural backgrounds to elevate interest in learning across our richly mosaic population of diverse peoples was an important milestone . . . then. Where we are now, for the sake of our children, the focus of education must keep pace with a changing society. Emphasis on educating students in the 21st century means embedding educational resources in all schools that will prevent us from leaving any students behind.

In Collaborative High Schools, academic classrooms would be connected to state-of-the-art career labs or workshops designed to mirror the workplace and allow for content learned in an academic classroom setting to be immediately applied into the career lab. This transference of information will serve to illustrate how information learned in one setting is directly linked to the hands-on, career-based projects designed to teach and equip students with skills related to a future worksite. For many students, the opportunity to acquire career skills through an experiential hands-on process may help them understand something that was taught in the classroom setting but had eluded them until they were given the opportunity to experience the information's direct application with their projects in the career lab. This "Aha!" moment of revelation sparked by the student's imagination creates a meaningful connection with something of interest and value to them in the career lab setting.

For many students, the ability to retain information learned in the traditional classroom setting is difficult because it is too abstract. One of the reasons many students underperform and lag behind is because schools do not provide opportunities for students to participate in projects that engage direct application of what they have been taught. One concrete example is the high rate of students applying to and finding great success in state-of-the-art vocational high schools. Vocational schools have enjoyed higher attendance rates compared to public schools because they are designed to couple learning with doing.

Transferring information learned from the academic setting into the career-training lab adds value to every student's educational experience because it helps them understand and value the purpose of investing in their education. Knowledge learned and directly applied to the real world results in students' having a meaningful and gratifying educational experience. It's how they find the purpose of education. Finding purpose motivates and inspires students to attend school on a regular basis, and this dramatically decreases the dropout rate.[15]

Embracing Innate Curiosity

I N GENERAL, TRADITIONAL EDUCATION METHODS IN MANY AMERICAN schools foster practices that push aside what students innately know or their natural tendency to be curious. This form of pedagogy is done under the mistaken belief that the purpose of schools is to treat students as empty vessels that need information poured into them, restricted to regurgitating only what they have learned to give proof of evidence-based learning. Students are tested on what they have been taught and not what they think about what they have been taught. Lessons are predicated on a one-dimensional approach of providing information. This approach asks students to demonstrate what they have learned, and they must mirror exactly what was taught, in the way it was taught.

When 21st century classrooms rely on methods of instruction and other pedagogical practices from the past, students are prevented from engaging more deeply in learning. We seem slow to discover that most students are generally prewired with the capacity to learn when they take some degree of ownership for their learning. In all classrooms across public schools, we undermine students' ability to use their imagination to acquire skills, learn content, and demonstrate the ways they are capable of learning. The learning process should be based on the belief that the driving force of learning is the propensity of all children, teens, and young adults to be innately curious. All students can and should be encouraged to contribute to their own educational learning experience through a process that includes their opinions, ideas, and perspectives, as well as their right to question what they are learning. Critical thinking and analysis happen when students reason their own way through challenging suppositions, making hypotheses, or crafting a thesis. Exploring how to prove or disprove an assertion enables students to arrive at their own conclusions, rather than being systematically led through a series of prescribed steps to an end that is pre-decided by the teacher. Learning should be fun and messy, and it should encourage taking risks through collaboration and intellectual discussions that stimulate curiosity. When students' curiosity is stimulated, it can heighten their willingness to go through a maze of the unknown, which, if they are trusted to learn through trial and error, will eventually lead them to the known.

Whether it be through self-discovery or contributions to group learning that require each student to think and rethink as many times as necessary to discover the answer, educators have to see students as possessing the ability to find their way through these cognitively challenging processes, in order for students to see themselves as capable of finding their own way. In this particular format of student-centered learning, students take on the role of teacher-learners. Teachers turn the lesson over to their students and become facilitators, incrementally scaffolding levels of more rigorous and cognitively challenging tasks to elevate intellectual thinking.

Learning something new should be similar to taking a stimulating and fascinating journey that is full of opportunities to use one's imagination and creativity in the pursuit of a new discovery. It should not be something that is simply told and then regurgitated. While there are times when memorization of basic facts and fundamental principles are necessary prerequisites for solving more rigorous tasks or problems, even that memorization can be done through a more fun and creative learning process created by the students. If they own the process of learning something new by making decisions for how they will learn it, they become fully engaged learners and owners of their education. We have to unlearn the habit of seeing adults as the only ones capable of educating students.

IV.
New Schools Alone
Won't Close
Achievement Gaps

How Failure Cultivates Apathy among Students

ARE *F*S TRULY OF ANY BENEFIT IF STUDENTS END UP DREADING attending school because they are filled with anxiety? In our current system of grading, when a student does not pass a class at the end of a school year, they receive an *F*. Earning an *F* also requires students to take the course over again the following year. Often it is not just the one or two courses they must repeat. Many are required to repeat the same grade. This places them in unnecessary double jeopardy. Why not dispense with assigning students an *F* and just require they do the work again, or retake the course?

Students who repeatedly get *F*s gradually feel they are incapable of succeeding in school. The initial or first few *F*s plant a seed of self-doubt. The continuation of failure increases and over time cultivates further doubt. If no effort is made by teachers to pause and then reverse these students' plight of what feels like the slow but inevitable progression towards the abyss of total academic failure, many students who are entangled in the continued cycle of failure internalize what they are experiencing by concluding they themselves are to blame.

Instead of feeling worthy of and entitled to an education, these students feel worthless. When they can no longer endure being left behind five days a week, they reduce the number of days they attend school; and this, then, results in mounting absences that make it all but impossible to catch up. On the few days each week they do put in an appearance, they notice changes in the quality of interactions between them and their teachers and peers. The changes can come in the form of students' politely accepting the reduction in the rate of eye contact with teachers while in class. Students hasten their transition through hallways to avoid chance encounters with teachers whose classes they skipped. The decision to attend class after absences causes discomfort, despite the teacher's joyful demeanor and a kind tone of voice when "Hellos" are exchanged between them. Students also are fairly astute at detecting sarcasm. Sarcastic utterances like, "It's nice to see you today." The insincerity of teachers who inquire, out loud in front of classmates, where there is no refuge from further embarrassment and humiliation, "Where have you been?" are not intended to elicit a response. The point is to publicly make clear what everyone already knows: the student has been a "No Show." The encounters, thankfully, are brief. Despite the student's outwardly appearing to be delighted to see their teacher and classmates, everybody knows differently. But if we develop alternative methods of assessing student errors and applying different and more effective instructional methods, we can discontinue the practice of blaming and failing students, by teaching them until they learn what they revealed they did not understand. When we fail students, we actually fail to understand that they require more, and maybe a different form of, instruction to address their learning gaps.

Changing How We Educate Students

R ESILIENCE OFTEN DRIVES OUR ABILITY TO ADAPT. ON THE very first day at the start of each school year, students generally arrive at each class, encountering stacks of textbooks on a table. Predictably, they then go through the process of being assigned a book. Most readers are very acquainted with the process, so they know what comes next. While the teacher reviews the topics covered in the table of contents, explains expectations for completing class and homework assignments, and gives information about weekly tests, eyelids begin to droop. But the teachers are programmed to persist in the face of students' signaling they are beginning to fade. Students are so familiar with the ceremonial start of the school year process and know where the one-way conversation will end: basically, it is going to be another year of input and output. And because most students are familiar with what to expect, they quickly adapt to the predictable ebb and flow of another year in another course where the textbook is the primary source from which they will learn and the teacher has made his or her intentions quite clear. Every unit will be covered by the completion of the school year and in pretty much the same manner courses have been taught for many years.

Does just thinking about it make you want to doze off? Or perhaps you were one of the students who mastered the art of appearing interested while doodling in your notebook or occasionally looking out a window and daydreaming while you patiently waited for the sound of the bell to signal the end of class. If you were lucky, the daily monotony of the same routines was interrupted by special events such as watching a film, taking a field trip, or having a guest speaker. But whether learning from a textbook, teacher instruction, film, guest speaker, or field trip, the process of learning was most often funneled through a one-way process of taking information in, and having your performance and grades based on how much you remembered and were able to retain from what you were taught.

Traditional education protocols were usually made clear in district-wide mandates based on state Department of Education policies: perform all instructional duties *by the book, using books, booking events* mirroring content *in the books,* and not being offended with the bell rings and you witness how quickly students *book it* out of the classrooms. Teachers are often working inside of guardrails and parameters where they are directed to adhere to state and district mandates regarding content, meeting timelines of what must be covered, and planning lesson based on content . . . not whether or not students are learning the content. The goal is to get to the yearly finish line having covered material, not necessarily having successfully taught the material covered. Evaluating a teacher's performance used to be influenced by the amount of content covered by year's end.

Thankfully, many educators have departed from the status quo of conforming to the old pedagogical norms where teachers only teach and students only listen. In many schools there has been a significant, or in some cases very gradual, shift towards placing greater emphasis on how students experience learning; generally planning lessons that actively engage students in learning through participation. The traditional methods of instruction and assessments never revealed what students truly learned, only their ability to memorize what they were told. As tests evolved and became more geared to finding out what and how much students truly comprehended, particularly in open-ended questions requiring evidence of deep comprehension as a means of measuring real learning, the results strongly indicated a need to significantly tailor instruction . . . and differently. The process of tailoring instruction has evolved and continues to do so.

But for many schools, while incorporating some incremental changes, it's as if they made minimal alterations to satisfy updated bureaucratic mandates which they can then check off in a box in the "Tasks to be Completed" column. That's no exaggeration. They actually must document and submit an inordinate number of records to their district, which are then forwarded to the state's Department of Education; presumably data and analysis embedded in reports are then passed along to the federal government, where it just sits in some space. Oversight of the public education system by each state's Department of Education is more about districts and schools keeping pace with an overwhelming volume of requests for records and documents related to the bureaucratic business of micromanaging the bureaucratic arm that regulates education.

Keeping up with the collection of various documents interferes with the time needed by underperforming and under-resourced schools trying their best to research and apply best practices that will enable them to keep their head above water to avoid being labeled an underperforming school. In the circumstances of underperforming schools, the volume of paperwork is even worse. It requires more time to prove they have completed specific tasks, so they can achieve and maintain the appearance of having met specific state-mandated, but not always well-crafted, standards that have not necessarily proven to be beneficial in improving the overall quality of education. Ironically, all schools—but especially underperforming schools—want to, need to, and should spend less time attending to filling out paperwork if it can be proven it is of no direct benefit to helping the school improve the delivery or method of instruction and advance their forward progress away from the rating of "underperforming school."

Schools are devoting way too much time to providing proof of implementation of haphazard and not always well-thought-out polices. In fact, many school leaders rightfully balk at the inordinate amount of time needed to fill out and submit documents because they see no connection with how those documents actually assist their efforts to improve the delivery and quality of education.

Many will claim—and there is some truth to the claim—that part of the reason for the snail's pace in adopting more progressive methods of instruction has to do with some teachers' resistance to change. But let's understand that, like many cultural norms in institutions such as college teacher programs, the current population of future teachers graduating from those programs were learning the instructional norms of their generation. Generations, by the way, that retained pedagogical practices passed on from previous generations. Progressive teacher training programs are appearing in many, but not enough, colleges and universities. Colleges and universities were, and still are, the primary institutional leaders at the forefront of training each generation of current and future teachers. Upon entering the teaching ranks in schools across the country, many of those same teachers arrived armed with instructional tools that were in vogue at the time, and they worked diligently to develop a high level of mastery in skills utilizing those tools.

Unfortunately, over a period of too much time, teaching practices and the public education system in general began to lag behind as other entities showed an ability to adapt new changes and were then able to advance forward. And despite many college teacher training programs' making advancements in education to improve the quality of instruction, they were disheartened to hear from recent graduates in new teaching positions, where they had arrived armed with enthusiasm and innovative ideas that were met with skepticism. In some schools, the new arrivals were politely informed about the instructional protocols used in that school, then were emphatically informed they were expected to provide instruction in the same manner it had been taught for many years in that school.

As an aside, we often hear about school districts' being challenged with retaining teachers, especially new teachers. Well, if they arrive eager and ready for the opportunity to utilize innovative methods of instruction and then are either explicitly informed or over time sense that their methods of teaching are incompatible with the traditional model used among the broad and highly outspoken majority of their colleagues, their welcome may be short lived. Many, but not all, veteran teachers who are inflexible about changes to their educational cultural values and norms, can find creative ways to nudge newbies to help them understand both the culture new teachers inherited and the expectations to follow the lead of those veterans. The irony is that it was the sharing of new and innovative ideas during the newbie's interview that influenced the decision of the principal and members of the interview committee to hire the newbie. When newbies with innovative ideas are fortunate to work for a leader willing to serve as a buffer between them and veteran staff who tend to be set in their ways, the longevity of newbies is far more likely. Such buffering also allows time for newbies to build professional alliances with veteran teachers willing to mentor their new colleagues; and it results in the mutual exchange of new ideas and exceptional traditional models that exemplify best practices. Strong staff alliances result in a higher quality education for all students.

Expand and Diversify Education Platforms

LEARNING PROFILES VARY AMONG STUDENTS. AND LEARNING profiles are usually ignored for the convenience of accommodating a teacher's instructional profile; often influenced by the teacher's learning *preference* . . . not the student's learning *profile*. Like their students, most teachers of previous generations were molded into one-dimensional consumers of information dispensed daily throughout their years as students in elementary, middle, and high school. All instruction for teachers during their years as students was done through one single method, where students sit, listen, and accurately recite back every word their teachers said, then pour those same statements onto paper and pass a weekly test. Their teachers conveyed "Job well done" by placing an *A* at the top of the paper with a happy face. Recalling the euphoria associated with receiving their teacher's approval when they were students, not all, but many veteran teachers expect their students to respond with giddiness when they receive *A*'s. But recent and current generations of students they teach don't seem to have the same level of enthusiasm they did. Today's generation of students do not yearn to be congratulated and to have their parents post their phenomenal achievement on the refrigerator for all to see. Earning *A*'s for being a passive participant in classes that reward good behavior, appearing interested in repetitive lessons that only require the students to eagerly raise their hand to be called upon as affirmation they are completely engaged, is an act of fulfilling a teacher's expectation. Appearing to engage in learning does not qualify as learning.

Learning opportunities beyond classrooms are limited to repeated visits to the same venues, that many students complain about having to visit for a third consecutive year because their school's budget limits funding for school buses for field trips and entry fees. Sixth graders who have already been to the same museums in their three previous grades don't want another year of hearing, "But the exhibits are new," because they know that usually means 1 or 2 exhibits among 50. They have seen the TV ads excitedly promoting the new exhibits, But the students often feel let down and victims of a bait and switch, because it took only 15 minutes to explore those two new, interesting exhibits. After that, they discover they have nearly three hours remaining to roam, once again, through spaces and other exhibits they have by now committed to memory.

Communities that invest in progressive and innovative models of education recognize students are not one-dimensional people. New education models are designed to engage students in learning using a variety of education platforms that are more appealing and interesting because they are aligned with the variety of learning profiles. The advent of various education platforms, including access to online courses, blended learning models, and Universal Design Learning tailored to each student's individual learning style, are among the latest acquisitions in more schools. Fortunately, the internet provides expansive instructional tools across the spectrum of educational platforms, making widely accessible to classrooms, highly creative tech apps that have shown success with increasing student interest in lessons. Evidence of technology's influence can be seen by the influx of tech-based apps currently used in more economically advantaged communities where educators see an enormous rate of success at engaging students in learning.

For many educators there is a reluctance to over-rely on technology inside and outside of classrooms. Online courses may be available to all, but not all student learning profiles are suited to consume information using text-based instruction, where volumes of written information about topics are provided, students read and then respond to questions about what they read, and then take a multiple-choice test at the end of each chapter. Both the assessment process, where students are actually tested for their ability to memorize information, and the one-way process of filtering information in—without the ability to interact with, challenge, discuss, share divergent points of view, or expand on information—limit the level of learning. Many online courses are designed to reward a student's ability to read, store it in a memory bank, and then respond by checking off the correct answer. However, for many students, online courses are beneficial, particularly for those who fall short of a few academic credits needed to become eligible for a diploma or college degree. The increasing number of colleges and universities offering online courses for adults is an entirely different matter. The availability of online courses at the college level has been a valuable resource for adults interested in earning college degrees without having to physically attend classes on campus. Adults caring for families and/or needing to work full time to maintain their jobs have benefited from the convenience of online programs that make it possible to pursue a college degree while managing other priorities in their lives.

Developmentally, to better understand topics being taught, students from pre-kindergarten through high school need access to a comprehensive range of educational experiences to stimulate learning, by engaging them in cognitively and intellectually challenging tasks. Active learning should foster curiosity about topics while providing students a process within which to exchange ideas, broaden their knowledge, and understand the importance of putting things into context (i.e., having access to background information). It is the need for students to be able to acquire learning skills that they can use to grasp the depth and breadth of concepts or topics being learned, not just go through the motions of providing responses that exactly match information written in the corresponding chapter.

Integration of Skills to Advance Learning: An Infographic Model

A S LONG AS THERE ARE CLASSROOMS WITH SHELF SPACE, THERE will continue to be textbooks. Textbooks in schools will never become extinct. But how they are used can and should be in keeping with our modern times. For example, many people are unaware that students not reading at grade level are not particularly enthused about textbook-distribution day. Fortunately, most, if not many, modern textbooks are also available as audiobooks. Or maybe students are reading at grade level, but they know at the completion of each unit or chapter is the obligatory essay-writing assignment. Like textbooks, essay-writing assignments have a long shelf life.

But the good news for students who experience essay-writing phobia is the invention of artistically cool, and more modern ways of illustrating what they have learned and how well they understand concepts. After reading a chapter in history, instead of assigning written essays summarizing the highlights, students can develop infographics—a less intimidating and more creative method of jumpstarting essay-writing skills. Templates of various infographic models can be distributed. Identifying categories students should include is important, but allowing them the freedom to decide what content will be embedded for each category facilitates trust in their ability to self-direct while thoughtfully engaged in learning. It's a student-centered model of introducing content by way of reading a chapter in the history book, then releasing students to freely explore, discuss, describe, and show their own interpretation of what they learned.

Infographic projects are a useful and painless instructional tool for launching research skills. Students start with identifying the essential key points, provide fact-based evidence with quotes for why they are the key points, include data accompanied by a graph, provide an analysis of data illustrated in the graph, prepare a brief but thoughtful summary, extrapolate a few key phrases from the chapter assigned, accurately cite references and other sources, include thoughts reflecting their opinions, and highlight discoveries they made that were previously unknown before reading the chapter. One of the many benefits of active-engagement projects such as infographics is the opportunity to work collaboratively to design them, which requires consensus building and other social skills.

Students who struggle with writing skills need alternative ways to show and tell about discoveries they learned. Infographics are a modern version of creatively designed brochures. As with brochures, selecting or drawing images that visually illustrate some key points, or listing different key points with short written captions, shows another way of demonstrating an ability to grasp information and the extent of their learning abilities. Students working in pairs or small teams to develop infographics is a safe and fun way to create paths for each student to participate in projects, propose ideas, and feel enthusiasm during the process of contributing.

Infographic projects have the capacity to expand to accommodate a versatile range of skills students can develop at each grade level and throughout their elementary through high school years. Introducing infographics in the early years lays the foundation of basic acquisition of reading, writing, researching, and presentation skills. The ability to integrate higher-level skills needed to keep pace with the increased volume of content taught and that students will be expected to learn, can be embedded in such tech-based projects as infographics; they are malleable and can be customized for a range of projects across all content areas. As each version of infographic project grows, so should post-presentation feedback sessions. Learning how to take constructive feedback can be valuable. But how teams demonstrate the way they heard the feedback should be reflected in subsequent designs showcasing a higher quality model with more sophisticated content. Constructive feedback is also beneficial for the continual development of healthy and productive team collaboration. Group-based projects replicate the team collaboration many current students will likely encounter in future places of employment, particularly tech-based media platforms. Preparing students for those employment opportunities requires them to learn how to take constructive feedback shared during their additional presentation, to broaden and strengthen their understanding about the topic. As students become more familiar with designing infographics, their level of sophistication will improve in the overall quality of their work product, while strengthening their presentation skills.

Infographics can merge into electronic portfolios with a series of infographics, featuring a combination of short essays with powerfully articulated statements in a senior research thesis project. Senior electronic portfolios that began with a seventh-grade infographic project to bolster the confidence of reluctant writers, have the potential of blossoming into a combination of eloquent and well-written compositions with illustrations, facts supported by data, and an in-depth analysis of the data that the student can defend in an oral presentation of their senior portfolio. Evidence of growth and the acquisition of more sophisticated vocabulary skills show in the student's paraphrasing key points, articulating opinions, making persuasive points in support of their opinions, and summarizing what they learned. Infographics are a gateway for starting at a place in which all students can demonstrate their ability to learn.

Infographics and other tech platforms can include a cachet of new vocabulary words or terms that become embedded into phrases presented as short captions displayed next to images students selected to help them illustrate their points. Students who struggle with vocabulary or writing skills need creative options such as infographics, or building popular mash-ups; another artistic process that allows for the integration of multiple sources of information, possibly including lines from poems, samples of musical lyrics, or short clips from films or videos related to particular topics. Mash-ups allow exploration of themes or topics using a combination of resources to support fact-based evidence, analysis, and opinions, represented in a series of artifacts selected by students and embedded in highly creative formats.

Since the advent of infographics, mash-ups, and other more sophisticated and creative technological tools, student engagement in learning has significantly increased. Those tools invite students to use their innate curiosity, which helps sustain their attention. Sustaining students' attention is essential in teaching them to learn how to learn; spending extended periods of time attending to tasks they enjoy learning about sharpens their ability to sustain their focus. Their cognitive learning can be improved by including lessons that also include scaffolding in more rigorous questions or tasks that require students to demonstrate or illustrate their deeper understanding of topics presented in projects. The key is to consider methods of instruction that deepen student investment in learning by allowing them to prove they can grasp essential information when they are presented options that allow them to artistically illustrate their understanding of content.

In an era of such an expansive range of technological options for students to showcase their true learning potential, merging content with tech platforms that invite creativity is a compelling example of why it is time to welcome new and diverse models of expressing ideas, thoughts, perspectives, and opinions in education.

We are witnessing a generation of students capable of accelerating the pace of their individual learning. They are also eager and poised for opportunities to unleash their imaginations, if and when we build a variety of educational learning labs and classrooms that invite them to experiment in surroundings that can accommodate the development of research and writing skills through cognitively engaging and challenging activities. Infographics and mash-ups are just a few among a multitude of other apps educators are using to advance student-centered learning models. As quickly as their world is evolving, some of the apps may already be obsolete or on the verge of extinction. But what is absolutely certain is the need to *divest* from models that students have no interest in and *invest* in diverse tech-based platforms that promote discovery through exploration. Adding tech-based platforms to public school curriculums is a more compatible method of instruction for classrooms populated with a broad range of different learning profiles. It's time to bring their technology skills into the classroom and allow their innate curiosity to thrive.

Disproportionate Education Funding Linked to Austerity Measures

OVER THE SPAN OF YEARS, WE HAVE SEEN THE INCREMENTAL reduction of public education funds, a sure sign of our government officials' diminishing commitment to provide all students access to quality education. We are witnessing our public education system dropping lower and lower on America's list of priorities. It will be up to us to intervene on behalf of our children and, without apology, to demand pro-education policies and reverse this egregiously detrimental trend.

Of course, there will be those against funding new and better pro-education policies. Claims of creating a funding source to improve our public education system will come in the form of the usual accusations of being tied to a social agenda to redistribute wealth. But the redistribution of the annual taxes we pay is really what is being proposed. And yes, the wealthy must contribute their fair share into our tax system; and, simultaneously, congress must stop syphoning money from our Federal Treasury Department for the purpose of big tax breaks for those who least need it. We have to be prepared to rebuff claims made by corporate leaders and other members of the 1% of America's wealthiest, who are routinely given enormous tax breaks from the same system average citizens are annually required to pay into. We need to "clap" back and tell them:

> We simply want a say in how to use the money we put into the system that we were promised would be given back. Your tax breaks are being paid with our contributions into our federally managed Social Security, Medicaid, and Medicare System. Your tax breaks came from money that everyone else had to contribute, yet you get to avoid making contributions, but have your hands out to be recused when your banks and businesses are on the verge of financial ruin due mostly to corrupt decisions resulting in expanding capitalistic ventures that benefit you and your stockholders.
>
> Are you aware that America's citizens are the actual stockholders of our Federal Treasury Department? Or how about the fact that every dollar taken to rescue your corporations contributes to enlarging our national debt? Debts then need to be replenished. Who is responsible for the repayment of those financial-rescue fiascos and tax-break giveaways? We the People. It is America's working and poor citizens who will have increased funds siphoned from our paychecks, or reductions in federal assistance programs for the poor, to rescue your companies from disasters of your own making. Those of us fortunate enough to earn incomes so we can make contributions to retirement funds never intended to be ATMs or bank accounts to the wealthy.

It's time that We the People make clear our expectations of how our contributions to our country's tax system are used. We the People can shift the narrative, and eventually the system, by conveying to our tax-collection agency and minders of our taxes to create new streams of funding for a new education system. If we need additional sources of revenue, let's have everyone understand that our public education system is experiencing its own emergency of being on the verge of collapse. We know how to financially rescue banks and corporations that have repeatedly been thrown life lines consisting of billions of dollars to prevent them from totally collapsing. Why can't the same case be made for our public education system, which should be regarded not only as too big to fail, but too important to fail?

The escalation of income disparities across many states, including an increasing number of communities predominantly populated by white citizens who earn minimum or below-minimum wages, is forcing more citizens to seek government assistance. Cities and rural communities with large percentages of citizens dependent on government assistance for subsidized housing and food stamps due to low-wage jobs are perceived as a financial burden by local and state government officials. And recent changes in government-funded programs designed as social safety nets for America's most vulnerable populations are being allocated less funding, which mirrors the defunding measures of our public education system.

It is apparent that our current economic culture is dangerously tilted in favor of the *haves*, which reveals our country is also at an economic and employment crossroads. Yet we are living in a time where increasing employment opportunities in the fields of technology call for a dramatic shift toward, and investment in, tech-based job-training programs for people of all ages. Basically, we need substantial investment in overhauling our public education system for pre-kindergarten through high school students, and funding to create new job-training programs for adults.

Retraining adults is needed for those currently employed in industries within which many economic experts are forecasting rapid rates of closure in the near future. An inventory of current employment opportunities across the country and globally makes it apparent that we are at the precipice of needing to ramp-up job-retraining programs to avoid an employment gap. We already have the needed volume of employable citizens to fill the volume of jobs currently available. We have to address the technology-skills gap that will prevent those citizens from accessing available jobs. The current and future labor force needs highly skilled workers for America's new industrial revolution: the field of technology.

Necessity of Comprehensive Counseling Resources

THE SUCCESS OF 21ST CENTURY STATE-OF-THE-ART COLLABORATIVE High Schools will depend on many important factors. One of these is the need to provide on-site counseling facilities for the large number of students who arrive at school with social, emotional, psychological, and medical issues related to circumstances at home and in their neighborhoods. So many children, teens, and young adults are born into or become the byproduct of circumstances beyond their control, but they still have to develop the ability to overcome what often feels like insurmountable obstacles. Schools may refer to these young people as *students* and plan academic instruction for students whom they expect to enter classrooms ready to receive instruction. However, the luxury of seeing these individuals as "just students" is an outdated myth because they arrive at school burdened with baggage that can and does interfere with their ability to be fully present and prepared to focus on learning.

Schools inherit behavioral issues when students lack the ability to access counseling that equips them with strategies to navigate life's problems.

These students are burdened with challenging situations within dysfunctional circumstances that manifest as behavioral problems. Whether these circumstances are within or beyond their control, one thing is absolutely certain: unless schools develop the capacity to provide comprehensive counseling services to help students address their complex social, emotional, psychological, and medical needs (often the result of years within the same school system that has shaped their development into troubled teens and young adults), it is highly unlikely that students will be able to learn. In turn, this will continue to perpetuate a self-fulfilling prophecy of low academic performance, and these failures will go on widening rather than closing America's achievement gap.

Part of the problem lies in the fact that students anticipate an unwelcome response to their real needs, typically a broad range of issues that are not created in school but are evident from the moment a student enters the building. Their inability to focus or interact appropriately with peers or teachers requires counseling, rather than discipline, when the source of these situations lies in a student's preoccupation with the enormity of whatever is bothering them related to circumstances outside of school.

The goal of closing the achievement gap in America's urban public schools will remain elusive if we continue to be unwilling to equip schools with the necessary resources to address the whole child. The responsibility of effectively educating children must include providing quality academic instruction concurrent with character-development instruction through on-site counseling centers equipped with staff qualified to help students learn how to cope with issues beyond their education—specifically, tackling the complexities of life's challenges. It is crucial to understand that students arrive at school burdened with baggage that shadows them everywhere they go, and that counseling can help them minimize obstacles that hinder their ability to lead a healthy and safe life, as well as help them achieve their optimum academic potential.

Studying and Learning Habits

S TUDENTS WHO DO NOT LEARN HOW TO LEARN ARE AT AN educational disadvantage. If they are never taught how to learn and then developmentally acquire more rigorous learning skills as they proceed from one grade level to the next, then they are likely to experience frustration throughout their years in school. Developing learning skills is one of the most overlooked yet highly significant assets necessary to perform well in school. Any effort to narrow and eventually close academic achievement gaps will require attending to learning gaps caused in part by neglecting a necessary prerequisite skill for consuming information across all content areas: *learning how to learn.* Never having been taught how to learn and never having had opportunities to integrate and strengthen learning habits from one grade level to the next are major problems that have continued to plague students in many schools.

For many students, learning gaps can be overcome by teaching students how to learn. From grades 4 through 12, schools focus primarily on teaching content. If we consider again how content and instruction progressively change, and the accelerated pace of learning between grades 4 and 12, it would seem fair to assume that each stage of advanced instruction requires a corresponding set of learning strategies that students must acquire to enable them to learn more progressively challenging content, delivered at an increasingly faster pace, combined with an increasing rate of independent study for completing assignments, by the time students reach high school.

Teaching students the tools for learning at each grade level will support their ability to understand content. Learning the tools for how to learn provides access to information and supports the ongoing process of students' being able to consume, absorb, and retain information. In addition to learning content, students should also develop ways to examine topics through a kaleidoscopic lens, enabling them to consider multiple and diverse perspectives. Learning cannot be restricted to a one-dimensional way of viewing and solving problems.

Learning how to learn is essential for the development of independent study habits. Teachers need to show and explain the variety of learning strategies and tools and help students distinguish when to use each one. For example, if students desire to be carpenters, how would they learn carpentry skills if presented only with a set of tools but never taught how to use them correctly? What if they were also never taught the necessity of distinguishing one tool from another, and which specific tool should be used under what circumstance? What if a plumber arrived at a residence with only a hammer to fix an overflowing toilet? In order to avoid these situations, people in the trades are required to be an apprentice or serve as a journeyman under the supervision of a licensed and experienced supervisor over an extended period. They are then assessed for their level of competency to determine whether they are eligible to advance from one level to the next, and to ultimately qualify for a license.

Since teachers are the facilitators needed to teach students how to learn, it is incumbent upon college teacher programs to embed the development of student learning skills in their training of upcoming generations of teachers. School districts will also need to revamp professional development training. After all, 21st century schools need updated curriculums, new technology resources, an expanded variety of education platforms, and more diverse methods of instruction to better accommodate the broad range of learners performing at different academic levels.

Those resources alone will not be sufficient for helping each student achieve their maximum potential. Teaching students how to learn and study is needed to help all students achieve their maximum potential. Similar to the process of teaching teachers how to use new resources or methods of instruction through a professional development process, students also need time to orient themselves and gradually master new concepts taught. Improving pedagogy (instruction) broadens understanding and expands a teacher's educational tool kit of resources. Teachers are afforded opportunities to participate in show-and-tell sessions followed by practice time. New curriculum initiatives are frequently introduced by professional instructors who walk teachers through a series of carefully prescribed, step-by-step procedures for how to correctly teach the material. Sessions are followed with those same professionals' being available for additional sessions for those teachers who request more time to familiarize themselves with the new content and time to gain mastery in understanding what they have been taught.

In some instances, where teachers value the importance of being entrusted to credibly represent the new curriculum and want to adhere to methods of instruction aligned with the curriculum's lesson plan, some districts allow for additional training sessions at the teacher's *request*, when their degree of competency is in need of strengthening. That is just a sample of a multi-tiered process where teachers working in high-performing school districts learn new content and methods of instruction. How great would it be if the same procedures were afforded to students? Why can't students request additional support until they too develop competency, then demonstrate their mastery of whatever they learn? Teachers and students need time and assistance to acquire new information. But they also need to learn how to consume, or learn, ways to learn new information. Learning strategies lead to healthy study habits.

Acquiring knowledge and strategies for learning and repeated use of those skills will improve learning in and beyond the classroom. Learning how to learn is vital to each student's overall success in being able to access content information, perform various assignments, participate in projects and discussions, and work independently. Knowing how to learn is also essential for students attempting to acquire good study habits, because students who do not know how to learn will not then go home and miraculously teach themselves how to do homework. If students are struggling in school, where they have access to teachers, it is unfair to expect them to perform school assignments independently. Without the skills needed to access and truly understand content, students feel incapable of completing homework and often do not even try. These students are at a disadvantage, and yet they receive failing grades for homework that is done incorrectly, incompletely, or not at all. For students who never had the benefit of learning how to learn, predictably substandard performance on homework assignments is evidence of their not having grasped or understood what was taught in their classrooms. Therefore, students are being unfairly set up for failure when they are expected to turn in assignments related to concepts they never understood in class.

Acquiring knowledge about and strategies for learning takes time. Opportunities to repeatedly use learning skills will improve learning. Once students know what learning strategies are useful for consuming and understanding what is taught, they are in a better position to acquire good study habits, particularly important for independent studying. Without the skills needed to access and truly understand content, students feel incapable of completing homework and often do not even try. Students anticipate being assigned failing grades for homework because they know what they don't know. Do we really think there are students who look forward to having their homework paper returned to them with a big red *F*?

Informing students about ways to improve learning and continuous, habitual application of learning strategies not only improves study habits but also strengthens their self-esteem. Heightening their self-esteem fuels their belief in their ability to do the work. Those students are no longer victims of education frustration, no longer made to feel miserable. Their misery and frustration are a recurring problem. It begins the moment they wake up each school day and are immediately filled with a sense of absolute certainty it will be another day of watching others who appear to "get it" while they feel stuck, and falling further behind. Then, adding insult to injury, students who are unable to do homework because they were not able to participate in learning during class, are at an even greater disadvantage when their parents hear their son's or daughter's complaints but feel powerless to help. Due either to their own lack of education or to their unfamiliarity with the "new math," the inability to help their children is a common refrain of parents. Parents who truly care and want to be of assistance find themselves placed at a disadvantage due to changes in curriculums and methods of instruction. We lay the disparity at the doorsteps of parents, who, unlike teachers, never attended a teacher training program or earned a master's degree in teaching.

After students acquire basic fundamental learning skills, eventually they will need to advance to a higher level of learning tools. The ability to learn how to use those learning tools will build their capacity to comprehend new and more complex information across all content areas, while also greatly improving their learning skills. Fundamental learning skills should be taught at the elementary school level and then progress, with increasing emphasis on teaching more developmentally rigorous methods of learning and studying, as students move through the different stages of middle school, high school, and college, where they will encounter more advanced levels of instruction and work. Without the benefit of some basic fundamental skills for learning, too many students begin to experience a steady or rapid decline in their ability to keep pace with lessons and the volume of work assigned. Their learning curve begins going in reverse, which then reinforces their sense of being unable to keep up. Falling behind triggers tremendous self-doubt and disappointment. If students experience prolonged periods of falling behind, with little to no opportunity (i.e., teacher intervention) to reverse course, they fail the course. Down goes their self-esteem; and most assuredly, what we should all be concerned about is how devastating it will be to their educational well-being.

Expanding every teacher's instructional tool kit with learning techniques and strategies will also improve student engagement in learning. Assessing whether or not students have acquired learning strategies is as important as testing for evidence of content learned. In fact, tests that show performance results generally are indicators of how well students understand the content and/or concepts taught. Substandard performance levels may be evidence that teachers need to examine the results through another lens: the possibility that the student's performance is being hindered by the absence of learning strategies. Weekly tests designed to test for understanding of content could also serve as indicators to strengthen learning skills.

One way to assess that theory is to embed lesson plans with explicitly stated learning objectives, first taught by teachers, then included in standards-based performance rubrics to reinforce what was taught. Rubrics are distributed among all students to allow them access to the teacher's expectations. Learning objectives, coupled with written standards-based assessments prior to doing assignments, provides transparency. Written and explicitly stated standards give students information they need about what components or elements will be required for successful completion of the assignment. Rubrics also reveal, in advance, how methods of assessing evidence of components or elements were included, as well as level of standard achieved in demonstrating depth of knowledge.

Many rubrics include a numeric rating scale that informs students how many points (usually from 0–10) they can earn, as well as what number of overall points will determine a final grade. Revealing in advance what is expected and the potential number of points a student can earn is often an effective motivational tool. Students have an incentive to do well. But what appeals to many students is being informed, in advance, about the highest number of points they can potentially earn because it places some degree of control into their hands. Teachers can also disseminate a chart revealing what grade is equivalent to number of points earned.

Not all students apply the level of effort needed to achieve the highest grade. Their preference for settling for a grade other than an *A* incentivizes them to make less of an effort. For teachers, the benefit of using standards-based rubrics to assess student performance prevents the practice of hiding from students both what will be judged or assessed and how their final grade was determined. A grading system that relies on objective and fair assessments benefits students and teachers. It builds trust in a grading system that is often perceived as subjective, placing too much power into the hands of teachers who some students rightfully suspect are influenced by how the teachers feel about them and not solely based on the evidence of their performance. Rubrics also provide evidence of what students learn, as well as the degree of how well they understood concepts taught.

Every parent-student-teacher conference should include student work samples and rubrics. Work samples accompanied by rubrics provide evidence of learning objectives, skills acquired, level of strengths, and areas needing improvement. Performance outcomes in standards-based rubrics can also be useful for identifying learning gaps because performance outcomes serve as a source of feedback regarding what students learned and how well it was, or was not understood. Learning objectives not understood or areas identified as needing improvement are the learning gaps that need to be closed. But teachers have to be cognizant of instructional methods used and assess whether the change needs to be made by students applying more effort or—and sometimes it may be a case of and/or—the need to consider using a different instructional method.

Eliminating Suspensions

ADDRESSING DISRUPTIVE OR INAPPROPRIATE BEHAVIORS IN schools is one of the most challenging issues, especially in many inner-city public schools. Disruptive behaviors in the classroom should not be tolerated, but suspending students from school because of disruptive behavior—which is different from dangerous behavior due to possession of a weapon—does not adequately address the problem. Removing students from school for disruptive conduct for a period of time does not guarantee they will have learned their lesson, nor can we rely on them to be able to independently reflect on their behavior and demonstrate a willingness to be more compliant with school policies when they return to school.

In many cases, students transitioning back to school after serving a suspension feel angry and humiliated. Often, the experience of being humiliated is so infuriating that they reenter school feeling more enraged and less likely to re-engage in learning. A report to Congress found that Black students, boys, and students with disabilities are disproportionately disciplined in school, leading to higher rates of participation in the juvenile justice system, and ultimately, higher incarceration rates later in life.[16]

It is time to adopt more fair and reasonable procedures and discontinue the current practice of prejudging and then imposing the harshest irrevocable sentence of expulsion in response to behavioral problems. Automatic expulsions perpetuate unjust practices that further disenfranchise those already at a major disadvantage. Not changing the policies and procedures for how we address school violations means that we remain committed to keeping the status quo of a system that mirrors the same level of injustice meted out in America's unfair criminal justice system.

Schools should not feed students to the criminal justice system. Yet, expelling students from school for behavioral reasons puts them at risk of entering the criminal justice system because the behaviors displayed in school will potentially become worse if there is no opportunity to receive guidance and support to change the behavior. Permanent removal from school increases the likelihood of entering on the pathway of the schools that release students to roam the streets, where they are in jeopardy of ending up entering the pipeline into the criminal justice system or prison.

Given the disproportionate suspension rate of black male and female students compared to white students in urban public schools, can we really pretend to be surprised by the correlation of school suspensions and expulsions being similar to the disproportionate number of teens of color serving time in juvenile detention facilities or the prison system? This seems to suggest that the conditions in both schools and prisons have a similar unfavorable and unforgiving track record. But it is the high numbers of black males being suspended, expelled, and/or jailed that clearly show America has a long way to go in dismantling institutionalized racial bias.

If we examine such school records as report cards, we find that black male students with a pattern of failing grades may have a higher tendency of being behaviorally disruptive in school because they are not attaining academic success. Instead of viewing the possibility that the behavior is linked to the humiliation of academic failure and then working with the student to reverse the trajectory of their academic performance, their conduct is seen through a disciplinary lens with a predictable outcome: suspension. Students faced with multiple suspensions find it easy to just give up and drop out. Suspensions and expulsions serve only to contribute to the perpetuation of a cycle of absenteeism from school, which then results in students' falling further behind while serving a suspension *because* they were suspended.

Expulsions are even worse if the student is not allowed to return to school under any circumstances for the remainder of the school year. Some districts restrict students from reentering school for more than a school year. And where do these students go to serve their suspension or expulsion? They sit at home unsupervised because parents or guardians have to go to work. Or they turn to the streets, where they are free to hang out and potentially pass the time engaged in unsafe or criminal behaviors. Suspensions and expulsions simply pass the problem of undisciplined behaviors along to even less supervised settings that place students at even greater risk of making poor decisions. Lack of guidance or participation in some constructive activity while out of school escalates problematic behaviors that school staff were unable to address. In other words, the problem gets passed on to where there are no responsible adults available to supervise dismissed students.

When students are dismissed from school to serve a suspension or expulsion, we are communicating that we have no other course of action, which is often true. Schools have limited resources to adequately address discipline. However, if we commit to no longer suspending or expelling students from school for disruptive behaviors, we would be forced to think of ways to address disciplinary issues differently. Reforming education cannot just be limited to the creation of new schools with updated curriculums and improved methods of instruction. Education reform must also include changing the methods of how we discipline students.

The first step is to discontinue the current practice of suspensions and expulsions for disruptive behaviors. That means our public education system has to adopt a new set of protocols to address noncompliance of behavioral standards and policies. It also means all students remain in school. If schools stop imposing suspensions and expulsions, it could provide an opportunity for school leaders and teachers to begin viewing discipline through a more humane lens.

Behavioral issues are broad and may require the need to roll up our sleeves and challenge ourselves to first reflect on the reasons for the behavior, rather than defaulting to the knee-jerk response of immediately imposing disciplinary measures. If we do not get at the root cause of disruptive behaviors and then recognize that they may be a manifestation of something more than outbursts or refusal to do classwork, we have missed a real opportunity to make behavioral transgressions a teachable moment. For example, a student's disruptive behavior may be manifested from mounting frustration due to an inability to keep up with the pace of instruction, resulting in their falling further and further behind. Eventually, the student's self-esteem begins to erode. Over time, the erosion of their self-esteem brings them to conclude that there is no longer any way to access learning; and this lays the foundation for seeing themselves as failures.

Now we arrive at the nexus of how so many students channel their experience of fragility due to continued failure. Academic failure is foisted solely on students, who are then blamed for creating their status. But masking failure for the sake of wanting to be with their peers, while many students will not admit it, takes quite a lot of effort. Some go through the motions of arriving at school and attending without participating in classes, and they are permitted to just stare off into space. That is the desired behavior teachers are willing to accommodate because the student's conduct does not disrupt lessons. Some students are left alone throughout the entire lesson. Others are not as compliant.

Teachers who do make an effort to assist and engage the student in learning may have their good intentions rudely deflected in front of the entire class. Eventually, the teacher becomes the learner. Students who rebuff teachers who attempt to engage them in lessons are conveying to the teacher how to avoid being humiliated. Teachers learn to keep their distance. More importantly, reluctance to interact with students is based on day-to-day cues from the student about how to address them and whether or not to approach them at all. This makes educating the student even more challenging because, when a student is no longer accessible, teachers are constrained from entering the student's space.

In poorly managed schools where rules and policies are clearly written and on full display in hallways and classrooms but never truly enforced, teachers are pretty much on their own. Some have wisely concluded they are on their own after witnessing one or more colleagues who attempted to hold students accountable and entered into confrontations with students that did not go well because the cavalry, meaning administrators, never came. Then, adding insult to injury, what could have been a small and contained situation quickly escalated into a bigger confrontation because the student felt amped up by the presence of peers, who cheered the student on as the student jeered the teacher.

When teachers work in schools that lack meaningful support from the administrators when problems arise, they adopt a posture of self-preservation. They take whatever measures are necessary to avoid confrontation with students. If they hear but decide it best to ignore incidents occurring in the hall, rather than getting involved and assisting a colleague who is trying to de-escalate a disruptive student, many teachers will simply choose to close and lock their classroom door. Students inside of classrooms witness the closing of the door through a different lens. They view their teacher's decision to ignore the incident as an abdication of their authority. Some students are sympathetic to the teacher's actions because it's no secret the school's culture is rife with tension. Unresolved issues create a tension that permeates entire schools; and if left unaddressed, these issues become an ongoing cause of concern for everyone's personal safety. Sadly, when students witness the collective impotency of staff, and school leaders willingly acquiesce to students' roaming their school with intimidating postures, the other students lose faith in those charged with the responsibility of ensuring their safety.

In any school, the degree to how well it is managed is a reflection of the overall culture, and it is often revealed through the conduct of the students, who are "environmentalists." That is, student conduct is generally aligned with whatever the school's environment allows. Students will rise to the occasion and act in accordance with expectations that are respectful, fair, and routinely enforced *if* the appropriate parameters and guardrails are in place. In well-managed schools, even when occasional mishaps occur, staff do not run to the nearest room and close doors to keep problems at bay. Staff members closest to the situation work collectively to intervene and take appropriate action. Students who are present witness adults taking charge by working together to address issues without showing fear or favor towards the parties involved.

There is no greater fear in a school than when students are present to witness critical moments that reveal they may not be safe. In less-managed or poorly managed school cultures, students observe that the adults nearest the verbal or physical altercations between students retreat and seek a safe space. Such actions make the student observers especially concerned about being able to survive peers who are permitted to be out of control. Seeing evidence to the contrary of what was said and promised at orientation on the first day of school, and repeated in artistically designed and beautifully written rules visibly displayed around the entire school, is the first indication that there is cause for concern. Anxiety can be triggered when students discover that behavioral policies and expectations assured during assemblies at the start of a new year are in reality invalid. One example is when, at the conclusion of a school assembly, conduct policies are reviewed; then, minutes after the assembly ends, another skirmish occurs that reaffirms students' cause for concern. Their justified concerns may be manifested in their declining attendance.

Students who frequently complain of not feeling well so they don't have to go to school may be suffering from anxiety brought on by feelings of being unsafe in an unsafe school. This may be especially true of students who had exceptional attendance throughout their previous years in elementary and middle school. For students who routinely comply with school policies and conduct themselves well at all times, lack of enforcement of school policies can lead to their being targeted for bullying. In fact, across many schools, students accustomed to getting along with others and enjoying their school experience during elementary and middle school generally identify a lack of adult supervision and management of students with challenging behaviors influencing their decision to stop attending school. Once they become targeted and experience being bullied, their previous stellar attendance record suddenly declines. Some students are left to fend for themselves and endure dreadful experiences for the whole school year.

Once the well-behaved students discover the pattern of inconsistent enforcement among faculty, staff, and administrators, they learn to brace themselves for the worst; they know that when students who have a tendency to bully others are free to conduct themselves in whatever manner the environment allows, it is going to be problematic for everyone.

It may be a revelation to many people, but the truth about students who take charge of their schools is that it absolutely frightens them too. Seriously, students who have more power than the adults who are supposed to be in charge, are uncomfortable because they know that with the absence of guardrails, they could spiral out of control. Their peers are terrified of any student's being perceived as the one that nobody, student or adult, dares to hold accountable for minor or major infractions. It's hard for students forced to witness the hands-off approach that results in bullies' being in control while acting out of control. Why? Because every student is raised with the explicit, even if unstated, expectation that the role of the adults in every school is to act responsibly on behalf of all students, particularly in ensuring their safety and well-being. Students who inherit authority usually do so because one or more people, however unwittingly, have abandoned their leadership role and responsibilities, making it possible for power to shift into the hands of students who never wanted the authority. Unruly behavior that is allowed to persist creates chaos that is extremely difficult to undo.

Once teachers and administrators discover that power has shifted away from them and into the hands of some students who behave ruthlessly, there is usually one of two immediate responses. One response is to make nice with the students in charge to curry favor with them because they have become too popular to take away their authority. The second response is to react by making an effort to take back authority, which is met with varying results. Usually, the credibility of any authority they may have once had has been diminished to the point where efforts to try to regain that authority lack authenticity and are met with resistance. Those school officials are usually branded as "a joke," and then treated accordingly.

On the other hand, the presence of fear among adults is evident in other ways. Some school leaders or members of the administration in highly restrictive schools are prone to deploying extremely heavy-handed discipline measures as an attempt to overcompensate for their feeling of powerlessness. Schools with an astronomically high number of suspension and expulsion rates are embedded in a culture of overly authoritative and unreasonable management. In those schools, even minor infractions are not tolerated. In other words, typical human mistakes are responded to as if they are equivalent to the students' arriving to school armed with a weapon. In essence, those who live in fear of students and those who fear showing their humane side to students do not possess a management style that benefits students.

Inside of classrooms, teachers do possess a range of options, but fear can overtake their ability to think of ways to approach students they fear. If teachers acquiesce by simply accepting the new ground rules dictated by students experiencing academic failure, we now have a classroom setting where the only lessons being taught are how frustration or intimidation become the acceptable vehicle to get the teachers to maintain their distance. Or, in some cases, failing grades create a different option for some students. While they don't necessarily want to choose to become the class clown, they have to find some way of hiding out in the open. Charismatic kids enjoy being at the center of attention. Not wanting their academic status revealed requires their redirecting the attention of the entire class away from instruction, which then helps them avoid the teacher calling on them. The range of behaviors used by some students to interrupt lessons through disruptions may be classic signs of languishing in failure. Students can become petrified when experiencing failure. While they try to appear indifferent, most are genuinely unhappy. Here's the truth about their predicament. The do not want to fail, nor do they take any joy in failing. The happy-go-lucky demeanor is a façade. Unable to reverse their continual academic struggles, they know they are headed toward an educational abyss where there is little, if any, chance of recovery. And they are silently crying out for help.

We tend to normalize some of the behaviors. Excessively funny and entertaining personalities are preferred much more than angry, disruptive personalities. However, this preference is a part of students' conditioning of replacing acceptance of failure with distractibility at the other end of the spectrum. When students who have a high rate of success become masterful at commandeering the class away from the teacher's control, they may also be crying for help. Classrooms and entire schools that have poorly maintained cultures where little or no learning is happening due to the frequent rate of disruptive behaviors often manifest with students' being in charge instead of adults. The question is, what contributes to the students' becoming so empowered that it results in their being able to take charge?

With the exception of weapons and severe physical altercations that place another person's safety at grave risk, all other school infractions should be handled through a process of in-school discipline rather than suspensions or expulsions. Students can and should remain in school to serve the consequences of noncompliance with school policies. Expulsions and suspensions do not work; therefore, it is time to shift our focus toward other means of addressing disciplinary issues. We may have to start with a new mindset about how we see misconduct. If we see patterns in the ways students are misbehaving—ways that are by now all too familiar to schools—why not retool our responses to more effectively address the range of behaviors that we can predict children, teens, and young adults typically display? These disruptive behaviors, poor attitudes, the tendency to become the class clown, and other behaviors are not new. Throwing students out of class only to have them return in the same condition that resulted in their removal has not effected change, so why are we still using arcane practices that do not work?

Here are the reasons:

- First, let's be absolutely clear, there is no point in expecting discontinuation of suspensions in poorly managed schools where high numbers of students are underperforming. In fact, the poor quality of education in many urban school districts, over a span of decades, has likely been a contributing factor of disruptive behaviors in poorly managed schools.

- Expulsions from school feed the growing flow of America's most disenfranchised and vulnerable population into and through America's controversial and unfair criminal justice system. The policies of handling disruptive behaviors in schools mirror how society responds to alleged crimes in the criminal justice system. The only difference is that public schools throw them out, while the criminal justice system throws them into jail. But suspensions and expulsions of high school students can serve as the first step on a path towards incarceration. One becomes a feeder for the other because both institutions unfairly target citizens from minority and poor communities.

- The long-standing tradition of suspending and expelling students is highly detrimental because temporary or extended time away from school disengages students from an essential pathway that can not only harm but completely derail their ability to attain any educational and career aspirations at a pivotal time in their young lives. Students who are suspended or expelled from school are often referred to subpar disciplinary schools or are funneled into the juvenile justice system. Consequently, students who are suspended or expelled have higher dropout rates than students who are not subject to higher levels of discipline. There is no research to support that black students act out at higher rates, but there is significant evidence that black students are disciplined at higher rates than non-black students. White students are also more likely to be referred to mental health services than to the juvenile justice system.[17]

- Uneducated and unemployed young adults are at the highest risk for becoming susceptible to engaging in poor behaviors that could be avoided if they are given the opportunity to remain linked to their education. In some cases, where the safety of others is at risk or has been violated, expulsions are warranted. However, students who are expelled should be allowed to continue their education in district programs that provide counseling focused on rehabilitation and possible reentry into a public school upon successful completion of the program and demonstration of conduct at the highest standards. Students allowed reentry should also be assigned to an adult mentor in the school to ensure a successful transition and to be monitored in their academic and behavioral performance throughout the remainder of their time in high school.

- Discontinuing any student's education can have negative consequences, but especially for students who come from low-income communities with access to fewer resources outside of schools to further their education. For many low-income students, it can be catastrophic to be turned away at a time when they most need to remain connected to their education.

- School administrators and staff members who respond to students challenged with undiagnosed emotional and/or mental health issues, solely as discipline problems, are doing a disservice to those students. Among all youths in juvenile detention centers, up to 85% have mental health disorders that would qualify them for disability services in schools, yet only 37%, or about half of them, receive those services. These students were deprived of an adequate education and instead were put into the juvenile justice system. Had the schools effectively intervened, there could have been a different outcome that would have reduced the school-to-prison pipeline.[18]

Lessons for Teachers: How to Avoid Humiliating Students

WHEN TEACHERS STAND IN FRONT OF A CLASS AND BEGIN TO teach, the assumption is that every student is attentive, fully comprehending the content, keeping up with the pace of the lesson and, judging from how they appear, performing well on class assignments, homework, and tests. Then, while grading papers, teachers discover that some students who appeared to be doing well, in fact were not. Given the lack of signs exhibited by students during the lesson, teachers wonder what they missed. Educators place a high premium on mastery. And while many students struggle with learning academics, most students have mastered the ability to appear engaged in learning. Recognizing the benefits of appearing engaged in lessons has served many students whose sole desire is to enter the class, sit, go through the motions of being present and engaged, and patiently wait for the thing that has become the most symbolic reward for enduring the class: the ringing of the blessed bell. But in an effort to look like everyone else, some students don't bolt out of the classroom when the bell rings.

Underperforming students generally appreciate not being reminded about their status by a teacher. And being the last student out can be a terrifying experience. No matter how politely a teacher utters a student's name, it does nothing to diminish the anxiety triggered when they hear their name followed by those dreaded words, "I'd like to speak with you for a minute." In that moment two things happen. The first is humiliation in the presence of their peers. The second is the need to find a way to save face. Social humiliation is created by the stigma of public requests to meet one-on-one. But there is a way to avoid humiliating students. Teachers can make one-on-one requests less terrifying by never conveying any sign that the request to stay behind is for a bad reason. It's just not cool. Teachers can respectfully request the student remain behind by stating, "I have something good I want to share with you. Do you have a few minutes?" Then begin the discussion with something positive. For example, if the student achieved 50% accuracy on a recent test, the teacher can start by highlighting what the student did correctly, then follow up with words of encouragement by identifying sections of the test showing that, while the final answer was incorrect, there was evidence of signs of understanding a portion of the problem. That alone reassures the student that the teacher recognizes their real potential, and, to the delight of the student, you can show how the category of "almost correct" answers could have achieved a passing grade.

Teachers will see how that kind of feedback lowers the student's defenses and lets them know the teacher is on their side. Lastly, when identifying portions that indicate evidence of not understanding, offers of additional instructional support can come in the form of a request to work in partnership with the student to help them learn whatever they did not understand. If you extend a hand with a smile and say, "Okay, let's meet after school for twenty minutes so we can get you on track" may genuinely lift the burden that matters most; they will not continue to be in danger of being left behind. Finally, the student sees hope and a pathway to working with the teacher to actually learn what may have eluded them. The tutorial process is a great idea . . . that is, if the teacher, after using the same method of instruction during the support session does not see evidence of the student's understanding, is prepared to use a different method of instruction that is tailored to the student's learning profile. Examining the effectiveness of a method of instruction, followed by a willingness to make modifications as needed until the student shows evidence of comprehension and is able to earn a passing grade of 85% or greater (which is in the range of showing mastery . . . and not just ability to pass at or near the 65% to 70% range), can be one way to end the failing of students. Failing the students is demoralizing and highly detrimental to the developmental growth of children who need and rely on adults to assist them through developmental, and sometimes fragile, stages of their young lives.

The need to be considerate of students when asking them, in the presence of their peers, to remain for a meeting is so important. It's also consequential when you don't take their feelings into consideration. The request is not what triggers the student's inner turmoil. It's how the request is made and who is present. We have addressed how a request can be made differently, but students who struggle with learning really feel embarrassed and ashamed, regardless of whether or not others are aware; because, truthfully, they know they are not doing well. They just do not want the added burden of being at risk of further humiliation by their peers, who likely suspect where the student's academic performance falls along the passing-to-failing spectrum. Many used to refer to it as the "bell curve." But regardless of how it is referenced, the existence of a performance scale, and where a student is perceived to be on that scale, sadly overshadows and, whether we like it or not, influences how students socially network with classmates or are judged by classmates and other teachers.

For those along the lower to lowest performing range of a perfor- mance scale, it is stomach-churning to suffer the indignity of a publicly stated request, made in the presence of their peers, to stay behind for a meeting. That's because, often, students witnessing these "requests" make the assumption that the request is because of the student's failing or low academic performance status. Some less sympathetic students who witness those requests don't help matters when they blurt out remarks teasing the targeted student. In fact, in that moment, peers who utter any response, let alone ones that signal the student may be in some kind of trouble, exacer- bate the level of humiliation. Whether their assertion is right or wrong, it's the arriving to the next venue that gets the attention of everyone because late arrivals to class or the cafeteria after meeting one on one with a teacher are equivalent to wearing a neon sign stating, "Stayed behind because ac- ademically I am behind." It's almost similar to being publicly summoned to the principal's office over the school's PA system. And that should be handled more humanely too.

V.
Closing Academic Achievement Gaps

What Teachers and Students Have in Common

MANY TEACHERS ARE UNAWARE OF HOW THEIR STUDENTS work so hard to not remind those teachers of their culpability in continuing the student's cycle of failure. But it's true. If teachers are willing to just stand by and continue to fail students, one cannot help but wonder: Is it because they lack the resources or the ability to teach students who are falling behind? And does the ongoing failure of their students trigger a sense of professional insecurity because teachers do not want their own uncertainty about how to fix it found out?

It is in this moment we need to recognize that students and teachers are mutually drowning in the same educational swamp and in need of a lifeline. If only teachers could understand that, just like them, their students do not want to be perceived as incompetent or less than proficient. But what keeps students' and teachers' heads barely above the surface of the educational swamp is that neither of them was ever made to feel safe about acknowledging they need help. Under the current failing education system, and in the absence of any signs by our government to provide the level of help needed to reverse the cycle of failure for students and teachers, We the People are going to have to intervene on behalf of our students and teachers to save our public schools. But we cannot save the status quo of a failed system. We must save and fix our public education system before city and other government officials dismantle the entire public school system and give it away to wealthy corporations. How do we fix our education system to make it safe for students and teachers to request and then receive support? Develop and professionally train teachers in new instructional methods to close academic achievement gaps.

If we do not fix the problem, then students, teachers, and their schools will incur the same consequence occurring in many other underperforming schools in poor communities across the country. State and city officials will continue downsizing school budgets. Smaller budgets will further impact each teacher's ability to provide quality instruction, hindering any chance of closing academic achievement gaps. Reduction of funding sources signals the rise of indifference to previous commitments promising to improve the quality of education in communities most desperately in need of better educational resources. If both students and teachers are at the same crossroads of uncertainty and have no specific roadmap for how to reverse course, they and we will continue giving big investors and corporations what they aspire to achieve: an erosion of the public's trust in our public educational system, in order to advance their goal of increasing the number of charter schools and closing public schools. Advocates of expanding school choice, vouchers, and privatization of public schools rely on the continuation of underperforming public schools to sway public opinion in their favor. As we witness the succession of successful efforts to privatize prisons and detention centers that house thousands of immigrants, it seems the growing interest in converting failing public schools into charter schools, funded by wealthy private corporations, is evidence that the government supports corporations' eventual acquisition of all public schools, where, coincidentally, the nation's highest population of disenfranchised citizens are easy prey. The privatization of public schools is also motivated by a desire to shrink and eventually decimate powerful teachers' unions, which just happen to be some of the nation's largest remaining unions populated by the highest number of women. Charter schools are able to hire nonunionized teachers and are often privately funded, taking away both bargaining power and the rights of parent voters.[19] Coincidence? I don't think so.

Closing Academic Achievement Gaps: How We Get There

THE QUESTION OF HOW TO CLOSE ACADEMIC ACHIEVEMENT gaps is the greatest challenge in reversing the current trend of widening academic performance gaps across America. However, if we endeavor to eliminate achievement gaps only for the purpose of leveling at least an equal number of the disproportionate minority students to the same performance levels as their peers attending public schools in more affluent neighborhoods as a means of assessing progress, we may be missing the real purpose of education: *educating all students at the highest standards.* Disproportionality of any population's underachieving simply means a higher number of those students are in need of more educational interventions. If the goal is to ensure no child is left behind, we must bypass the rule of contending with just catching up and bringing the number of students failing to an acceptable rate.

Raising performance levels is absolutely necessary. And initially it may be beneficial to use the high-performance levels achieved by successful students as benchmarks. But shouldn't we want a quality education that results in each individual student's truly achieving at the highest academic standards based on their individual abilities, instead of just settling to catch up with the performance of others? Our mindset of attaining performance levels equal to how others do is not aspirational enough. Once changes in the way we educate all students occurs, we have to resist the temptation of being content with academic achievement levels attained at a predetermined performance bar of success. If the goal of determining success focuses on matching the same performance levels of another student or population, we will be creating a new meritocracy where the educational glass ceiling establishes a status quo of encouraging attainment of "sameness" rather than encouraging students to achieve at levels that reflect their true individual potential. In other words, those who have had access to a lesser quality of education may in fact be capable of performing at levels that surpass their peers attending schools in affluent communities. Therefore, it may be in each student's best interest to not just raise the bar but remove it so we can allow them to accelerate their individual learning capacity to achieve at their highest level. One cannot help but wonder about the potential number of overlooked geniuses in educationally neglected communities across the country.

The mission of closing academic achievement gaps is possible if we are willing to invest in several changes. Among those changes are three very important initiatives that could have an immediate and positive impact as well as accelerate forward progress in overhauling our education system. The first initiative is to divest from the standard default response of blaming students for failing to learn. The second initiative is the development of a new education system that promotes learning through discovery and active engagement, where the process of educating students is a multifaceted interactive experiential process. The third initiative dovetails with the first two initiatives in that it goes to the very heart of what ails our education system: identifying a process of assessing and closing academic learning gaps. Implementing steps to identify and remedy learning gaps will help discontinue the practice of blaming students for what they do not learn. More importantly, if addressed in a timely and consistent manner, the process of identifying and then remedying learning gaps as they occur could prevent students from being left behind or excluded from participating in lessons. Focusing on closing academic achievement gaps could be the start of a new era of educational success that leads to future employment and economic prosperity for every student enrolled in public schools.

Educator's Instructional Oath

THE GOAL IN EDUCATION IS TO TEACH STUDENTS, NOT FAIL them. One way to attain that goal is to consider creating and holding all educators accountable to an Educator's Instructional Oath and require adherence to the promise to do no harm. The Educator's Instructional Oath would obligate all education professionals to discontinue the practice of holding students accountable for not meeting academic passing standards. Assigning a failing grade for students experiencing challenges with learning inflicts unnecessary harm and ignores one of the most basic rights all students should be entitled to: the freedom to demonstrate what you know and don't know, without fear of judgment or failure. Educators must regard errors as revelations about areas in need of additional, or a different method of, instruction. When errors are found, every student must be guaranteed access to additional academic support. The academic support should be delivered in a compassionate and constructive manner that is without judgment. Measures taken to remedy areas in need of additional support should persist until students demonstrate evidence of mastery at the highest standards in subsequent assignments and assessments.

In our current education system, students who perform poorly are perceived as responsible for schools' receiving unfavorable performance ratings and negatively impacting their teacher's evaluation. These conditions shift the focus away from education and onto self-preservation for schools and teachers. Let's commit to stopping self-preservation in education.

Discontinuing the Policy of Failing Students

S CHOOLS CAN AND SHOULD TAKE MORE MEASURES TO BUILD each student's self-esteem rather than continually trigger feelings of uncertainty, insecurity, and failure during the most formative years of childhood and teen development. One way that schools can avoid inflicting the shame and humiliation students so often associate with academic failure is to stop failing students. Schools should replace the policy of failing their students with a commitment to help them learn and succeed.

Commitments need the support of policies and practices that actually do help students succeed. In recognition of that fact, a process is needed to identify and address learning gaps. Equally important is the need to exchange the letter grade *F* with *NC* (*No Credit*). Receiving no credit would have the same result: the student would need to repeat the course until he or she earns a passing grade. But the most essential difference between receiving an *F* versus *NC* is that earning an *NC* does not have a numerical weighted value. It is completely neutral and therefore cannot negatively influence or devalue passing grades earned. It simply means no credit has been earned and the student must retake the entire course until he or she earns a passing grade. Discontinuing the policy of assigning students *F*s will help students feel less threatened about the possibility of receiving judgmental and punitive feedback. The current grading system incentivizes dropping out of school. It also further demoralizes minority students in poor communities who are already vulnerable to entering the school pipeline-to-prison path.

Instead, students see schools as institutions meant to educate the "smart" students while messaging to the rest of the population that they matter less and therefore deserve to receive less. Some teachers can and do use the grading system to unfairly wield their authority over students. Assigning students an *F* without producing evidence—information about standards or criteria not met—to justify giving a student an *F*, enables assigning of grades to be subjective. Of even greater concern is how some teachers may abuse their authority by weaponizing *F*s. When students sense they are not liked by a teacher or perceive they are being unfairly and repeatedly targeted for even minor rule infractions, they generally are not surprised when, at the end of a term or school year, and likely too late, their teacher exercises and sometimes abuses the power to determine whether or not they are eligible to advance to the next grade, by assigning an *F*. In urban school districts, ongoing concerns are legitimate, regarding racial bias influencing the grading process. This is another reason to discontinue the failing of students.

The potential of a new grading system of *No Credit* may be an insufficient fix for the disproportionate numbers of minority students currently failing. But any measure that eliminates a subjective practice in which those in positions of authority—who may hold racially biased opinions about black and brown students' academic capabilities—can decide who gets to pass or fail, is a step toward a more equitable and fair means of assessing all students. Ensuring a more equitable grading system is also needed in urban schools predominantly staffed by minority teachers and school leaders. The potential to abuse one's authority is a problematic occurrence across many schools and teachers from diverse ethnic and racial groups. However, in districts that lack interest in truly (and not just rhetorically) investing in the creation of healthy school cultures, the lack of oversight enables the adults in charge to freely wield unchecked power that leads to abuses in disciplinary practices, excessive targeting of students they don't like, higher rates of suspensions and expulsions, and—the ultimate, most injurious abuse of authority—deciding who passes or fails. Preventing any teacher from failing students can mitigate the potential abuse of power.

Schools should require transparency about all criteria used to assess academic performance. Teachers should use competency, performance, and academic standards-based rubrics with rating scales that clearly identify specific areas in which students need to improve and how their performance is judged. More importantly, standards-based rubrics should be shared with students prior to completing an academic task, so they have an understanding of what is expected and assurances that their ability to demonstrate what they know and the depth of their knowledge will be determined by points earned at various levels, and not by their teacher. In addition, they understand that their teacher must provide a completed copy of the rubric indicating what level of performance rating was achieved by a student and how the final grade was determined, based on their individual performance and not at the teacher's potentially subjective discretion.

Samples of students' work and performance rubrics should also be shared with parents at parent-teacher conferences so that parents are provided access to evidence of the teacher's assessment, to justify the merits of their assertions of their son's or daughter's academic progress. Standards-based rubrics for determining levels of academic competency and performance achievement are transparent, and student work samples provide concrete evidence of a student's progress, which should be followed by a show-and-tell discussion of remedial steps taken by the teacher to address areas of learning gaps revealed in the rubric. Parents should receive copies of work samples, rubrics, and a list of remedial steps used to improve performance, as well as recommended guidance they can provide to support and encourage their son or daughter to continue making academic progress. Parents' interest and participation in their child's education is one of the most important signals they can give to assure their sons and daughters that they value their educational aspirations.

If we invest in more humane and compassionate methods of conveying to students and their families that schools want to find and fix learning gaps and divest from the practice of failing students, schools will no longer be complicit in the continuation of branding poor students and students of color "failures." A more compassionate method of assessing academic performance will also help foster positive self-esteem during each phase of maturational development for students in pre-kindergarten through high school.

Eliminating failing grades at the high school level will increase the number of poor and minority college applicants. Updating our grading system will prevent the continuation of a practice that is so injurious to high school students. Despite the maturational growth many students make from the time of their freshman year to their senior year, earning *Fs* at any time during their four years in high school debilitates a student's overall grade-point average. Instead of appreciating changes they invested in during their junior or senior years, where many do remarkably self-rehabilitate their overall performance by improving their attendance, transforming their learning habits and applying themselves more seriously to improve their chances of achieving their aspiration of attending college, the *Fs* earned in their first year or two haunt them throughout high school. Sit with a junior or senior sincerely interested in applying to college while they are calculating their overall grade point average (GPA), and watch the change in their demeanor as it dawns on them how deeply *Fs* earned in the first year or years have come back to haunt them and overshadow the gains they spectacularly managed to achieve in their later years, when they finally grew up. Rather than there being some form of, if not rewarding them for successfully rehabilitating themselves, at least recognition of what they achieved and the *A*'s and *B*s earned in their final two years as proof, they feel cheated. The gains they made are not being rewarded. All of the *A*'s and *B*s are at the mercy of *F*s that equate to a numerical value of zero and seem to have a weightier force of gravity; pulling down the value of every high grade earned . . . regardless of the change in circumstances.

Okay. Let's pause here and acknowledge most students arrive to high school not always grounded in . . . well, anything. They are immersed in a social experiment that is often highly distracting and generally consumed with things other than seriously applying themselves. Basically, they sometimes need time to get it together, and to this day most of us who were once high school freshmen still don't know exactly what that means because we were afflicted with the rollercoaster effect most first-year high school students experience. Yet eventually we came to our senses and became more grounded. Miraculously, the turnaround high school students eventually make aligns with the goals and aspirations of educators and family members who remained steadfast in their belief that eventually the students will snap out of it and become motivated to take their education more seriously. And the majority of them do.

This is why schools have to dispense with the failing of students. Schools and families need to allow time for the social experiment to progress along each student's individual learning curve. Let's embrace the fact that students are not one-dimensional beings. They are students and human beings wired to socially engage in a range of behaviors that are part of the natural exploratory stages of development. Lessons learned from social experiences do help shape the content of one's character. But everyone must be given the time and space to experience growing up through trial and error, discover how some decisions have consequences, and have time to recover and learn from their mistakes *without* the school's piling on failing grades from which they can never fully recover. When we fail them academically, we are imposing a system of never forgiving them for their past mistakes and denying them the ability to fully recover from those human errors. And we do that because we have not yet understood the need to view every student's educational experience more holistically. Instead of adherence to policies driven by a system that promotes failure, shouldn't we be more invested in a system that permits our humanity to step up and provide assurances to students that schools will provide a safety net of humane resources without ever condoning policies that allow them to fail in a time when they need us to appreciate that the arc of their educational growth is dependent on their social progress too?

Whether or not schools are aware of the magnitude of what students are experiencing, we should endeavor to make schools a reliable anchor of support students can hold on to, sometimes for dear life, when faced with a crisis or other teen-related complications. Teenage life *is* complicated. Failing students is so counterintuitive to a school's effort to ensure the well-being of every student.

Discontinuing assigning an *F* will reduce educational anxiety at a time when teens and young adults are consumed with other more vexing or complex issues—like needing to boost their personal profile "likes" on social media. *We get it—we see you!*

How Blaming Students Leads to Shaming

I F A STUDENT COMPLETES A TEST THAT SHOWS HE OR SHE KNOWS 40% of the material represented on the test, that's actually beneficial information. No student ever deserves a failing grade when he or she demonstrates additional instruction is needed for the other 60% of material covered on the test. The 60% should serve as a window into specific areas in need of either additional instruction, an alternative method of instruction, and/or differentiated instruction. Academic assessments should be used as a system to identify what has been learned and specific areas in need of additional instruction. Then, after additional instruction, assess the student again.

The standard for determining quality instruction should be reflected in 90% or higher achievement on the final assessment and the ability to retain that same level of performance on subsequent tests that include the same concepts. For example, math requires some level of mastery of prerequisite skills needed to successfully perform math problems at the next level. If a student achieves 90% accuracy in a test for multiplication skills on a previous assessment, yet when those same multiplication skills are embedded in the ability to successfully complete a long division problem and the student achieves only 50% overall on the test, the question to ask first is, "Was 90% of the multiplication correct?" If so, you have evidence of that student's having mastered a skill previously taught and evidence of the need to intensify instruction to master other skills necessary to successfully solve division problems. Scaffolding is the introduction of a gradual incremental series of steps that require mastery of a previous concept or skill in preparation for the successful understanding and acquisition of a new skill for the subsequent series of more rigorous and challenging levels.

Grading a student's overall performance based on a final answer's being incorrect is insufficient. Mistakes made by students ought to be perceived as a teachable moment rather than a failure. Missteps or errors are simply an indication of areas less understood. Fostering an educational culture where students no longer have to fear punitive outcomes for making mistakes will help narrow the achievement gap. Schools that promote the practice of seeing errors as a teachable moment will bridge one of the most significant gaps that has influenced how students experience education: trust. Students will trust an assessment process that places emphasis on simply showing what they know—not whether their answers are correct or incorrect.

Teachers should communicate to their students that the goal of any assessment is to use each student's answers as indicators of where there may be possible gaps in their instruction. In essence, students' responses help facilitate a genuine exchange of teachers and students' learning from one another. In fact, teachers should think about ways of communicating their appreciation to students for taking the assessment and allowing the teacher to use their responses to inform them about the quality of their instruction. We often hear many in the education profession committing themselves to be lifelong learners. What better example of living up to that creed than by demonstrating a willingness to continue to professionally grow through a process that welcomes mistakes to help improve the quality of instruction, while teaching students the value of their truthful responses, rather than devaluing their effort to show you what they know and don't know?

Identifying where and how mistakes were made by pinpointing, with accurate precision, where something was done incorrectly, combined with remedial instruction, is a more constructive method of assessment. In addition to the remedial instruction provided to help students understand and then correct errors, students should also be challenged to demonstrate mastery of areas previously not understood by consistently providing correct answers on subsequent assignments and tests. Adopting the practice of using errors as teachable moments will lead to a willingness to be more engaged in learning. On the other hand, the continued practice of failing students and not addressing the real issue not only deepens mistrust but also widens the achievement gaps as teachers move further along the curriculum, introducing new concepts requiring mastery of skills or concepts that were taught but not learned, begetting more failure on subsequent assignments and tests. Assigning failing grades to students who really are demonstrating a need for additional support places the burden of *not getting it* on students rather than providing additional instruction and/or a different method of instruction.

Students who failed a subject at one grade level will likely experience failure for that same subject at the next grade level if not provided access to remedial instruction. The cycle of failure gets repeated, resulting in students' continued discouragement and fear of a particular subject. The longer that fear lingers, the more it fuels their mistaken belief that they will never be able to achieve passing grades in that subject. But if not properly addressed, continuation of failure does successfully teach them something: fear of that subject. After a period of time, experiencing failure happens so often that it feels normal, and apprehension becomes less of a concern. It's been replaced with an expectation of failing. Failure in one subject can be so devastating that, when a student is academically challenged in one or more other subjects, their overall academic self-esteem begins to decline.

Okay. We know this, right? *But then why have we allowed it to continue?*

Assessing Learning Gaps Is Vital for Rehabilitating Our Education System

I F WE EVER INTEND TO RESTORE TRUST IN OUR EDUCATIONAL system, we have to commit to a process that ensures educators have the time, training, and resources to prevent students from falling behind and failing. That undertaking will require drastic, but very doable, changes in our education system. Ongoing consternation about how to address academic achievement gaps can end when our public education system sees the responsibility of educating all students as its most important priority, and then develops and institutes a real plan for closing academic achievement gaps. We have to stop viewing academic failure as the responsibility of students.

Rehabilitating our education system has to begin with how educators view student performances in assignments and assessments. Instead of teachers' leaping from finding errors to applying a final grade, there should be a different purpose for identifying errors. The purpose ought to be to first perceive errors as a means for revealing what students did not comprehend or learn. Their errors may be an indication of their difficulty in grasping what was taught, due to the method of instruction that may have prevented their ability to fully access the information taught. We have normalized acceptance of academic performance gaps confirmed by data revealed in assessments. But we have yet to figure out the real root cause of those academic deficiencies. Until we discover what is causing academic deficiencies, how can we ever expect to find the correct remedy that has the greatest potential for closing achievement gaps?

And then let's go one step further and ask, given the historical pattern of our public education system's providing less-than-adequate—and at the very least inequitable—educational resources to those living in poor communities and neighborhoods predominantly populated with people of color: "Was the public education system ever designed to ensure the fair and equitable distribution of resources to all of America's children? Or was there some nontransparent but implicit decision that became repeatedly folded over and across several generations where poor citizens were always perceived as being worthy of less, which then made academic achievement gaps predictable and acceptable?"

Those questions are relevant in determining the effectiveness of whatever measures are proposed in our attempts to proceed forward because we will need to see efforts to move forward as a twofold mission. First is the need to remove the racial inequities that have impeded the ability of people of color to fully access quality education at the highest standards across all communities, enable forward progress in their ability to attend and complete a college education, and/or obtain employment that would pay quality incomes. All of these are linked to an educational tracking system that had its own racially and economically unfair line of demarcation. Removing those barriers that laid the foundation for keeping Blacks at the back of the line is essential to convey a new commitment to end all policies that oppress any citizen of color or are based on economic status. Eradicating barriers from our public education system will be extremely beneficial to the process of implementing new, equitable, and more effective education policies and practices devoted to providing access to quality education for everyone. It will also enable forward progress in advancing opportunities dedicated to helping all students achieve their academic potential.

In addition to removal of racial barriers, we need to implement measures to prevent the continued widening of achievement gaps by dedicating our efforts and the resources to eliminate learning gaps. This second aspect of the twofold mission will require investing in a system of routinely looking at long-ignored evidence of academic struggles many students experience, implementing a series of remedial intervention steps to prevent the students from falling further behind, and helping students catch up or accelerate their learning to enable full participation in all classes.

Routine monitoring for the purpose of detecting learning lapses means students will not have to incur the burden of fearing failure, nor will teachers perceive students in need of additional support as a strain on their time, resources, or reputation. When students fall behind and no remedial intervention steps are taken, lapses in learning may be an indication of lapses in instruction. In any classroom, at the first signs students are falling behind, remedial intervention should be the first priority. Instituting a policy of remedial intervention to prevent students from failing requires the development of an integrity-based system of checks and balances that ensures teachers are trained to proficiently utilize techniques for identifying learning gaps, applying instructional remedies, and preventing further. lapses from occurring. (See Appendix A.)

Education leaders in every district, across the entire educational chain of command, have to be committed to taking ownership when educational safety nets weaken or become ineffective. Each individual has to be educationally qualified in order to be a reliable and knowledgeable resource who can be looked to, without fear or intimidation, for support in finding and closing educational learning and instructional gaps. Placing emphasis on measures to close achievement gaps will end the cycle of failing students. It is also a more compassionate way of educating students.

The integrity of our educational system will be greatly enhanced when schools set a priority on eliminating learning gaps. Early identification of learning needs and referrals to support networks are an evidenced-based method of supporting students who are falling behind. By using multi-tiered systems of support, the development of learning assessments and interventions does not fall solely on one educator; instead, it is a collaborative effort.[20] (See the Resources section of Appendix A.)

The elimination of learning gaps in a school can occur through a practice in which every teacher routinely looks for indicators that students are falling behind and provides immediate remedial intervention. Remedial intervention is the safety net that will enable educational rehabilitation for students in need of additional time and instruction.

In a classroom setting, preventing students from falling behind will require an understanding that equity is not defined as the teacher's equally dividing her or his time among all students and then expecting it will result in every student's learning at the same pace. That practice has proven ineffective because students do not learn at the same pace, and students with learning gaps that were never previously addressed will need additional academic support. Equitable education in a classroom has to be based on a system of delivering additional time and instruction proportionate to each student's individual learning pace. Providing students with additional time or instruction, or access to an alternative method of instruction, will need a teacher and teaching assistant in every class as well as attention to size of student population assigned to a classroom.

Some consideration has to be focused on the burdensome and sometimes unfair expectations of teachers to cover the volume of content, which then requires the need to provide instruction at a pace that may contribute to leaving many students behind. In addition to teachers' needing to meet district requirements to cover specified amounts of content within a school year, teachers also learn to fear the consequences of their students' underperforming on standardized tests. The result is an entire school where leaders, teachers, and students become consumed with the preoccupation of failure.

Learning gaps are the responsibility of schools. Therefore, schools are obligated to take measures to ensure all students can access learning.

Students in danger of falling behind cannot be ignored or vanquished to a section of a classroom designated for those perceived as unteachable.

Daily educational rehabilitation should include short-term remedial interventions to address academic learning gaps as they occur. The learning gaps may be attributed to instructional lapses or to teachers' being continually subjected to the dumbing down of instruction driven by lowered learning expectations.

High schools can address learning gaps by devoting time at the start of each school year administering prerequisite academic assessments across all content areas. The purpose of the assessment would be to detect level of content knowledge and gaps in knowledge, and assess baseline performance levels for reading and writing skills. Assessment results revealed could help teachers develop a rigorous remediation plan to address academic gaps from the start of each school year.

To rehabilitate our education system, we will need to revise the process of how and why students are assessed. Typically, assessments are relied upon to determine whether or not students need 504-classroom-based support services supervised by their teachers or a different and more involved level of supportive intervention from trained special education teachers. (See "IEP vs. 504 Plans: What's the Difference?" at *Understood.org/articles/en/ the-difference-between-ieps-and-504-plans.*)

The current process of assessing, analyzing and determining level of resources needed to improve student academic performance is as follows:

- Student work products and class tests

- State-mandated standardized tests

- 504 Assessment

- Special education needs assessment

Generally, data gathered from student work products and class tests are used as the first indicators of whether students are experiencing academic learning challenges. In many states, mandated standardized tests are given annually; and if students are designated as "special needs," they have the right to receive accommodations or, depending on the severity of disability, may be granted an exemption from taking the test. The state-mandated standardized tests are listed second in the sequence of tests partially because the data related to performance is perceived as viable and useful for identifying areas in need of improving. However, the last topic within Chapter X, How Standardized Assessments Amplify and Perpetuate Class and Racial Bias, describes reasons student's performances may be impacted by circumstances inside and outside of school. State examiners, while determining whether answers are right or wrong, do not take into consideration the challenges students may be experiencing. It is rather curious that the number of students performing so poorly in so many urban schools never piqued the curiosity of the state or local districts to open the hood of the car, inquire why, and allocate the real resources needed to address students who repeatedly underperform. This book is dedicated to going beyond inquiring why, and getting to *what can be done about it* as one of several measures needed to rehabilitate our public education system.

First, I propose adding a new assessment and changing the sequence of how we measure academic performance. The revised process and assessments would be as follows:

- Student work products and class tests
- **Learning Gaps Assessment** (see the Process and Start-Up Tools sections of Appendix A)
- State-mandated standardized tests
- 504 Assessment
- Special education needs assessment

The addition of the learning gaps assessment is directly linked to student work products and class tests. When learning gaps assessments are routinely deployed in classrooms across all schools, it will not be business as usual in the way we currently assess, grade, retain, and repeat students in the same grade for another school year, or make referrals for special education or other services. Performance results on state-mandated standardized tests, if we use the data in the way the federal and state level educational leaders initially promised when they rolled out the exams in the first year, will be indicators related to the level of efficacy in the Learning Gaps model. (See Appendix A.) Students, teachers, and school leaders will have no reason to fear, when we can view the standardized test through a lens of being helpful and not punitive. In the first year, teachers were assured there would be no punitive outcomes attached to student performance data because it was intended to be a tool to identify areas in need of improving, and the state Departments of Education would allocate resources to school districts to improve performance outcomes in subsequent years. Learning gaps assessment will alter how teachers review the most important assessment tool routinely utilized in every classroom: work, activities, tasks, and a range of other valuable artifacts assigned to students. Learning gaps assessment will also stop the glut of referrals for special education services. When learning gaps are detected and a process for remediating those gaps is put in place, fewer students will require the resources of 504 or Individualized Education Programs.

What to Do Before Proceeding with Special Education Evaluations

T HERE IS NO DOUBT THAT MANY STUDENTS REQUIRE AND benefit from special education services. However, many other students who have been placed in these programs may instead simply need remedial assistance with their day-to-day learning processes. Conducting a Learning Gaps Assessment is a good first step to significantly decrease the rate of students receiving special education services who don't truly need them, and it will reduce the disproportionate number of students of color, particularly black males, who have been referred for special education evaluations.

By making sure special education programs consist of students truly in need of the resources the programs were designated to provide, we can restore trust in a poorly managed and substandard referral system that has resulted in the disproportionate and overpopulation of minority students. If we manage to adhere to those principles, we will not abuse the trust of students and families who want to believe that the evaluation assessments truly indicate a need for services, and are not the result of one or more teachers finding it difficult to academically or behaviorally work with a student and therefore thinking the situation warranted a referral for special education services.

But another important benefit is reducing the number of special education students who do not need to be placed in those settings. When we reduce the flow of referrals and transitioning of students from general education into special education services, budgetary costs will go down. Decreases in the number of students accurately identified as needing special education, will benefit districts tethered to years of allocating funds needed to cover the high and costly range of special education services. Transportation in urban communities, as well as the expense of special education services themselves, are among a school district's most costly annual budget allocations. So not only will districts see a decrease in costs associated with special education services because there will be fewer special-needs students needing them, but the transporting of special needs students will also be significantly reduced, for the same reason.

That having been said, it must be emphatically stated that saving money must *never* be used as a tool that negatively impacts students who truly do need special education services. The number of special education students may be reduced as a result of the new assessment process, but for many students there will always be a need to provide special education and transportation services in accordance with special education assessment findings and recommendations. *No* monetary master plan should purposely reduce funding sources for transportation, or any other area of needed services benefiting the educational, social, emotional, and physical well-being, and overall developmental growth, of all special needs children, teens, and young adults. Reduction in funding at the expense of those most in need would also result in negatively impacting services needed by, and in accordance with, each student's Individual Education Plan or 504 Plan, and required by law.

Most importantly, it would be morally reprehensible and detrimental to reduce much-needed quality-of-life funding resources and deny access to resources to our citizens who are differently able. Equitable access to resources that enable differently able citizens to live a quality life is an imperative, not a choice. Removing funding sources to assist citizens most in need of support and already at a disadvantage would only further exacerbate their quality of life by viewing their need for support as too costly or a strain on budgets.

VI.
How We Close
Academic
Achievement Gaps

(See also Appendix A)

Aligning Teacher Evaluations with Closure of Learning Gaps

A NEW EVALUATION OF TEACHER PROFESSIONAL PERFORMANCE levels should be based on how effectively learning gaps were addressed and remedied. After teachers develop competency with the process of analyzing student work products and assessment results to identify learning gaps, they must respond with an individualized instructional remedial plan that requires evidence of student mastery as the criteria of proof that the learning gaps have been closed. Teachers' developing the habit of applying instructional remedies will close learning gaps and advance students along their individual learning curve, instead of impeding their educational growth. Applying instructional remedies to advance student learning will accelerate a teacher's professional development along their professional learning curve.

Teachers will need professional guidance to develop proficiency in applying steps to ameliorate student learning gaps. One of the essential goals in the teacher evaluation process has to be for teachers to provide quality instruction to effectively address learning gaps. To achieve this goal, teachers need to develop proficiency with observing student participation in daily lessons, and examine student work and test results in search of concrete evidence and indicators of whether or not students are learning. Capturing evidence in those areas, followed by a thorough analysis of what the student's performance reveals, is essential to detecting learning gaps. Once learning gaps are identified, the process shifts to examining the method of instruction used, objectively assessing its degree of effectiveness, and determining what more is needed to close the learning gaps. (See Steps VII and VIII of Appendix A.)

Sounds simple, right? Well, to get there from here requires some monumental changes in the way teachers are taught how to teach in college programs and professional development sessions provided to current staff members in their school districts. The chapters devoted to closing academic achievements gaps provide a detailed road map for how to break the cycle of failing students by focusing on educating them when errors are detected.

Diversify Assessments to Capture Range of True Potential

THE ASSESSMENTS THAT SCHOOLS USE TO MEASURE LEARNING are of equal importance. The ways students learn are as diverse as the broad range of learning styles and levels of performance in every classroom. In fact, not enough attention is given to understanding students' learning styles and learning profiles. Both are essential in understanding the assets students possess and rely on to process information. They are also necessary for planning lessons tailored to be fully inclusive of the broad spectrum of learning styles and profiles. (See Preparations, Task 1, of Appendix A.) If we overlook the different learning styles and learning profiles, we further limit the ability to accurately assess student performances. It could be argued that the absence of competency- and performance-based assessments hinders our ability to capture a fuller and more holistic analysis of what students are capable of achieving. It is also why limiting the range of assessments and investing total reliance on one-dimensional sets of testing measures, such as standardized assessments, restrict schools from measuring all of what each student has learned or is knowledgeable about. Standardized assessments are designed to measure outcomes of only a portion of what each student truly knows or is capable of performing.

Our range of assessments has to include a competency-based series of demonstrations and performances that enable students to showcase what they learned and the depth of their understanding of what they learned. For example, students who assess well on a standardized math test are never required to show evidence of a broader understanding. Understanding—being capable of performing computational tasks taught in isolation—does not mean they can apply their understanding of the elements of math in a broader context. Addition and subtraction of numbers in an isolated abstract classroom setting will not promote the transference of what is learned to broader applications, such as understanding supply-side economics, balancing a checkbook, or making informed decisions about how to manage their finances. Frankly, it's time to include financial literacy courses that are separate from the standard math curriculum. Financial literacy is one of the most undervalued and critically needed subjects in our education system. Educating students about how to personally manage money and develop healthy financial habits should not wait until they receive their first paycheck, where they will instantly seek to gratify every whim, purchasing things they do not need. Money interlocks with every facet of their lives in the real world. Preparing them about the broad scope of money's influence while in school is one of the greatest preparations our education system could bestow upon every student. Let's appreciate the many ways financial literacy courses at all grade levels can enhance future generations of young adults' ability to financially survive and experience economic prosperity for the rest of their lives. Often referred to as financial literacy, simply expanding math curriculums to include a few chapters devoted to making and managing money does not result in students' being financially smarter, adequately informed about, or better prepared for what they will encounter in future financial matters. Determining the value of a potential investment, purchasing a home, gauging the performance of a portfolio, and monitoring investments are skills currently not taught alongside algebra and geometry in math courses. Financial literacy courses should also be included among the list of foundational core subjects of science, English language arts, math, history, and technology.

Rather than relying on state exams, we ought to set a priority on offering financial literacy courses, if we expect students to survive in the real world where a different level of math aptitude and skills will be required. How are students supposed to know how to manage their personal finances if we do not provide the range of information and opportunities to, at a minimum, expose them to survival skills? Schools exist to educate students. Managing one's personal finances requires the cultivation of skills and understanding of how to manage and build healthy financial management habits from elementary school through high school. Acclimating students to concepts related to income earning, saving, and spending habits before they get their first job will enable them to be informed about how decisions they make, from the day they earn their very first paycheck to every paycheck thereafter, will impact their potential prosperity in their future. Students are always advised to plan for their future. We need to support that advice by giving them financial literacy programs in school that will allow them to financially plan and succeed in their futures. Math is a separate content area from financial literacy. Both require students' ability to demonstrate true competency in understanding math through real-world applications. However, most students do not comprehend the multiple facets of money, assets, income, savings, loans, retirement, credit, and many other financially related matters people encounter in their daily lives. Because these students are currently ill-equipped to fully understand the availability of resources for how to manage their finances, they are at risk of being victims of financial schemes and opportunistic predators who have always relied on the ignorance and naiveté of their prey.

A standardized test that requires demonstration of math skills using a single problem-solving task does not show evidence that they have learned how to use these skills beyond a computational task. It only measures a student's ability to do what the test was designed to assess, a single computational task that can only be assessed in a pencil-on-paper or electronic-survey response. Some states have made modifications in requiring students to show more evidence in how well they comprehend what they have learned. In humanities portions of assessments, the addition of open-ended questions requires in-depth explanations, and math requires students to show their problem-solving skills and explain how they arrived at their answers. But overall, it seems most assessments were designed to lend themselves to quick and easy scoring. Assessing performance outcomes takes volumes of time and financing, which tends to motivate scorers of exams to churn out information as quickly and expediently as possible. Learning is not a one-dimensional or expedient process; learning is a multidimensional and sometimes labor-intensive process that should not be judged through one single form of assessment to determine a student's authentic level and degree of understanding and overall competency. For example, students can easily demonstrate the fact that one plus one equals two, but can they also demonstrate that they have learned the meaning of interest rates and how they impact one's credit history?

A combination of measuring instruments and performance-based assessments that determine true competency and understanding of how each student individually absorbs and processes information is absolutely necessary. The process we currently use determines only the level of education, not quality of education, and does not take into account the cognitively and developmentally complex spectrum of each student's learning process. Competency-based assessments will require orienting curriculum and instruction to place greater emphasis on experiential learning, which includes each student's individual learning style and learning profile, and less emphasis on rote learning.

Favorable Outcomes of Pedagogy Done Well

GRAPPLING WITH INEQUITIES IN PUBLIC SCHOOLS HAS NOT been successful. Decades of academic performance disparities between racial and ethnic student populations, combined with the disproportionate number of minority students failing, being suspended from school, and dropping out of school, on the surface appears to be about race. While many more in minority populations historically have underperformed, the inequities in the quality of resources, methods, and delivery of instruction, as well as the absence of high standards and expectations, all influence the quality of education across many low-income communities and communities of color. Those are the conditions responsible for educational inequities in public schools in our most vulnerable and disenfranchised communities. Race, ethnicity, and poverty are the scapegoats for an education system that undervalues the need for quality education in low-income communities.

Our public education system is underserving students and then blaming those being underserved for substandard performances. Performance outcomes in public schools are the result of inequitable educational resources, not a student's race, ethnicity, or economic status. Yet it is the students who bear the brunt of performance outcomes—outcomes that were highly predictable due to the absence of quality educational resources and equitable access to them. Blaming ongoing failure on students of color and those living in low-income communities is and has always been the default response, and one of the main contributors perpetuating our country's racially divided system. It also underlies the foundation of America's preoccupation with the need to improve education by addressing racial bias in classrooms.

Educators can get beyond the quagmire of how to address racial bias in classrooms by focusing on delivering quality instruction. Teachers can improve the quality of education for all students by using student performance assessments to assess the level of effectiveness of their instructional practices. That starts with divesting from the current practice of assessing student work to determine whether they passed or failed. Using student performance to gauge the level of efficacy related to methods of instruction, and applying alterations when needed to improve the quality of instruction, will have the positive result that no student will ever earn a failing grade. In fact, no final grade should ever be the initial conclusion.

The first round of assessing a student's performance, for all assessments, should be to inform teachers about the degree of effectiveness of their instructional methods used in lessons. Analyzing test results and other samples of student work demonstrating what was learned and how well they learned, reflects the quality of the teacher's instruction. Shifting the focus of judging performance outcomes, and years of blame, away from the student and onto how students are educated in school, may inject more fairness and equity into an inequitable education system.

Pedagogy done well can be devoid of racial, ethnic, economic, and any other bias. In fact, it can be the very thing that mitigates the continuation of constraining academic achievement among student populations underserved in public education. Besides determining the degree of instructional method effectiveness, there will also be the need to assess the level of a teacher's content knowledge of subject and method of delivery/communication used in lessons. Assessing the level of effectiveness of an instructional method can be done using the current assessments. Qualitative instructional-based assessments to determine level of effectiveness of instructional methods, which can be modified as needed, are a more equitable way of educating students.

Instructional-based academic assessments will enable teachers to capture what students have learned, show areas in need of strengthening, and inform teachers about whether or not the method of instruction resulted in every student's achieving academic success. But for students who do not achieve academic success, there will be no need for alarm or panic. The instructional-based assessment is doing exactly what it was meant to do: reveal learning gaps. Learning gaps identified in the assessment are not the responsibility of students, and therefore they should not incur the blame for showing what they know and do not know on the assessment. Neither should teachers be put in a position of fearing the results as a reflection on them or their ability to teach. Assessments have to be given a status of neutrality, where no one is assigned blame for the outcome but instead teachers embrace whatever the results reveal as an opportunity to analyze the method of instruction used, determine the degree of effectiveness in benefiting every student, and, for those whose results indicate learning gaps, prescribe remedial steps. Any of this may require alternative methods of instruction to ensure that students achieve academic success. The bottom line is that instruction must persist until learning is achieved.

Transitioning away from the current practice of failing students who don't meet passing standards is an attainable goal. Educators from across the spectrum of novice to seasoned veteran may need professional development and time to learn a more equitable and fair process of assessing performance results. Partnering with students and families to engage them in the remedial phase will require orienting them about the overall academic achievement plan, which must include both the awareness of the students' learning profile when determining the effectiveness of instruction and the devising of steps to improve the quality of instruction. (See Appendices B and C.) Following are the steps involved:

1. Develop teacher familiarity with, and proficiency in, using uniform standards, understanding the criteria for determining whether or not standards were met, and verifying evidence of level of strength achieved for each standard (rubric scale of 1–10, where 1 = weak and 10 = exceptional).

2. Thoroughly examine a variety of student work samples and assessments to identify areas of insufficient knowledge or incorrect responses. (This step will likely reduce cheating.)

3. Engage teachers in the analytical process of cross-referencing student work results with criteria and standards-based performance rubrics.

4. Identify reliable indicators of specific learning gaps or patterns of learning gaps and the extent of the learning gap deficits.

5. Prescribe remedial strategies.

Assessing the quality of instruction will significantly improve how students and teachers perceive and experience education. Fortunately, there are many highly competent and passionate teachers who truly are dedicated to improving education for all students—and we could certainly use more of them. Whenever you encounter them, express your appreciation to them for the great effort and work they do 180 days of each school year, and many of their weekends too.

Focus on Closing Achievement Gaps Instead of Schools

MANY EDUCATORS MAY RESENT A STUDENT FOR MAKING THEM look bad and then adopt a posture of indifference, which puts the student at greater risk for continuing to fail. Failure begets more failure when teachers wrongly conclude there is no point in providing additional or different instructional support that might prove more effective. Instead, their lowered expectations continue to perpetuate a status quo where it has become acceptable to condemn students to the status of "underperformers." Underperforming students are casually discarded and left to join so many of their other undereducated peers who get ensnared in the continual cycle of academic failure.

The persistent rate of underperforming students is and should be alarming. But even more alarming are the remedies deployed by school districts struggling with the question of how to close achievement gaps in underperforming public schools in—you guessed it—many low-income urban communities. Instead of placing the focus on providing improved instruction and other resources needed to better educate underperforming students, many school districts have directed their focus on how to misuse their standardized test data to target underperforming schools for closure, which reduces the overall number of underperforming students and ultimately reflects more favorably on the district's reputation. There seems to be little to no interest in using test outcomes to academically address and close academic gaps revealed, which is supposed to be the goal of the mandatory statewide standardized assessment. That goal appears to have been swapped for an entirely different purpose: identifying and shuttering persistently underperforming schools solely for the benefit of enhancing the appearance of the district's own performance profile. But districts have also discovered a financial benefit for closing underperforming public schools.

The number of public-school closings in low-income urban communities shows a pattern in which districts have a greater interest in finding measures to reduce the size of underperforming student populations by closing their schools. The purpose appears to be to discontinue the cycle of the district's persistent failure to provide quality education for all of its students and thus alter the public's perception about how the data exposes the truth, that districts are still grossly underperforming. Unfortunately, many other public schools not underperforming but in the same zip code as the schools that have been underperforming for decades, are being caught up in the same net of massive school closures.

Flipping public schools into corporate-run charter schools has become one of the fastest growing and economically profitable industries that may one day rival the economic boom amassed from the privatization of prisons. Many urban city leaders across the country are drinking the Kool-Aid promoting the false claim that charter schools are outperforming public schools. That narrative became the prevailing doctrine when city officials discovered the financial benefits of making empty school buildings available for sale or as rental properties to corporations eager to take over public schools. The financial windfall to cities partnering with corporations invested in expanding charter schools in low-income urban communities has also resulted in shrinking budgets among the remaining public schools. The per-student funding formula that states use in determining how much each city or town receives is also contributing to the shrinking of public school budgets. When students transfer to a charter school, their funds allocated to support their education follow them from one school to the other.

Failed efforts to close the achievement gaps have resulted in targeting and closing schools with high rates of underperforming students, and this adds further degradation and reduces resources to low-income communities in need of better-quality schools. Replacing old dilapidated schools and outdated curriculums with new schools and contemporary curriculums in low-income communities could potentially become symbolic beacons that generate pride among the residents and a valuable anchor in communities long neglected. Decreasing the number of schools populated by high numbers of underperforming students, as a remedy for responding to decades of expanding academic achievement gaps, is a blatant dereliction of responsibility and educational malpractice. It reveals that districts have no real interest in closing achievement gaps but are instead willing to use the lack of academic progress in public schools as an excuse to replace them with charter schools.

In America, citizens residing in poor urban and rural communities are subjected to all manner of social experimentation. Sustained periods of neglect or shrinking resources turns those communities into social petri dishes where long periods of the gradual or sometimes swift and massive reduction of a school's budget and/or institution of ineffective educational reforms result in educational neglect and stagnation. The lack of academic progress reflected in district and statewide assessments has become justification for abandoning public schools and handing them over to corporations. We now have become a nation dependent on the failure of the poor in order to justify turning public institutions over to wealthy corporations under the guise of school vouchers and school choice being in the best interest for underserved children. Public schools, including those that were not underperforming, are randomly and mysteriously slated for closure, and at the same time communities see an expansion of charter schools. Now families really have no choice but to enroll their children in so-called choice schools, because they are the only ones available in their neighborhood.

School choice may give the appearance of being the preferred choice of poor families; but when public schools are disappearing and being replaced with charter schools, is there really any genuine open selection process going on if the only schools available with open enrollment are charter schools? The messaging in promoting school choice and charter schools has been effective, and quite deceiving. Privatization of prisons and public schools is the social experiment inflicted on low-income communities.

Public Schools Must Continue to Evolve

GIVEN THE LIKELIHOOD OF AS-YET-UNKNOWN ADVANCEMENTS in technology and other areas related to education, public schools must be durable and open to accommodating advancements to ensure they do not remain stagnant. School stagnation is how we inherited our current system that is driven by decades of outdated educational policies and practices. Any chance of improving our education system will require a departure from our reliance on outdated methods of instruction based on curriculums and standards from past eras. If our education system does not continue to evolve, students will once again become the victims of outdated educational practices.

Educators and public school district leaders have to resist whimsical decision making to chase and adopt the next education reform highly recommended and deemed acceptable simply due to its receiving popular acclaim. The cycle of continually chasing the next best thing, which then is quickly discarded and replaced with another thing, based solely on the preference of a new leader of a school district, is often the cause of chaos and uncertainty if the installation of the new thing is done without extensive research and careful analysis proving it is the real thing and not simply a whimsical decision to replace another thing.

Districts should instead invest in creating a brain trust of highly competent educators representing elementary, middle, and high schools and tasked with the mission of brainstorming innovative ideas and researching best practices based on proven results of improvements in education. More importantly, the team should create and distribute a well-articulated rubric that identifies the specific standards and criteria that team members will adhere to in determining whether or not the practice aligns with rubric standards. Members of the brain trust team should cultivate norms that adopt and maintain oversight of current advancements in the expansion of education platforms that enhance and broaden the scope of methods of instruction, as well as explore newly discovered information across all content areas.

Staying current in the changing world of science, math, arts, technology, and other subjects will enable alignment with, and the ability to keep up with, advancements that benefit the entire society. Maintaining fundamentally stable foundations while also remaining flexible will enable new cycles of technological and other advancements to be absorbed in as they occur. But changes have to be rooted in stable and reliable foundations, like members of a brain trust, to maintain a link between educational goals and pragmatically sensible alignment with new ideas and measures in the broader society, in order to ensure that schools are keeping pace with other industries. The continual cycle of evolution in education has to have the capacity to grow, but within reasonable and sound decisions that always reflect what is in the best interests of students.

VII.
Focus on School Culture

What's the Alternative? Improve School Culture

EFFORTS TO CLOSE ACADEMIC ACHIEVEMENT GAPS IN URBAN public schools will be impeded if we neglect to also improve school culture.

Collaborative High Schools would provide counseling, mentoring, and advocacy resources to address disciplinary issues. Collaborative High Schools' administration and support team will be guided by and committed to utilizing a disciplinary process that lets students learn from their mistakes while retaining their dignity. It is the school's responsibility to educate students who are experiencing a broad range of complex issues typical of teenagers trying to navigate their way through developmental stages.

Various behaviors, such as continued physical bullying, intimidation of others, and ongoing disrespect towards others, are disruptive to learning and negatively impact a school's culture. But instead of suspending or expelling students for violation of policies related to nonviolent disruptive behaviors, Collaborative High Schools include alternative spaces equipped with education resources, as well as social behavior and academic counseling resources, to support the continuation of a student's education while participating in a behavioral rehabilitation program aligned with the school's mission to rehabilitate and eventually reintegrate students back into their regularly scheduled classes.

The use of technology in Collaborative High Schools places education on the vanguard of closing the academic achievement gap and, of equal importance, paves a way to eliminate the detrimental practice of suspensions and expulsions. Discontinuing practices that temporarily or permanently separate our most disenfranchised student populations from continuing their education will ensure they retain a firm and stabilizing grip on the rung of America's still most reliable ladder to obtaining future career and economic success. Retaining and ensuring the continual elevation up the education ladder is imperative, regardless of any disciplinary, medical, legal, family related, or other issue, because circumstances and conditions eventually change. A student's journey from teen years to adulthood is transformational and goes through different stages. Who students are today, and the conditions they currently face, may be formative, but it does not always predetermine who they will become. Therefore, instead of branding students, we should focus on the behaviors that impede their forward progress by helping them understand and then take responsibility for their decisions. This will increase the probability of getting them to see the root cause of their behaviors.

Normalize Resources for Social and Emotional Needs

G ENERALLY, PUBLIC SCHOOLS ARE DESIGNED TO FOCUS SOLELY on the development of academic skills, to the detriment of students, teachers, and school leaders. In fact, across many urban public schools, one of the most vexing challenges preventing teachers from teaching and students from learning is the alarmingly high number of behavioral incidents that daily shift a teacher's attention away from instruction to classroom management. While we have known this for so many years, schools have been unsuccessful in identifying effective ways to fix the problem.

Education in 21st century schools must expand to include the development of social and emotional skills. If schools can be responsible for promoting the well-being of the whole child, based on the premise that academic success is interconnected with and greatly influenced by physical, social, and emotional fitness, we can enhance a student's education experience, which would likely result in improved academic performance. If we learn to find ways to safely and without judgment or condemnation approach them before the potential of an incident occurs, we benefit from preventing a student's committing of a violent act that leaves hearts forever broken. Sadly, when perpetrators of massive violence are asked why they commit such acts, they often cite such factors as being bullied, ridiculed, and/or ostracized, and having a sense of loneness that leads to social isolation. Being subjected to prolonged periods of bullying and ridicule is liable to push our fellow citizens closer to and, for some, eventually over the precipice of imminent danger for so many innocent people. If we learn how to help them and save them from harm to themselves or others, we save lives.

Physical, Social, and Emotional Fitness Linked to Academic Success

N AVIGATING THROUGH THE NORMAL DAY-TO-DAY TERRAIN OF teenage life is a challenge for most students. But for those in a fragile state of experiencing life without definitive boundaries or guidance on how to handle self-identity issues, judgmental social barriers that fuel insecurities, the need to belong, and the yearning for approval by their peers, it is worse; they live in a perilous and vulnerable state in and out of school. The current 21st century schools can and must be equipped with prevention and intervention resources for guiding students through the peaks and valleys of teenage life. But there are other factors, such as the influence of social media, which have become weapons for cyberbullying. On social media, cowards anonymously post injurious and debasing statements, and do so with impunity. While generations have been told the best way to ignore unkind words is to keep in mind that "sticks and stones may break my bones but words will never hurt me," the advent of social media and the internet have completely obliterated that sage and once-useful advice. In fact, the impact of social media has dramatically shifted the pendulum away from those catchy phrases that once assured and comforted us when we felt hurt and pain and convinced us that, if we ignored unkind remarks, we would diminish the sting of the taunt and all would eventually be well.

There is a human cost for remaining oblivious to the harmful impact of those who seek to weaponize social media into a cyberbullying platform. Schools no longer have the luxury of ignoring the serious pain and devaluing of generations of children, teens, and young adults who are ardent consumers of social media. Even the teens who appear to have it together and seem capable of withstanding minor taunts can be easily influenced by hateful remarks uttered and then unleashed in the public domain, which goes viral. In fact, a correlation between poor mental health outcomes and cyberbullying was found in a study that included 31,148 students from grades 6–12.[21] So it turns out "sticks and stones *can* break one's bones," and words *do* have the power to inflict great pain. Kids of all ages are susceptible to humiliation, but when degrading comments are put into socially unforgiving and highly toxic platforms accessible to the public, it can become too much to endure. Exploring options, including contemplating suicide, to escape what for way too many youths feels so cataclysmic and simply too much to bear, is a crisis-management issue. Schools and families must expect to contend with, and prepare in advance, intervention measures to help these kids safely and successfully navigate their way through those situations.

All schools must advance their technology to include the ability to track and detect the origins of those who engage in cyberbullying. IP addresses should be traced, and those who are proven to be the authors of bullying should be held accountable. Schools should also inform students they have the ability to detect authors of cyberbullying as a means of preventing or at least significantly reducing cyberbullying. Another resource to prevent bullying is the inclusion of an anti-bullying staff position. Students can report incidents or electronically forward messages they received, which can then be investigated without revealing the source of the person reporting the incident. (See Appendix D.)

With the exception of those who could potentially endanger their own personal safety or the safety of others, all other issues can and should be addressed by the school staff charged with the prevention and intervention of behaviors that do not comply with school policies.

Those who exhibit dangerous or mental health issues that could endanger their own personal safety or the safety of others, need to be referred to mental health counseling services. However, finding and honoring a pathway for successful re-entry back into the school after receiving counseling, and a formal process that verifies the student is ready for transition back to school, is also the responsibility of the school. How the school handles the transition into counseling, and what gets conveyed to the rest of the school's community while the student receives treatment, is both important and consequential. Students who need counseling also need and are entitled to retain their dignity. An open and transparent policy of providing counseling without judgment whenever any student is in need reflects a culture of acceptance, and it declares unequivocal support and readiness to be supportive through compassion if and when any student is in need.

Embracing the entire student population means accepting the foresight that students across a broad spectrum of needs will require, and are entitled to receive, a responsive and compassionate range of resources to help them successfully navigate through some unforeseen academic, emotional, psychological, financial, and other challenges. Schools that adopt a culture of genuine collaboration of caring and concern will not fear the unforeseen but instead, through planning and prepared readiness, show students that not only are schools prepared for whatever may happen but that they are also unafraid when the need to address any mental health issue arises.

Conveying messages encouraging students to seek assistance when suffering from depression may significantly reduce their reluctance to ask for help. Policies clearly stating that resources are readily available for safe and confidential intervention, accompanied by an outlined process students can expect if and when they need support, will serve as a welcoming invitation to "Come on in and let us work together to help you because there is no crisis too big that we are not prepared to handle." Schools must also commit to a promise to retain the student's seat at the school during their absence while issues are being addressed. Do that, and you build trust. Keep your word, and you will be trusted.

Preventing Schools from Becoming Incubators for Bullying

I F BULLYING IS A PREVALENT ISSUE IN ANY SCHOOL, YOU CAN BE sure the adults who are charged with ensuring the well-being and safety of every student, while physically present, are actually missing in action. There is no consistent enforcement of posted rules implying "Zero Tolerance of Bullying" and zero efforts are applied to address bullying. These situations create the worst conditions for any student, but especially students who are the victims of bullying, and innocent students who are forced to watch other students openly torment their peers.

When bullying becomes a normal part of a school's culture, all students are forced to coexist among the few who are free to select a random target and make an example of them. At the end of any given day, students not targeted are relieved they were not singled out to be publicly humiliated on that day; but they know, intuitively, they can be singled out at any time and for no reason. *Schools become the incubators for bullying when the adults in charge fail to take charge and intervene to stop it.*

Provocation by those in positions of authority is also problematic. Bullying among students is usually the focus of zero-tolerance policies. But some staff and school administrators who routinely subject students to a disproportionate amount of criticism, or who continually accuse innocent students of violating school polices, maybe abusing their authority. Abusers of authority publicly admonish students using an aggressive tone of voice and are prone to speak sarcastically. Some staff members purposely initiate confrontations with students and then convince others that their version of what took place is more credible than what the student alleges. Those actions are intended to set up students and frame them for some form of punishment. A school's inability to ensure the protection of all students is one of the most grievous derelictions of supervision. It also contributes to a reduction in student attendance. If a school's culture permits bullying with impunity, would it be fair to expect students to continue attending if there is no ability to get out of harm's way?

Even more perplexing is when students share with their parents how they witnessed incidents of unjust behavior by staff; parents then reach out to school leaders to convey their concerns and are either met with denial or receive no response at all. Many incidents go unreported, leaving students to contend with growing discomfort. One particular study showed that students do not report bullying due to fear of being labeled a narc or in fear of retaliation for "getting others in trouble." It also found that teachers who get to know their students are key in reducing bullying.[22]

Student-teacher rapport or lack of a good rapport is determinative in how students experience life in their schools. A lack of rapport does not necessarily equate to poor chemistry between students and teachers. But students who have a neutral rapport with teachers are placed in an awkward position when they witness the ways the teachers interact with other students whom the teachers make clear they do not like. If given an opportunity, many students will confide feeling fearful and mystified about how it is possible that such unprofessional behavior among teachers is permitted. Witnessing teachers abuse their authority places students at the same level of risks as being around students who bully. In schools where students and staff are permitted to unfairly target and abuse students, the rest of the population may watch with a sense of alarm but also see the need to be strategic so as to avoid becoming a victim of bullying in a place that provides no protection or any chance of escaping. Even those who manage to escape by simply leaving school to avoid conflict know what trouble likely awaits them on the day they return. Bullying, or the inability to effectively stop bullying by students or adults, leads to absences, which then become the gateway for dropping out. In the minds of students who are victims of bullying, there are few if any options available to stop the cycle of abuse. Most people may view school bullying as an isolated problem that can be remedied if brought to the attention of school administrators. Victims of bullying have to contend with the consequences of reporting bullying.

Not all schools understand the importance of protecting students who report being victims of bullying, which then places those bullied students at greater risk of further incidents. Knowing there will not be adequate protection to ensure their safety, students conclude the safest option is to stop attending school. Those who remain become focused on how to get through a school day without enduring more pain. Consumed with thoughts of strategic ways to keep a low profile, they do whatever is necessary to become and remain invisible in an effort to remain below a tormentor's visible radar; and this diminishes their ability to focus on instruction, which prevents them from learning. How are those students expected to perform on any test, but especially standardized tests, as they keep one eye on their tormentor sitting a few seats away, but still feeling so close, causing them to repeatedly read the same question over and over again because the mere presence of their predator makes them lose their train of thought? The presence of bullies impacts every square foot inside of schools. There are no safe spaces to hide.

Academic performance levels are sometimes linked to students targeted for bullying by other students. Proficiency and exemplary performances in academics can make a student a candidate for valedictorian and resented by peers interested in teaching a lesson to those who wear their academic achievements like a badge of honor. But students who struggle with learning can also fall prey to bullying. If all teachers, staff, and students can honor a pledge to promote mutual respect for others and have zero tolerance for bullying, it will result in a healthier environment that enables all students to feel safe and welcome. Healthy school cultures can exist when everyone works collectively to achieve common goals of respect, like applauding the efforts and contributions of students socially willing to lead by example in areas beyond academic performance or athletic ability.

Remediation of Learning Gaps Can Reduce Bullying

YES, LEARNING GAPS MANIFEST IN MULTIPLE WAYS WE generally do not think about. Learning gaps are linked to bullying. While there may be little awareness of how the practice of failing students is linked to the issue of bullying, think of the academic and emotional relief it would provide students who do struggle with learning, if teachers were proficient at detecting and remediating learning gaps. The potential of removing judgmental stigmas related to how one's level of academic performance is perceived would be beneficial to many students who are singled out and bullied for experiencing learning challenges. Sometimes schools inadvertently cultivate circumstances where students develop grievances, like experiencing academic failure, which morphs into social embarrassment and humiliation. In an attempt to avoid being labeled "stupid," students who feel the need to deflect attention away from their academic failure may be prone to making their presence felt in other ways. For some of these students, bullying behaviors can gradually emerge as a means of resistance to earning a reputation based on academic frailties and deciding they will dictate the terms of how they are perceived by reinventing their persona and appearing invincible in other ways. Adopting a more aggressive and intimidating posture forces everyone's attention away from judging their academic performance by shifting everyone's focus on their new persona and making others reckon with them on their terms. Saving face requires inventing a status that garners respect, even if it is out of fear. Schools are not always good at understanding the different ways students handle failure. Inside of schools, a segment of the student population may be manifesting bullying behaviors due to academic frustration and failure. It is why they too would benefit from learning gap detection and remediation support.

Survival Strategies to Avoid Bullies

Students of all ages want to succeed in school. They thrive on positive feedback when they do well. For most students, doing well really matters. For many students transitioning through developmental stages of social and emotional growth in a school setting where academic exceptionalism is expected and rewarded, academic performance influences social status. No student ever wants to be wrongly perceived as incapable of learning. But even more worrisome is the potential social consequence of having their peers label them as "dumb" or slow. Conversely, in many urban public schools, students who are perceived as "smart" develop protective radar due to their well-founded fear of being targeted and bullied. In many inner-city schools, students are penalized for earning a reputation for being "smart." Their need to cultivate an appearance of being uninterested or lower their level of class engagement is a means of survival. Having witnessed the harsh treatment of others identified as "smart" in schools where various groups of students are given the freedom to target and abuse academically aspiring students is sadly indicative of the student-run social construct in many middle and high schools. All schools serve as a microcosm of the values and expectations in their surrounding community, and to some extent our society.

Staff Positions to Prevent Bullying

Given the unlikelihood of students' being able to resolve issues among themselves, or those rare occasions where students perceived they are the victims of a teacher or other staff member's abusing his or her authority, the presence of a skilled conflict resolution counselor may be a necessity, and a way to cultivate positive school culture. No school is immune to bullying. Therefore, the presence of a skilled conflict resolution counselor, familiar with strategies to effectively respond to bullying incidents, provides credibility to the school's policies of not permitting acts of bullying and ensuring the safety of all students. Minor incidents of early bullying can be extinguished before they escalate into further and more serious levels of bullying, by a process of resolving conflicts between the students involved. Initial and minor altercations between students are the potential first signs of bullying. It is those moments, not yet perceived as bullying, that need immediate and effective intervention to prevent circumstances from evolving into more problematic situations. Using respectful and effective conflict resolution models that enable students to address what may appear to be small incidents, while they are in the earliest phase of what could potentially become tumultuous if left to fester, is where schools often can and should take the initiative to stop the seeding stage of bullying behaviors. During my tenure as a high school leader, I created the 9 *R*'s for Resolving Conflicts (see Appendix E) to address a range of disagreements between students. I was at my wits' end with finding a way to address these. I didn't want to use the default response—dismissal from school or reviewing a list of repercussions for inapproprate conduct, but never addressing the real problem or applying a pragmatic solution to prevent any recurrence of problems. I had to think of a process that enabled problems to become teachable moments that would lead to all parties' resolving to work towards peaceful coexistence. The 9 *R*'s process worked every time, and this is why:

The 9 *R*'s for Resolving Conflicts
Viewing Mistakes as Teachable Moments

This model works because it takes students through an accountability process that . . .

- **Promotes fairness**
  Enabling the examination of consequences of decisions through a series of non–pre-judgmental steps.

- **Focuses on learning from mistakes**
  Using role reversal to conceptualize pain inflicted on others.

- **Develops compassion and empathy**
  Understanding and acknowledging the impact of words and behaviors.

- **Teaches the difference between intentions and perceptions**
  Clarifying how those on the receiving end of hurtful comments and behaviors feel.

- **Achieves mutual reconciliation**
  Revisiting, reviewing, reflecting, and taking full responsibility.

- **Respects and maintains everyone's dignity**
  Recognizing accountability does not require loss of dignity while learning how to ask to be forgiven.

Note: Elementary school teachers are welcome to modify the language in the model to make the content developmentally appropriate for age group.

VIII.
The Prosperity of Inner-City Schools' Reliance on Safe Neighborhoods

Neighborhood Reputations Influence Public Perceptions of Neighborhood Schools and Residents

REGARDLESS OF HOW SCHOOLS PERFORM, THOSE LOCATED IN neighborhoods with a reputation for being unsafe are judged through the same lens. So are the people who live in those neighborhoods. Think of two key selling points real estate agents most often refer to when showing property to potential buyers: the reputation of the neighborhood and the reputation of the schools in those neighborhoods. Potential buyers earning high incomes are in a position to pay to live in safe communities and enroll their children in high-performing schools that are located in neighborhoods with a safe reputation. If you live in government housing, earn a low income, or barely have enough to make a down payment on a home, like many other working-class citizens, your options are based on what you can or cannot afford. Public-housing residents are assigned to locations *supposedly* based on space availability, regardless of conditions within the neighborhood surrounding them. Most of the time, they are forced to take—and express gratitude for being assigned—an apartment unit in a housing project and enroll their children in schools in the same neighborhood. Others often make wrong assumptions about quality of housekeeping within these apartments. In reality, many residents maintain meticulous homes. In fact, the level of cleanliness and standard of care they devote to their homes and how well they attend to the needs of their children have always been overlooked. It is also true that, similar to what can be found in other, more financially stable communities, there are also families living in disorganized, chaotic, and less-well-kept dwellings too.

But is a comparison between project housing and more financially stable communities really equitable? Living in poverty, and being constantly surrounded by it, never stops being hard. Poor appearances in the projects are more likely the result of the ongoing stressors relating to having to make do with far less in low- to no-income circumstances.

That said, there are many more unheralded families led by parents, single parents, grandparents, or other guardians who manage to set and maintain high standards and expectations for their children, regardless of income status and often in spite of the conditions in their neighborhoods. These families take extraordinary measures, doing their best within a challenged budget, to maintain a stable home. They work hard to maintain adherence to rules they put in place to inoculate their children from the influences of others who have the worst of intentions. And many, despite numerous potential dangers beyond their control outside of their

160

immediate homes, successfully stay the course as they usher their children, teens, and young adults through life and school. Their hope is to help them transition into young adults who are prepared to use their best judgment and maintain their sense of self and resiliency as they travel forward into unchartered territory: a life of unknown obstacles yet potentially promising opportunities for those who continue to work hard and are willing to earn every ounce of success they endeavor to obtain. Their parents know that content of character is the one thing, without exception, their children can own; it supersedes income level, skin color, and the way others may attempt to define you as a person.

These same successfully run households surrounded by less-than-desirable conditions they did not create but are forced to live with due to their income level, are subjected to the perils of co-existing inside of unsafe neighborhoods. Whether right or wrong, perceptions fuel rumors, which elevate apprehensions about the level of safety many feel while traveling to schools in neighborhoods labeled as "unsafe."

Because the day-to-day ability of any school to function is impacted, to some degree, by the type of activities in their surrounding communities, it is vital to the well-being and potential prosperity of a school that we recognize the important link between schools that are safely nestled inside of stable and economically more prosperous communities and schools that are not. First, let's openly acknowledge that unsafe communities acquire negative reputations for a reason. Schools located in neighborhoods associated with numerous crimes that contribute to the status of being deemed "unsafe" may do all that is humanly possible to distance themselves from being branded as unsafe. But their efforts are hindered by the pervasive crime-related incidents that serve as a reminder that neighborhood schools are not encased inside of impenetrable safety bubbles. Since that is a fact, it may be time to finally address one of the root causes impacting the ability of many public schools to perform at higher standards: the lack of safety in their immediate community or their surrounding neighborhoods.

The ineffectual and poorly managed investigations lead to high numbers of unsolved crimes. That opens the door to tentacles of retribution and retaliation when the offended feel the need to seek revenge, and this leads to still more instability. When violence is allowed to persist, communities forfeit any chance of finding some equilibrium resembling peace. If there is no ability to stop the violence before it can spread, schools are the most likely places in the path of further incidents, because they represent a cross-section of kids from different neighborhoods, with opinions and grievances that mirror those in their neighborhood. Volatile situations that arise across neighborhoods and eventually seep into schools demand an inordinate amount of attention, and this siphons valuable time away from instruction. When the level of school safety becomes the most important priority, it distracts from the learning experience; it is unsettling to not only see increased presence of security personnel and police at higher-than-normal alert levels but also to hear, even from within classrooms, their constant chatter on walkie talkies while roaming hallways. When concerns about safety arrive at the front door of schools, and everyone anticipates the much dreaded "School Lockdown" announcement to prevent the escalation of whatever ignited outside the school's front door, such reports of dangerous activity inhibit everyone's ability to focus on instruction, never mind their ability to learn. Now imagine that scenario taking place during the mandatory statewide exams, where performance outcomes will determine the graduation fate of high school students expected to focus on learning in some of the most unsafe conditions that exist inside many urban public schools.

To be fair, not all public schools in all inner cities are under constant safety watch. However, those that are exist under such ruthless and unruly circumstances that the constant need to monitor violence in their schools is a normal part of the daily school operations. And now safety protocol measures taken in those schools are spreading across the country in response to mass shootings. In our current culture of the spread of violence, almost all public schools lock every door around an entire school except for one. And that one single door that allows access to the school is completely inaccessible without the individual's first passing through a series of steps that include verifying one's identification on video cameras mounted at the door. That door takes on the presence of a military-like level of a highly secured and closely monitored entrance. The single entrance is also locked. Video cameras are mounted at the entrance and, for schools that can afford them, posted around the schools' outer perimeters. Visitors ring a doorbell announcing their presence; they are asked who they are and what is the purpose of their visit, which is then confirmed by the staff expecting them, before the sound of a buzzer precedes the unlocking of the door and permits them to enter.

There has been an alarming number of incidents of high school shootings and mass murders in schools located in communities once thought to be immune to violence. This has significantly raised concerns and outrage about mass shootings. The national spotlight about the potential dangers of mass shootings in any school, regardless of zip code, has added the responsibility of heightening safety protocols to the long list of other school priorities. In fact, because we have now become a nation consumed with anticipation of another impending massive shooting incident, for most schools ensuring the safety of everyone is the single most important priority—as it should be. Other countries took immediate gun-safety measures to eliminate any potential threat of additional mass shootings to ensure the protection of every person. In this country, the absence or lack of willingness to follow their lead forces communities to unnecessarily live under a state of constant anticipation of the next incident. Schools are under siege and consumed with expectations of the inevitability of being the next school in harm's way, which fuels ongoing insecurity. Being a nation of resilient people, we eventually find ways to recover, move away from a period of paralysis caused by disbelief, and ultimately adapt by accepting another level of new norms. The new norms, dictated by a sense of helplessness and fear, lead us to adapt by considering the adoption of a range of more stringent safety protocols. Does this really have to be our new norm?

Nationwide concern about the safety around and inside of all public schools is warranted, yet little attention is paid to the level of daily violence filtering into schools located in unsafe neighborhoods. Instead of our being equally alarmed by the high death rates caused by guns in inner-city neighborhoods, it feels like there is an unspoken acceptance for the tragic loss of life that occurs in "those kinds of neighborhoods." People living in areas designated as too poor to care about are at even greater risk because income or lack of income leads many to conclude our society tends to devalue the lives of "those people" from "those neighborhoods." Many inner-city schools are subjected to a constant and even higher level of helplessness and fear than their peers consumed with mass shooting events in safer neighborhoods. The main difference between the two worlds is that people living in poor communities have had to develop many layers of self-protective measures over a span of many years. The entire physical landscape of many poor inner-city neighborhoods bears the scars of crimes committed over decades. These scars, along with the other wreckage of violence, serve as a daily reminder of how dangerous life is right now for those living there. And it's also a daily reminder that political officials never allocate sufficient, if any, funding needed to make all neighborhoods safe. The lack of empathy for people forced to co-exist in unsafe communities serves to perpetuate the negative stereotypes that too often stigmatize citizens who deserve better. Many people aren't even aware of the significant decrease in crimes in many urban communities. But who can blame them for being unaware of the reduction in violence, when communities continue to bear the existence of boarded-up buildings, broken windows, and building edifices pockmarked with bullet holes from another time? The remaining presence of eyesores, incurred years ago but never even cosmetically upgraded, continues to fuel mistaken perceptions of ongoing dangers. Contrary to what most of the public think, many citizens living in poor communities are not receiving credit in the media or on social platforms for initiatives they have taken to reduce crime rates in their neighborhoods.

In communities where the spell of violence continues unabated, it is unfortunate that we have not yet found a long-term solution to addressing and ending the reign of terror caused by gang violence. Allowing unimpeded violence, committed by a small segment of people affiliated with gangs, to continue terrorizing the majority of citizens in those neighborhoods enables their ability to expand by inducting new generations into their ranks. With each new group of inductees, their gang membership grows, as do their reputation and influence. The territorial feuds between gangs in adjoining neighborhoods also contribute to the perception of their elevated power. The perception of elevated power, combined with tactics of intimidation, is used to wield influence across entire communities. Wisely, citizens dissatisfied with the presence of gangs find ways to adapt in order to survive. Adherence to unspoken but clearly known expectations of neighborhood gangs is quite common. Gangs have become so territorial that no trespassers are allowed entry into or passage through their neighborhoods.

Citizens who are familiar to gang members feel a sense of relief when they pass the *recognition test* that allows them safe passage to their residence. However, students attending school in neighborhoods outside their own community, because it's where they were assigned by the district (which has no understanding of the unsafe conditions that exist between neighborhoods), face many perils. As just one of the many safety measures these students use to avoid traveling through well-known violent areas in their own or neighboring communities, they arm themselves with maps of the city and schedules for buses and trains used to transport them to and from school. But the stress they endure is perilous while they anxiously wait for trains and buses to arrive in unsecured stations. Also perilous is the convergence of students from diverse neighborhoods wearing clothing displaying colors that intentionally signify allegiance to their neighborhood gangs; these students flow into those same stations at the same time to attend schools they were assigned to. Students do not choose to linger in public spaces like stations, for fear of drawing the attention of others who may like a student's athletic gear and then become intent on possessing it. If a brawl between gang members breaks out, innocent students take flight to avoid skirmishes where weapons are likely to be drawn.

The number of funerals held for innocent students who were among the collateral damage in the aftermath of gang-related incidents shows just how perilous conditions are for those traveling to and from school. Common spaces, like stations, where teens and young adults from many different neighborhoods converge to catch their train or bus to school, are particularly perilous for vulnerable first-year high school students trying to acclimate to new transportation schedules. But generally, any student is in a perilous condition when caught in the throes of unexpected gang activity, or by others who are easily set off by the appearance of someone they recognize and have an unresolved beef with, in stations or en route to school inside of buses and trains that feel like traps. And for many subsequent days, attendance rates at many schools across urban communities show a precipitous decline. That is why so many students having the misfortune of their school being located in one of those "No Trespassers Allowed" zones, are faced with the option of either requesting a transfer or deciding not to attend school. The concerns of so many innocent youths not returning home are real. It's time we took them more seriously.

Did you know some students base their decision to attend school on seasons? The joy felt by many as winter turns to spring and the eventual arrival of warm weather, is perceived quite differently in some neighborhoods. Our delight in weather forecasts announcing warm and sunny conditions absolutely terrifies many students who reside in certain inner-city neighborhoods. While we bask in the luxury of appreciating blooming flowers and the warmth of a sunny day, those in unsafe neighborhoods feel anxious about the warm weather forecast's ushering in a season of gun violence. Like bears and other species that emerge from a winter of hibernation, so too do the bullies and thugs who terrorize their neighborhoods. Seriously, their fear of the anticipated spike in violence is palpable. And they are not wrong. Statistically, many cities have records of increased deaths during warm weather. Innocent people, whose level of income determines where they live, have to manage their daily struggle for the right to wake up the next morning enshrouded in an invisible layer of combat safety gear, just so they can live through another day of their daily fear of guns; that is a part of their routine existence.

It would be an understatement to say citizens living with the lowest incomes in America pay the biggest price. Being dependent on government subsidies should not be synonymous with increasing one's statistical probability of becoming a crime victim. But everyone knows the life expectancy is shortest for people who cannot afford to live in safer neighborhoods.

In neighborhoods where law-abiding citizens are constrained by the inability of law enforcement officials to restrain criminal behaviors, whole communities of citizens are forced to rely on their own survival instincts. They invest time thinking about and adopting self-protective measures against sudden random or planned acts of violence. Having no other options available, generations of residents have had to become self-reliant as a means of adapting to unsafe conditions. The hardship of trying to live in impoverished communities where the constant threat of violence is deeply woven into the fabric of their lives is the plight of those earning incomes too low to relocate to safer environments.

Students sitting in classrooms within those same neighborhoods wear layers of invisible protective gear. Burdening children with the responsibility of developing lifesaving skills isn't a matter of choice, it's a necessity. But sitting in a classroom does not reduce their concerns about life and death. While they sit in classrooms, their learning is interrupted by the constant backdrop of sounds outside their classroom windows, serving as reminders that the daily violence continues just beyond the protective walls of their school. Students and staff develop an immunity to the constant piercing sounds of police cars and emergency responder's sirens.

The familiar sounds are a natural part of the daily co-existence of violence while receiving instruction. The instruction comes to a pause because it gets drowned out by the emergency vehicles rushing past the school. And as alarming as the sounds of sirens are, even more alarming is the sense of a foreboding helplessness that resonates among the students. They sit in classrooms plagued with thoughts about the possibility of those sirens signaling the potential loss of someone in their community because they have normalized the expectation of sirens' being synonymous with a tragic ending, most likely a death. For too many, death is an all-too-common occurrence in their community. But what isn't said, at least out loud, are the students' sincere hopes that, whatever level of danger those sirens signal, it does not involve someone they know. Remember, we are talking about children and teens' being subjected to the daily reminders of living in domestic zones of terror where they attend school and then navigating through those zones while traveling to and from school. *Let's just pause a moment and try to imagine the mental, emotional, and psychological toll we have quietly acquiesced to and allowed our children to live with.* I don't say that for shock value. I say that because I am shocked that we don't take action to prove to our kids how much we value them and their right to be safe, regardless of where they live.

People who live in safe neighborhoods cannot imagine and, fortunately for them, never will have to imagine the daily interruption of instruction that is replaced with students' thoughts of "Please don't let it be someone I know." They have become good at appearing to remain focused on learning, but their hearts and minds are elsewhere. The fact that they succeed under those conditions is astounding and remarkable.

How do we make the life of every student sitting in every classroom in an unsafe neighborhood as uneventful as the lives of their peers living in safer communities? The goal in both types of schools is similar: take action to shield their kids from violence and to provide protection, by whatever safety means available. But the difference in what both communities are able to achieve is attributable to the difference in availability of resources, not their desire and passion to protect their kids. Schools are perceived as one of the resources available to protect kids, provided they can safely travel to and from their schools.

Statistically, students released from those safe schools into unsafe neighborhoods at the close of each school day are just as much at risk as their peers attending less-safe schools. Safe schools in unsafe neighborhoods do not protect principals from receiving phone calls informing them that one of their students was the victim of a violent attack resulting in their death. The finality of the unexpected loss of anyone unleashes untold sadness and grief. But when school leaders have not only relished but gone out of their way to create opportunities for genuine interactions with their students daily, those positive interactions influence the ebb and flow of each school day. The privilege of mentoring and caring about students as people in need of friendly interactions and guidance, makes being the recipient of a call about the abrupt and unexpected end of their life a very jarring experience. When that call comes, compassionate school leaders who took the time to get to know so many of their students well, just cannot comprehend what is being said. Over time—which really becomes timeless because the resurgence of the pain is right beneath the surface of whatever layer of shield one creates to move forward—they grieve less, but the memories of previous interactions continually, and often at the most unexpected moments, surge to the forefront of their thoughts. The absence of those students makes school leaders miss their presence even more. Gradually and over a period of time, if they are lucky, the memories become more welcome. The quality of conversations the leaders shared with them are now a small treasure trove of indelible impressions, or gifts, they left for school leaders to remember them by . . . and always appreciate. The sudden departure of a student who is a victim of senseless violence is a sad reminder that the leader has absolutely no control over, or ability to predict, when an interaction with any student may be the last. All the more reason leaders enjoy letting them know they are loved and how much their being at school also made the leader's day special. *Full disclosure, which may be evident by now: this author was one of the school leaders impacted by the unexpected loss of students whose lives were abruptly ended by a senseless and flagrant act of violence.*

Reducing violence is an ambitious goal. The total elimination of violence in any community seems absolutely insurmountable, but it nevertheless should be the standard all communities aim to achieve. Striving for total elimination of violence recognizes the value of every single person's life. Any effort to completely eradicate violence in communities requires actionable steps beyond the typical slogans proclaiming "No more violence!" while marching in protest of the senseless loss of another life. Something is needed other than rhetorical promises and assurances by community leaders, politicians, and law enforcement officials, who truly mean well, stepping up to declare for the umpteenth time that they will do everything possible to make sure members of communities are safe and never have to attend the funeral of another member of the community. Then in the most definitive and convincing manner shout for all to hear, "B*ecause the violence has to stop!*" But they never make clear how. It's usually because they just do not know how. In fact, when communities are recovering from the aftermath of losing, burying, and saying their final goodbyes to someone, within days they turn on the news and are left shaking their heads upon hearing the devastating news of yet another victim of deadly violence. Whatever happened to those assurances by elected government officials and members of law enforcement to step up efforts to back up their rhetoric of "Zero tolerance for any behavior that results in the murder of another life . . . ever again . . . *period!*" Those eventually become photo opportunities and sound bites with no real teeth. It isn't due to lack of effort. It may be more to do with identifying a different way to address the issue. But like any solution, particularly in systemic and deeply under-resourced communities used to going without, it may be time to look within for the answers.

Okay, we've all heard that safe neighborhoods and communities are the responsibility of everyone, including our political leaders at the federal, state, and city level, as well as every person living in unsafe neighborhoods. Similar to safety concerns and our need to prevent mass shootings in schools, it is equally imperative that we make it a national priority to save communities that are under the constant threat of gun violence. There is a definite link between student academic performance in schools and preoccupation with safety in schools and surrounding neighborhoods. Sadly, the one way to prove the existence of that link is the decrease of school attendance by students who simply don't feel safe enough to attend their school. Then there are those whose premature deaths inflicted by gun violence or a fatal stabbing, decreased that school's population of potential rising stars. Yes, this author is still not over those who are gone. But especially those taken under circumstances that still cannot be fully comprehended.

If we are serious about closing academic achievement gaps in schools, closing employment gaps in low-income areas, closing economic equity gaps, closing health and wellness gaps, and improving other areas that negatively impact the lives of so many—then providing everyone the benefit of living safe plays a role in improving their quality of life. Addressing violence in ways that net and sustain meaningful results could also have a positive impact upon efforts to close academic and numerous other long-neglected gaps. The rate of concern for personal safety among citizens living in safe communities is astronomically less compared to that of people residing in areas that are less safe or totally unsafe due to high crime rates. Their physical health and emotional well-being are consistently better too. More importantly, the benefits of being healthy and well influence their quality of life, which is directly tied to the overall stability of their communities that are healthy and vibrant. The privilege of citizens who can afford to live in healthy and safe communities also empowers and rewards them for earning high incomes. They have a say in, and financially contribute to, the cultivation of achievement by setting standards strengthened by community norms, particularly the maintenance of safety guardrails inside their suburban communities. The mastery of careful forethought displayed by community developers and civil engineers, who envisioned suburban communities, then worked diligently planning and building large networks of interlocking suburban communities, was never replicated in poor communities. Although many of the initial suburbs were not gated, the level of income required to purchase homes there gave them a feeling, and created the perception, of being gated. High-income suburban communities also benefited from zoning policies that enclosed and protected vast acres of land surrounding their schools, shopping malls, playgrounds, town centers, and meticulously manicured community common spaces. The existence of utopian-like prosperous communities does instill thoughts in my mind of what access to equitable resources can do to uplift neighborhoods out of poverty. And it led me to think about a wider point of view, which I eventually began to ruminate out loud. What would it take to educate children in safe schools nestled inside of safer urban communities? The next chapter will explain how I reimagined whole neighborhoods through a different form of urban renewal.

A Different Form of Urban Renewal

ERADICATION OF TERMS LIKE "SLUMS" AND "GHETTOS" AND replacing them with aesthetically nice-looking homes made of quality material for people earning low or no incomes would have a profound impact on the overall quality of life for citizens living in those neighborhoods and their schools.

Perhaps it would be advantageous to think more broadly about transforming both old outdated schools and the poor neighborhoods in which they are located. Unfortunately, urban renewal projects disrupt the lives of poor citizens whose residences are located in highly desirable areas. Their neighborhoods are in the direct path of city planners interested in creating upscale housing to attract high-income earners. Citizens currently residing in those areas are receiving notifications about their homes being replaced by new homes, which they will be unable to afford. Eviction notices mean that most, if not all, current government-assisted residents will be displaced so plans for urban renewal projects can proceed. Public school buildings that are owned by cities in neighborhoods targeted for urban renewal will either be shut down and rented or sold to corporations funding charter schools.

The volume of inner-city residences will be reduced but not totally eliminated, requiring some schools to remain open. But as their populations decrease, those who remain will be forced to make one of two decisions: enroll their children into charter schools or attend one of the remaining public schools. That will lead to a return to school segregation. Across many cities and communities, desegregation might have once been an aspiration, but it never came to fruition. In some, but not all, communities where desegregation was perceived as being forced upon generations of residents, many years later there are still reminders of those designated as "others" not being welcomed. Public school closures will inevitably contribute to further segregation by forcing the migration of remaining families of color to enroll in predominantly black and already poorly funded public schools.

Let's dispel the myth about poor families having options. While much is made of the availability of "school choice" to any and all families who truly desire to enroll their children into high-performing schools, the truth is that families only appear to have access to a range of choices. School choice and vouchers are frequently asserted as options, but there are hefty fees associated with enrolling a child into high-performing private schools. Unbeknownst to most families, vouchers provided to support those who wish to transfer their child into private schools cover only a portion of the overall cost of enrollment. The difference between the amount covered by a voucher and the remaining cost is the responsibility of the family. The reality of income's restricting access to school choice and the voucher system benefits the charter schools because they are free to boast about improved academic performances and outperforming public schools, which some have achieved, but many charter school populations are, in fact, performing at or below student populations enrolled in public schools.

Since the introduction of what for many has really been a *false* school choice, supported by inadequately funded vouchers preventing families from transferring their children into highly desired private schools, educational migration toward charter schools has been on the rise. While technically states place a cap of the number of students permitted to be enrolled in charter schools each year, political leaders and businesses have found ways to get around those policies. Two very useful strategies bolstering enrollment in charter schools, which are also public schools but do not require vouchers, are annual underfunding and closing of public schools. It's a matter of reducing the supply of public schools to increase a demand for charter schools.

It may have taken the appointment of a very incompetent person, who was quite transparent when she announced her intentions to transform our public education system into a more school-choice, voucher, and charter-school-friendly landscape across the country. Deregulations and proposed changes in funding formulas reflected the sincerity of intentions of the Secretary of Education to begin dismantling the federal government's responsibility of supporting public education in America. It seemed the arrival of an inexperienced corporate executive with obvious allegiance to dismantling public education was the clarion call needed to warn us all about the potential extinction of public education. And it ignited an overwhelming response of exasperation that fueled demands to do something different. The educational needs, ignored for centuries, of particular populations were in serious jeopardy of never being a priority. The citizens who recently took to the streets across the nation declared a need for dramatic change across many institutions; they maintained that the barriers preventing the advancement of all citizens over so many centuries could no longer be tolerated. Substandard public education in low-income urban and rural communities was among the list of institutions in dire need of change.

But let's be clear. The people who have wanted the change more than anyone else are those living in impoverished neighborhoods. After years of begging and pleading for resources to improve safety, which is directly linked to quality of life, it is not necessarily their voices that are finally being heard. It is the voices of wealthy suburbanites wanting to migrate back to city life that are heightening interest in investing in communities to make them safer. But everyone knows there is absolutely no chance of their returning until those neighborhoods are made safe and provide more desirable and upscale housing aligned with the interests of high-income earners. Fortunately, the recent emergence of urban communities' finding ways to retain longtime residents to co-exist with high-income citizens migrating from the suburbs, is part of the socially responsible experiments invested in maintaining or enriching the mosaic contributions of diverse populations.

Resources within Neighborhoods

MIGRATION TRENDS OF PEOPLE DESIRING TO LIVE CLOSER TO culturally diverse venues of entertainment are increasing the footprint of gentrified neighborhoods needed to accommodate the volumes of high-income earners interested in living in or near the city. Many of those same potential future citizens interested in migrating back into cities are welcoming opportunities to coexist in or near diverse neighborhoods if they meet two important criteria: *safe neighborhoods and high-quality schools.* Imagine that. They want the very same thing current residents in those communities want and have always wanted, and whose previous generations of family members also never deviated from listing among their highest priorities hundreds of years ago.

If decades of funding resources and adequate support from political leaders have not proven beneficial, it may be time to look elsewhere to bring the dream of safe neighborhoods to fruition. But the residents haven't disappeared. The vibrancy that does exist in their communities is so often overshadowed by periods of unrest, sometimes but not always due to violence. Erroneous assumptions are made about the quality of life of millions of residents who routinely live normal lives, despite having to sometimes, but not always, coexist with less desirable or even dangerous conditions. Media attention frequently captures events that fuel the perception of lawlessness done by many, when in fact they represent the few.

Changing those perceptions will require use of the innate gifts of resiliency, combined with a sense of urgency, to retake the reigns of strong and unyielding deciders committed to taking back their communities. First, it may be useful to reimagine what their neighborhood could become *if only . . . .* If only what? Might they dare to create a blueprint of how it could be? Then draft a road map to show a way of transforming the entire community from what it currently is, at times a bit of a mess and unsafe, to what the members of the community aspire for it to become. Here's a helpful tip: Identify a meaningful and developmentally appropriate role and specify responsibilities every person can work on, in unison with others, toward achieving just one goal: total investment in creating a safe neighborhood.

Establishing safe and stable communities should be a national priority. But like politics, where all things are local, the best chance of improving safety in all neighborhoods in urban cities is to be willing to "do it yourself" . . . and with the support of others. For too many years, citizens have watched, waited, and periodically felt compelled to protest about the tyranny of guns in the hands of those who roam freely, behave lawlessly, and terrorize others with absolute impunity.

Enough time and evidence have shown the job of making neighborhoods safe will have to be the responsibility of those who live in them. It may have to start with courageous declarations to end tolerating the tyrannical conduct of those robbing whole neighborhoods of their material possessions and access to a better quality of life. Developing and implementing a strategic plan for eradicating violence will be taxing work. It also relies on humans' being willing to come together, to invest in a willingness to fight to take charge and transform their communities. It starts with declaring zero tolerance for ongoing violence. Say "No More!" and then support it with a community rebuilding action plan. We are people of resiliency. Even if residents living in a given community don't earn high-enough incomes to purchase property, they can still influence what happens there. Just because they don't have the means to pay property taxes, doesn't mean they don't get to have a say in the quality of life they live while residing in any property, whether owned, rented, or government-subsidized.

Quality of life is determined by the quality of the conditions inside of each person's neighborhood. And if residents make a choice to responsibly and safely take reasonable and constructive measures to eliminate obstacles preventing them from accessing a quality life, where's the harm in finally instituting changes that could result in safe neighborhoods on a path of achieving their aspirations to not just survive, but truly thrive?

The Good Will of Social Custodians in Communities

L IKE SO MANY VIBRANT AND THRIVING COMMUNITIES, CITIZENS living in poor neighborhoods will need a committed network of Social Custodians to reclaim and make safe their neighborhoods. Social Custodians are synonymous with guardians, defenders, upholders, overseers, protectors, and keepers; in other words, "people responsible for something valuable." America's children, teens, and young and older adults all qualify as *valuable and worthy of being valued*, regardless of level of income and the zip code in which they reside.

So, Who Can Do What?

L ET'S START WITH THE MOST OBVIOUS—AT THE NATIONAL level—and work our way down into communities and schools.

Nationally and statewide

- Follow Australia's lead: enact laws that prevent mass shootings in schools
- Amend gun laws

Cities

- Completely remove guns and other weapons from inner city communities

Neighborhoods

- Establish Neighborhood Peace Corps
- Expand networks of Neighborhood Peace Corps, interlocking surrounding communities
- Establish Neighborhood Watch groups promoting self-policing
- Establish Neighborhood Disputes Councils to resolve internal issues

Neighborhood school partnerships with community organizations

- Create middle and high school internships with community partners
- Unify networks of responsive community organizations in the pursuit of one single mission
- Develop Social Custodian programs in support of communities

Parents: in and around your homes

- Take responsibility for removing guns and other weapons from your own residences
- Conduct neighborhood searches for guns and other weapons stashed in hidden locations within the community

Police departments

- Conduct Community Matters police training to *end* police shootings of unarmed and innocent black males

Local hospitals—mental health and counseling agencies

- Identify, administer to needs of, and monitor citizens with mental illness, as well as *those with chronic and acute symptoms*

Building Bridges in and beyond Neighborhoods

THESE ARE STEPS THAT CAN BE TAKEN IN THE COMMUNITY AND beyond:

- Partner the economic minded with organizations that develop start-up companies for youths
- Develop micro-loan programs in economically depressed communities
- Transform the sale of illegal drugs to the sale of legal goods in exchange programs

- Transition gang members away from illegal activity by appealing to their economic acumen, skills, and profit-earning aspirations through the sale of various forms of art, patented inventions, clothing and sneaker designs, and other creative ideas

- Establish a good-deeds mentoring program to promote outreach and compassion for neighbors; pair young adult males with a network of younger kids and their families to guide and support as a means of caring about and for others.

- Hold community gatherings to promote community pride

- Establish urban farmers markets selling the wares of community members

- Cultivate community-based networks of *"Good News Around Our Neighborhood"* media producers and promoters. Citizens who perform good deeds are worthy of, and tend to enjoy, being in the spotlight. And since good deeds often beget more generosity from others, more good news will follow.

Link Community Initiatives to Influential Messengers in Sports and Art Industries

Professional Athletes Advocating for Better Lives in Communities They Came From

PROFESSIONAL ATHLETES FROM ALL RACIAL AND ETHNIC backgrounds across all sports are expanding their mission to include raising awareness about the corrosive impact of systemic poverty, high unemployment, lack of quality education, gang violence, illegal sale of drugs, and the flow of guns and drugs in poor neighborhoods. They, like many advocacy groups, are amassing calls to look beneath the surface of problems and address the root causes. Improving education and the economic prosperity of the disenfranchised is directly linked to measures that successfully remove the obstacles constraining our country's ability to close academic achievement, employment, and economic equity gaps. The professional athletes' enormous popularity can be a driving force in influencing the hearts and minds of fans by urging them to cheer on efforts that will lead to improved quality of life for all citizens, but especially for those who they know don't earn the level of income that would allow them to purchase tickets to attend games. Over the course of many years, professional athletes have successfully instituted mentoring programs in communities they came from. Increasing the presence of athletes to personally sponsor annual youth events several times a year will expand interest in youth programs that contribute to stabilizing neighborhoods. Mentoring social custodians of communities and linking to Neighborhood Peace Corps will bring a lot of clout and respect to those community-based organizations devoted to safety in your and their neighborhoods.

Contributions from Hollywood Executives and TV and Film Producers

The financial success of highly rated movies and television shows filmed in neighborhoods showcasing the blight of inner cities with boarded-up buildings and broken windows captures the authentic conditions of people living in the low-income housing. Portions of the vast proceeds generated from using images of impoverished communities in those inner cities should be earmarked for the urban renewal of those same locations. Ideally, every urban community's filming contract with producers of TV shows, films, and documentaries should contain such clauses.

The production team selects these various sites to depict the challenges of living in gritty and unsafe-appearing neighborhoods. Unfortunately, the filmmakers capture and reinforce, as well as normalize, the false stereotypical perception of how the majority of Blacks and Latinos live. It is a very profitable, even if deceptive, tactic. Characters are hired to appear to participate in the daily consumption of violent behaviors that include the sale of drugs, routine engagement in reckless gunfights that result in the loss of innocent lives, and a variety of other criminal behaviors. These characterizations cast entire races of people further in a negative light and reinforce the rest of America's perceptions that this is how all inner-city minorities live.

How beneficial it would be if those same populations were subjects of socially uplifting and aspirational lives! Recent discussions related to reparations provide an opportunity for socially responsible deeds. At the very least, executives in the entertainment industry making huge sums of money filming in poor neighborhoods can repay those residents by requiring city or town officials to invest funds earned, *and at the expense of furthering the perpetuation of racial stereotypes,* into a community reparations fund that will directly create nice homes and improve the quality of life. Those gritty community conditions captured on film increased the wealth of entertainment executives and their industry. Those who make substantial money filming in communities that are in dire need of urban renewal, should commit to leaving it in better condition than the way it was found. After all, when they finish filming, would any of them choose to remain and live under those conditions?

The list of safety measures consisting of community-based actions can be supported by middle and high school youths' paid internships. Internships can partner students with community organizations in the development and supervision of Neighborhood Peace Corps (NPCs). Neighborhood Peace Corps could consist of a network of community-based organizations working in unison for one single purpose: creating and maintaining safe communities.

Neighborhood Peace Corps can be utilized to support self-policing. If the NPC organizations included adults assigned to mentor high school and middle school student interns, students could gain meaningful experience as they work collaboratively with agencies linked to the mission of ensuring neighborhood safety. With thoughts of neighborhood safety and ending shootings, community-based policing would be an opportunity for youth members of NPC and their adult mentors to be trained on self-policing techniques.

Joining initiatives that link advocacy to actions promoting community safety, can be achieved. In addition to teaching youths how to contribute to community safety in NPCs, young teens and adults also need constructive outlets that will serve as countermeasures to the gang activity that otherwise appeals to their sense of belonging. Gangs promote and romanticize a life injurious to the well-being of themselves and others in their communities. While numerous tactics are used to recruit and retain members, three of the most central tactics, and highly successful elements, that make gang life appealing are a *sense of belonging* for those who feel a sense of abandonment, *power and intimidation* by imposing their will over others, and *instilling fear* using various forms of bullying, physical violence, or weapons. Accumulating money is also an incentive used to recruit naïve youths into gang life. So, the challenge has to start with creating innovative and enterprising ways to accumulate money in ways that contribute to the new mission of making and keeping neighborhoods safe.

The most challenging element communities must grapple with are messengers with charismatic personalities and the ability to persuade others . . . to do the *wrong* things. Identifying those individuals and successfully reorienting or convincing them to cross over into positive leadership roles that will benefit the vitality and safety of neighborhoods is a monumental challenge. But consider the high stakes of living with the continued erosion of neighborhoods plagued with violence. Recognize it will require the collective efforts of every unemployed, non-school-attending, able-bodied citizen to target those who habitually target others, to assist communities in reversing course, and to imposing new norms that will result in reclaiming and restoring their neighborhoods into habitable and friendly communities.

We need to find a way to recruit all youths in a mission to build a new foundation of permeating new norms in which youths use their natural leadership gifts for the good of their communities. If we can see a way of valuing youths through deeds that will allow them to choose peaceful measures to make community safety one of their highest priorities, we need to invent sustainable roles whereby their efforts are revered and respected. Addressing their sense of belonging can be done by communities' finding overt and intentional ways of showing children in their respective neighborhoods that they live inside of one of those villages we often hear it takes to raise a child.

Any serious attempts to create safer neighborhoods will require attention to the well-being of every citizen, including veterans, those differently abled, and members of LGBTQ. Any and all citizens who are homeless must also be a priority. Paid job-training programs and eventual employment, coupled with finding housing and transitioning homeless adults into long-term living facilities while waiting for housing to become available, is an absolute must. Because fixing one area while allowing others to languish without being properly attended to diminishes the sustainability of the one area fixed. Homelessness, unsafe neighborhoods, substandard schools, and poor health care are byproducts of inequities inherited by people raised and living in poor communities.

Homelessness is just one leg of a chair in need of fixing, but the sustained stability of any four-legged chair requires equitable distribution of long-term and adequate support. In this instance, the metaphor refers to the need of creating and maintaining a safe and vibrant community. If only one of the multiple measures required to ensure the safety of neighborhoods is implemented, the burden of over reliance on the one measure while neglecting the others will erode enthusiasm, trust, and a belief in the system you are responsible for creating and maintaining. Undoubtedly, like all community-run organizations, adequate funding resources will be needed to support all measures that contribute to the community's ability to thrive. If only one leg, or measure, is functioning while the others are neglected, that one leg, or measure, will eventually no longer be capable of enduring the added weight it must carry to make up for the absence of support for the other legs.

Financial incentives may need to be the first of many building blocks to steer youths away from the temptation to join gangs or participate in other criminal related behaviors. Some communities successfully launched social experiments focused on luring known influential leaders, who sometimes engaged in criminal behavior, away from bad choices. Those experiments succeeded by providing better options that included financial stipends for participation in job-training programs, attending counseling sessions to address their issues and concerns about their lives, and creating leadership roles to use their influence as positive messengers to appeal to others and recruit other youths. The new recruits were cycled into programs through paid employment-training programs and helping them find employment opportunities after school and during weekends. Expansion of successful programs to attract and include additional neighborhood youths is key to retaining levels of safety achieved in neighborhoods that found ways to entice youths to live more constructive lives.

The vibrancy of a strong community can be established and maintained through other unique initiatives, like introducing a cross-section of residents, from adults to middle and high school students, to various community-based economic opportunities that build skills in self-reliance, linking to banking programs. One example is microfinance-banking programs. The creation of microfinance banks in communities can entice youths and adults to create start-up small community-based businesses run by a system of self-governance. If youths can be shown how to build entrepreneurial businesses and taught how to make and manage their financially profitable endeavors, using microfinance-banking and other investment tools, it could be a way of building long-term investment in things that matter to them. Opportunities to learn about the "Benjamins" that matter most to them will take a different kind of schooling tailored to their real area of interest.

There will also need to be a coalition of parents willing to declare and then make good on a promise to get rid of guns in their homes, followed by a declaration that they will never permit any guns inside of their homes. Mothers are the ones who bury their children. They commiserate together to comfort one another when one loses a child. Why not choose to be proactive and work together to find ways to remove weapons from their homes, and then institute and adhere to taking action to keep guns out of their homes? While not all guns are stashed inside of homes, many are. To reduce and eventually eliminate the murdering of kids in neighborhoods, parents have to take direct and unequivocal action to prevent use of guns, hidden in their homes, being responsible for the loss of life. Parents can be the most influential arbiters of resolving conflicts in their communities by establishing and enforcing new norms in their homes and intervening in potential conflicts. Parents working in partnership with *community intervention and counseling resources* can and must be on the front line of taking power back from those who seek to destroy their family.

Neighborhood Safety Groups

E STABLISHING A NEW NARRATIVE ADVOCATING NEIGHBORHOOD safety has to be backed up by new behavioral norms that establish what are unacceptable behaviors for those who live, visit, or are just passing through a peaceful and safe community.

Parents are key to neighborhood safety. It may hurt to hear this, but the parents have to show a willingness to be held accountable for the loss of another life taken by their son or daughter. Promoting safe communities and neighborhoods requires the adults to launch initiatives to take back the power owned by the few, and reinvest their talents in activities enabling them to learn how to care for and about, instead of killing, one another. Perhaps start by having individuals create a list or inventory of innate talents, career aspirations, artistic interests, or other untapped and previously unknown skills, to assess their assets, if they really yearn to be on a better path outside of the rigors of academics. They may very well benefit from opportunities to develop their skills in areas of interest to them. If a need exists to form different and innovative education programs tailored to individual aspirations of community members of all ages, those aspirations need a chance to be achieved outside of traditional school settings. To create safe and vibrant neighborhoods, it is essential to have a society that embraces expansion of programs to accommodate hidden talents typically not seen or that are unable to fit into our traditional education system. For many kids in a community, non-traditional programs that capture the interest of youth have to be strongly considered as an option worth investing in. It may be the best way to engage a greater number of kids in something they can find purpose and enjoyment in pursuing.

Everyone has to unequivocally refuse to allow the persistence of an all-too-common perception: that they *can live with fewer casualties*. Really? What if, instead of accepting few casualties, we lowered the number of casualties we find acceptable to zero? That can be achieved by instituting measures listed to make neighborhoods safer. But besides those measures, let's imagine another contribution schools can make to create safer communities. Since schools help raise children from pre-kindergarten through high school, they can start training students of all ages in ways they can be Social Custodians in their communities. Identifying the attributes of what Social Custodians can do—particularly starting with elementary-grade-level students inside of their schools, which gradually evolve to community-based internships in middle school and paid apprenticeships during high school—could bring one of the greatest returns on investment (ROI) in any community. Social Custodianship could be maintained through the continual cycle of students over the span of their thirteen years in school.

Universally, if given the resources, the majority of communities want safe schools, playgrounds, libraries, places of worship, and all of the other places that make up a community. The mission of improving the safety and overall quality of life for all citizens across many communities is possible. It just takes the ability to first imagine it and then a willingness to commit to supporting ways for multiple agencies and organizations to work in concert with one another to achieve one single mission: restoring and maintaining safety in neighborhoods. It could be similar to America's Peace Corps, where US citizens were deployed to regions around the globe to perform humanitarian deeds on behalf of others in need. Peace, prosperity, and safety are worthy missions in which neighborhoods and communities can invest to perform humanitarian deeds of kindness and promote respect among those who live with and around them. Peaceful coexistence is an aspiration that can make neighborhoods safe and save lives.

Neighborhood Peace Corps: Networking with Surrounding Communities

N EIGHBORHOODS DO NOT INDEPENDENTLY EXIST ON ISLANDS. Often, conflicts between neighborhoods instill so much fear that many residents hesitate to travel through neighboring communities. Realistically, safety initiatives in one neighborhood alone cannot ensure vibrancy and safety in surrounding communities. The need to address safety in one community depends upon the conditions of the communities they border, as well as those that may have the only grocery store or popular restaurants shared by members from multiple surrounding communities.

Neighborhood schools could be the link in reconstituting healthier cross-community relationships using friendly and carefully planned rivalries in sports, e-sporting competitions, and various invitations to cultural events. But school-run Neighborhood Peace Corps (NPCs) can expand into small collectives of three to five Neighborhood Peace Corps designed to share the same mission of ensuring community safety and celebrating the prosperity achieved by neighborhoods that interface with one another. Each individual NPC has a collective of community leaders and residents in partnership with community organizations, businesses, agencies, schools, places of worship, hospitals, police departments, and small businesses. The ability to interlock with and work as a network of NPCs that are devoted to achieving the same goals—safe neighborhoods through advocacy of and active participation in measures resulting in achieving sustainable peace— expands a sense of everyone's being welcome and being assured of safe travel through all of those neighborhoods. Students would no longer have to plan alternative and lengthier routes around neighborhoods through which they once feared traveling to get to and from school. Tardies and absences would no longer be of concern.

While each citizen, business or organization member, and student has responsibilities they attend to in their respective roles, each will have to embrace a dual identity and another responsibility as an active contributor within a collective engaged in networking to advance safe neighborhoods where all are allowed to enjoy the ability to peacefully and safely coexist with one another. All are linked to one mission but are free to create measures they can institute, in a way suited to their organization, to contribute to the mission. Imagine the benefits derived by all participants if everyone is free to create their own way of contributing alongside many other equally valued contributors devoted to achieving the same aspiration of neighborhood safety for everyone. Each person, organization, agency, and other institution located in neighborhoods is a potential positive anchor for a safe and stable community.

Students located across different communities within a city can be brought together; they can establish positive alliances with peers they had previously learned to fear. Those alliances can start with organizations located in safer communities and designated as magnet programs, where students from different schools embedded in different neighborhoods assemble on a weekly basis to share experiences, as well as ideas their organization uses to promote safety; to create a weekly newsletter about each community's efforts and progress; to provide a catalog of safety protocols and strategies that work; and to sponsor community-based events hosted by neutral magnet organizations to celebrate safety-related goals achieved across all neighborhoods.

Creating healthy, vibrant and safe neighborhoods is often a hallmark of pride among the citizens living in those communities. It provides a positive sense of identity in belonging to a neighborhood that knows what it feels like to live in a community where people care about one another—even those who may not like one another. The desire to live in peaceful coexistence is something everyone has in common, and it is a great motivator for cooperation, which contributes to cohesion. Cohesion is rewarded by the improved quality of life that comes from living under conditions that make safety and a respect of others a preferable way to live. Some communities earned the distinction of a great reputation due to the ongoing and sustainable dedication and work of many within the community. The presence of adult role models, linked to community-based organizations that are committed to fostering socially educated and well-informed young citizens to become future stewards and advocates working to maintain safety, helps contribute to the improved quality of life for all citizens living in and beyond their communities. Those community-based initiatives can be replicated across neighborhoods in and around urban communities.

Given the need for establishing peaceful coexistence between and among neighbors faced with the same fears of lawless behavior from some living among them, many of the citizens may be interested in forming community-based Neighborhood Peace Corps dedicated to developing academically educated and socially responsive young citizens, starting at the elementary school level and continuing through young adulthood. Developing age-appropriate initiatives to engage children of all ages through their young adult years in making some form of monthly contribution to their communities, could help normalize habits of good citizenship.

Communities across many inner cities plagued with gun violence and daily loss of life under such meaningless circumstances need to redirect the attention of their kids away from the appeal of joining gangs and other destructive groups that inflict harm on others. Replacing the perpetual cycle of violence that results in a constant state of living in fear of losing their life or a loved one's will require a monumental shift in attitudes and behaviors. Developing alternatives to violence, such as aspirational programs that promote excellence in and outside of school, and preparing students for college and careers, is where the focus and energy can be placed in establishing new community norms that lead to safe neighborhoods aspiring to achieve a better quality of life for all who live there.

The very survival of communities depends on their residents' becoming academically and socially educated, linked to aspirations to see themselves as social custodians of their neighborhoods through developmentally inspiring programs aimed at a collective contribution to elevate pride in the places they call home.

Neighborhood Peace Corps or comparable initiatives that have the potential to unite everyone for the greater good of their community may likely accelerate community safety first. Then in time, as citizens finally experience being unshackled from constant foreboding, the freedom from fear may gradually be replaced with a real sense of hope and joy. Being free from violence and the fear of violence over a period of weeks and then months will lead to a real sense of safety. Sustained absence of violence over many months may be enough to ignite a sense of comfort among neighbors who have long desired access to open community spaces, to have the ability to travel through their neighborhood and surrounding neighborhoods without fear, particularly for their children. So many generations of children in inner cities who are born in high-crime neighborhoods have had to learn to adapt in order to survive violent conditions they did nothing to create but nonetheless inherited.

Initiatives like an NPC could also signal a change in how communities of color self-police through a process of compassion and counseling, and not regarding every interaction as "combative," as is so frequently the case in the manner most communities of color are policed. Young adults and parents can be the role models for children. Children seeing successful measures by members of their own communities will cultivate a desire to want to emulate the behavior of the adults. That can set in motion positive change, which then can be the public relations recruitment tool for future generations raised in those communities. As more people in the community see and experience community self-governance and safety models that work, over time, all citizens will begin to truly trust the change. Perhaps having a taste of what could be would infuse a desire to never allow the re-emergence of unsafe communities. If people recognize that living in healthy and vibrant communities can be achieved when true safety has been restored and for a sustainable period of time, maybe, just maybe, they will embrace what they have, to the point of refusing to ever relinquish what they once thought was impossible: the restoration of faith and hope in their communities.

In unsafe neighborhoods, schools that make their students feel safe and welcoming are to be commended. However, despite the accolades and well-deserved recognition for the improvements in school safety, as long as schools are embedded in unsafe neighborhoods, providing a safe haven for each student for only six or seven hours of each school day does not ensure a student's safety after school hours. The sirens students and teachers hear during the school day periodically disrupt instruction and learning, and remind them what awaits them when the school bell rings at the end of each school day. While the sound of school bells signaling the end of class, especially the bell before lunch, may be welcome for some or many students, that last bell of a school day, signaling dismissal, does make some students pause. They are likely the ones having to pull out the transit map to review the arrival times at various stations of trains and buses added to their route that will extend their travel time but ensure their safe arrival home.

I have seen the hesitancy in the eyes of students who confided their reasons for being late, and I refused to mark them tardy. I was rooting for their strategy to work so they could continue not only to come to school, but to arrive safely each day.

IX.
Policies Preventing Forward Progress

Removing the Glass Ceiling in Education

INSTEAD OF REPEATING A GRADE IN ELEMENTARY OR MIDDLE school, students should be allowed to pass on to the next grade and retake only the courses they did not pass. Enrollment in different grade-level courses aligned with performance levels can be achieved through flexible scheduling. For example, a fourth-grade student who needs another year, or portions, of third-grade math could be assigned a third-grade-level math course while being enrolled in other fourth-grade-level courses. Socially, placement of a fourth-grade student in a third-grade level course should not require the student to sit in a third-grade classroom. It would be demoralizing to the student's self-esteem and educational well-being. If there are other fourth-grade students needing to retake all or portions of a third-grade-level math course, they can be assigned to a cohort or special group of *Math Achievers* who meet in the school library for math lessons.

Critical to building trust in the process among the students will be acknowledging their progress using a system of integrity; honoring the students' right to immediately advance to the next level when they consistently demonstrate the ability to achieve at mastery level. To not allow students to move on when they truly are ready is to allow the continued perpetuation of a system that forces the retention of students despite irrefutable evidence of their being ready to advance to the next level. Discontinuing that practice can be done by developing a reliable system of assessing and then promoting students when they show progress. The continued practice of ignoring a student's readiness to advance to the next level is equivalent to condemning students to an educational glass ceiling that prevents access to what ought to be a student's educational freedom, and right, to progress along their individual learning curve at their own learning pace.

If multiple forms of assessments, including classwork and test results, repeatedly indicate a student has mastered all third-grade-level skills, indicating the successful closure of the third-grade-level learning gaps detected in the initial assessment, the student should be eligible for immediate transition into the fourth-grade-level math curriculum. The advancement should occur when criteria are met and without regard for the time in the school year. Generally, students placed in a grade at the start of a school year are retained at that grade level for the remainder of the school year. That implies that learning is a regulated process where progress is only worthy of promotional consideration on an annual basis. Annual promotions suppress each student's educational freedom to learn and continue to advance into higher grade levels at their own pace, because our education system is restrictive and inflexible.

Also, the results of the initial third-grade-level math assessment should detect the learning gaps but also narrow the scope of the remediation plan to specifically target instruction for skills related to learning gaps. The key for determining a student's readiness for a successful transition into their fourth-grade math class with their peers is to first be sure they possess the skills aligned with where their fourth-grade math class currently is, and ensuring the student is prepared to fully participate upon entering the class. Flexibility is an important factor. Another possibility may be to keep the 3/4-grade-level cohort together throughout the year, but transition students who are ready to the fourth-grade level content. Conversely, accelerated learners who perform above grade level, but whose social and emotional development would benefit by remaining with their same-age fourth-grade group, should have access to whatever grade level curriculum and instruction their assessments show as appropriate level of academic placement. Similar to the 3/4 math group, a group of fourth-grade students could be placed in a 4/5+ group, with curriculum and instruction tailored to their grade level of ability, or enrolled in individual classes aligned with their performance levels.

Bottom line: no student has to be held back if they are ready for higher-grade-level content, and no student has to suffer from the humiliation of retention when in need of more time to master content at a previous grade.

Individualized Educational Continuum

WITHIN ANY CLASSROOM, THERE IS A BROAD RANGE OF learning levels. For example, students assigned to fifth grade are likely to have several learning levels; but some students may not perform at the fifth-grade level in one or more subjects. All students are capable of learning, but not always at the same rate or pace. When students do not keep up with the pace of instruction in a homogeneous fifth-grade classroom of same-age students, they are burdened with the responsibility of falling behind; and when they do, they develop a sense of inadequacy.

As exciting as the start of each school year can be, this time of year places so many children at risk for falling behind once instruction begins because the presumption is that all are equally skilled and cognitively ready to consume instruction in the same way and at exactly the same pace. We also assume learning occurs along a linear pattern, whereby one method of instruction and the pace at which it is delivered are suitable for every student. It's as if education takes place in a factory of student robots where education is dispensed one way, and all are expected to keep up. Fortunately, the use of recent student-centered educational models, designed to individualize instruction in accordance with a student's learning profile, have proven successful because they enable each student to progressively learn along their individual academic learning continuum *and* at a pace that is compatible with their cognitive development.

Another benefit is the variety of methods of instruction available to students who, in the 21st century, consume information through many different mediums, including electronic devices and technology platforms. While many endorse the availability of a variety of technological resources, efforts to continue to improve education will require additional alternatives. These alternatives include methods of instruction, expansion of educational resources to enable each student to cognitively progress along their individual learning continuum at their own pace, and resources aligned with each student's learning style and profile across all content areas. Educating students can and should include group instruction and tasks that collectively engage students in the sharing of ideas to solve problems while developing social and communication skills among their peers.

However, there is also a need to modify lessons to include individualized learning time. The majority of America's children growing up and traveling through our public education system have experienced what it feels like to sometimes become invisible and be left behind. Typically, the majority of children who perform well and at grade level in one subject may perform at a higher or lower grade level in one or multiple other subjects. It was never due to their inability to learn. But unfortunately, our educational practice was designed to force teachers to follow a quota-driven system, where expectations were made clear that a volume of topics, chapters, or units had to be covered within the ten-month school year or the teacher would incur a performance evaluation based on amount of material covered. Those mandates of what and how much was expected to be taught shifted their attention away from emphasizing instruction and onto amount of content completed. It is a pressure-driven system where the criterion for assessing quality of teaching is based on amount of information covered, rather than each student's truly having the ability to learn and achieve mastery. It's an education model that does not benefit students or teachers. It is simply a status quo(*ta*)-driven system that deprives students of a real opportunity to learn.

To not individualize education means to continue to keep students stuck, consequently constricting the pace of their learning. Students who learn more quickly experience boredom when teachers repeatedly review content already learned.

Forward progress in their individual education is hindered by continued adherence to education policies and practices designed in an era focused on bureaucratic regulations that permit students to advance only one grade level each year. The outdated policies and practices that perpetuate the bureaucratic status quo impede advancing more beneficial student-centered educational practices that are tailored to allow students to progress along their individual learning curve at an accelerated or slower pace, using methods of instruction aligned with their learning style.

Grade retention is associated with higher dropout rates as well as students' failing again. A literature review conducted by Huddleston in 2014 looked at test-based grade retention, and found that holding students back due to test scores is not necessarily beneficial or effective.[23]

X.

The Detrimental Impact of Politicizing Education

Blatant Efforts to Undervalue and Underfund Education in Public Schools

FAILURE IN SCHOOLS CULTIVATES APATHY AMONG MANY STUDENTS. One thing those students do comprehend well is the absence of a teacher's enthusiasm to put forth a continued effort to provide instruction. Many of those teachers may use failing grades to reinforce their belief that students who earn failing grades are incapable of being taught because they are incapable of learning.

Why are they perceived as incapable of learning? They see decades of research that shows a consistent pattern of a disproportionate number of students of color from low-income communities doing poorly in school. It's a problem of epidemic proportions. A 2014 study by Rauschenberg found that differential grading does occur: grading varied based on student characteristics, and income of students was the strongest predictor of differential treatment when controlled for test scores.[24] Is there a probable link between the expanding rate of declining academic performance levels of students from predominantly minority and poor communities *and* unresolved racial bias that continues to show up in various forms across our educational landscape? According to a 2001 study by Dee, teachers were complicit in the widening of the achievement gap when they lowered their academic expectations due to racially biased beliefs about black students' being intellectually inferior to white students. This study found significant results to support the hypothesis that having an own-race teacher does improve test scores.[25]

School districts and political leaders who annually underfund public school budgets in poor communities are even more complicit in perpetuating racially biased policies that undercut programs in their most vulnerable communities. Students from rural and urban poor communities need a significant infusion, not a reduction, of educational resources. When teachers find themselves at the mercy of declining school budgets that were decided by policy makers who obviously do not care about the children raised in their poorest communities, they frequently offset the reductions by paying for materials out of their own pockets.

Teacher Salaries

T HE ENORMOUS SCOPE OF RESPONSIBILITIES ASSIGNED TO teachers 180 days of the year is undervalued, and they are underpaid. It is grossly unfair and ironic to have a system that reveres and pays enormous salaries to professional athletes who were educated in grades K–12 by teachers earning far less than those they helped elevate to their professional status. America worships sports and entertainment, while showing an increasing inclination to decrease public school funding, particularly in our poorest communities. This represents a nation's commitment to elevating the status of sports figures and a willingness to ignore the plundering of an educational system in need of overhauling and rebooting to align with the 21st century.

In a country of so much wealth, how is it that fact of underperforming schools in poor and working-class communities has not received the same level of indignation as that expressed at stadiums and arenas across the world when home teams lose a match? Why are we not equally adamant about demanding better-performing schools? Quality, high-performing, and dedicated teachers and other school staff deserve support and appreciation for their role in cultivating those same athletes we unabashedly root for during the frenzy of competitions.

During middle and high school, when signs of certain students' potential exceptional athletic prowess begin to emerge, too many schools allow the gravitas and accolades attributed to those select few students to overshadow the academic needs of the many other students, who are in dire need of educational support. What became of the real reason educators and students are brought to their institutions—to fulfill the mission of educating *all* students that will uplift and elevate *every* student's potential prosperity?

Enthusiasm for future superstars of sports is a great thing. But wouldn't it be wonderful for schools to embrace, with the same level of enthusiasm, and show up *en masse* in equally significant numbers, as fans do for football and basketball games, to debate team competitions, science fairs, spelling bees, or departing buses carrying students selected to represent their school as high school interns in Washington, DC or young ambassador leadership programs?

If we really wanted to re-examine professionals worthy of higher praise and higher raises, it's time America saw teachers, who are responsible for the education of all of our children 180 days a year, as being among those who are long overdue for a significant hike in their annual pay. At the very least—given the amount of wealth available for America's wealthiest, who were recently given tax breaks that will make them even wealthier—it appears that our nation can in fact locate funding sources to overhaul public schools as a part of the long-promised infrastructure upgrades and pay all first-year teachers a baseline salary of $75,000. Those who excel and demonstrate their ability to provide quality education during their first three years should be eligible for an additional $25,000 salary increase at the start of their fourth year.

And, yes, if we increase the baseline annual salary for new teachers to a minimum of $75,000, we must also adjust the annual salary of veteran teachers who should be paid incomes in accordance with the number of years of outstanding service. What that particular dollar amount could or should be has to be determined by a teacher's evaluation performance, by number of years in the profession, and in adherence with union contracts. Districts hiring veteran teachers with more than ten years of service from another district should base their salary on total years in the profession; not salary that only rewards them for a pre-determined number of years that is well below the total amount of years they have worked. It has to be a fair meritorious system, rewarding the *total* number of years worked. Their years of extraordinary service to other districts—and, by the way, the same reason your district decided to hire them—should count.

Frankly, much like the tactics corporations deploy to entice top-notch performers as a way of recognizing prospective candidates' credentials, school districts possessing evidence of a candidate's proven credentials should explore ways to attach incentives teachers can earn at the end of each year. In a time of teacher shortages due to exoduses of new and veteran staff, combined with enrollment droughts experienced by numerous college teacher training programs, it may be necessary to reconsider the criteria currently used to determine teacher salaries. Restructuring teacher salaries may help stem the flow of teachers making early departures and attract other potential prospects to the profession. One important proviso needing consideration in determining annual salaries for teachers is aligning salaries with annual increases in the cost of living. This likely will mean increasing base rates of annual salaries to keep up with cost-of-living fees as well as increased health-care costs. We have to view their worth at a level comparable to that of highly regarded corporations that pass out bonuses based on performance and longevity.

How to Attract and Retain Quality Teachers

THE BEST WAY TO ATTRACT AND RETAIN QUALITY TEACHERS IS to incentivize interest in joining one of the most honorable and demanding professions; to show them how much the work they do on behalf of your children matters and is appreciated, by raising salaries and providing income-growth increases each year. For districts trying to attract and retain new teachers, start by offering a higher base salary, one that will not require adding another job or two to try to keep up with current daily cost of living.

Orientation for the top potential candidates should include a few meaningful visits to the schools in which they wish to launch their careers. Among the visits, school staff may want to consider one or two random unscheduled visits to allow transparency about how the school functions. Having a sense of the school's culture may be better seen during impromptu visits, to give candidates a chance to develop, first hand, their own impressions of a school they are considering for potential employment. Prospective teachers should also be encouraged to attend staff meetings and professional development sessions and have informal discussions with teachers about a range of topics related to the teachers' experiences at the school, length of time they have worked there, and why they stay. No single interview will be sufficient to allow a prospective and impressionable new teacher to gather a more accurate and complete profile of a school than to be invited to make several informal and unscheduled visits to the school. Invite them to prepare and teach a lesson.

At the conclusion of their interview and while on the premises, candidates should also be required to write a response to a statement or question related to the position they are applying for. Requiring a writing sample helps to ascertain whether or not they are capable of composing a well-written and grammatically correct essay that demonstrates specific knowledge related to the content they will be teaching; and it reveals their level of ability to be a role model for their students. Students need educators who can demonstrate mastery in written communication skills.

Interviewers should share innovative approaches the school has most recently adopted, as well as the results of those recent initiatives. Potential newbies might also be interested in how and when teachers are encouraged to take on leadership roles. Assigning new teachers an in-school professional mentor is an important and valuable resource. Probe candidates about their interests, ideas, and resources they might need. Inquire about their professional aspirations for the first year; and, for the candidate selected, be sure to let them know they and their aspirations were heard by making good on promises made to them to convince them that their talents and skills would be a perfect match for your school.

Allow candidates to appreciate the openness of the school's culture and welcoming staff by allowing them to view the interview process as a mutual form of both parties' willingness to be interviewed. After their visits and conversations with staff, invite them to return and have a discussion about what they observed and ask clarifying questions. Attracting and retaining quality teachers may be worth whatever effort a school staff can extend to candidates to help them experience authentic opportunities to become better acquainted with a place that is willing to welcome them to view the school from many different perspectives.

How Public Schools Become Charter Schools

PERHAPS YOU ARE AMONG THE MANY CITIZENS WHO NEVER received the memo from city officials and district leaders about plans to eliminate public schools and replace them with charter schools. That is because no memo exists. In fact, school districts across urban communities generally do not want the public informed in advance. They fear the overwhelming resistance of a well-informed community who have been advocating for so long for real improvements in education but, as is so often the case, discover that the district and they, the citizens whose taxes provide a source of funding for education for their children, are on divergent paths.

Those taxpaying citizens discover it when various, and previously unknown initiatives, like school choice and vouchers, are randomly rolled out in a highly orchestrated avalanche of media coverage. The media then reports what it is told, which is often exaggerated content containing fabricated claims of how their plan benefits school improvement in every school in their community—at least among those schools that remain open. Unbeknownst to the community, while its attention is being drawn to how to process what is happening, including how to recover from the nontransparent and political decision to steamroll the public, things are proceeding forward as planned by those in power.

But wait. Aren't schools funded by taxpayers? And aren't the actual properties on which the school buildings are located also funded by taxpayers? So how is it that the citizens, who actually pay taxes and therefore may be equal partners in ownership of both the schools and the properties they are built on, are given no say in how those properties are used, or whether they are permanently closed, or become rental properties for sale and are sold to corporations to convert them into charter schools? Was there an undisclosed public forum resulting in the creation of a political policy waiving the rights of citizens to participate in any and all decisions? Was the public notified about the planned dissolution of one of the most highly coveted democratic oaths—to always include citizen input on matters related to the development of policies that require funding from taxpayers?

Many have suspected that the origin and successful evolution of expanding schools for profit, also known as charter schools, was the creation of the 2001 "No Child Left Behind" education act, which launched school choice and vouchers. The initiative has blossomed into a covertly profitable non-profit industry throughout many poor urban communities. City officials may as well come clean and post signs announcing "Public Education for Sale by This School District."

There seem to be ideal conditions that coincide with charter schools' successful and unabated encroachment of public schools. Unnatural takeovers of entire districts happen after natural disasters, such as what occurred to the entire Louisiana Public School District after Hurricane Katrina. Another event that enabled private corporations to swoop down and take over an entire district included the disaster in Atlanta. While not a natural disaster, it was quite unnatural in how many teachers, following the orders or lead of their superiors, were prosecuted and jailed for illegal conduct related to a cheating scandal on the statewide assessment, and how quickly a network of charter schools took over an entire district in an inner-city community.

When a former president was running for the presidency, the State of Texas manufactured data that falsely claimed high passing performances among students across the state, who had in previous years not performed as well. A journalist who pursued the story eventually revealed the data had been manipulated to boost the former Texas governor's favorability ratings to heighten his profile and make him a more credible candidate for the presidency. After the facts about that scandalous deed were revealed, no one was held accountable. Why the disparities in holding one group accountable but not the other? Sometime after taking the office of President, that same former governor began promoting charter schools.

Are those events actually an indication of a bigger plan for charter schools to overtake public schools in beleaguered inner cities where kids are trapped in underfunded and underperforming public schools?

How Standardized Assessments Amplify and Perpetuate Class and Racial Bias

WHAT IF THE RESULTS OF MANDATORY STATE-STANDARDIZED academic assessments are not for the purpose of improving student academic performance? To improve academic performance requires increasing school budget funds. Appropriate levels of school budget funds are essential for the survival of all schools. But, as evidenced in test performances in schools within most poor communities, the highest priority must be a more equitable funding system that allocates more to schools in dire need of more educational resources to improve academic performances.

But let's pause to consider *why* there is a justified reluctance to inject additional funds into schools that have received increased funding in past, though not recent, years, yet showed little to no improvement in student performances on assessments. We cannot continue to advocate for additional, or any, continued funding of a public education system that never provided adequate funding for public schools in poor neighborhoods. The widening of the academic achievement gap is a result of the evolution of less attention and even far less funding to adequately address the broad scope of problems in public schools in poor communities. So, while there may be universal agreement to stop providing funding resources for languishing underperforming schools, because it will not be a good use of those funds, we cannot abandon those students who were forced into an inequitable education system that was always underfunded from the first days of their school's existence.

The mission of *America's Educational Crossroads* is to urge our nation to reconstruct our entire public education system into one that works for every child. We are approaching two decades into our current century but are using an educational framework from previous centuries. As we watch the rebuilding of our nation in the midst of a new technological revolution, we will need a new and more comprehensive education system that has to include a new list of "absolute must-haves." The list of "absolute must-haves" includes building new schools in poor neighborhoods throughout every inner city and rural community in our country. Another "absolute must-have" is a new funding system no longer based on inequitable social and economic barriers from the past. Those outdated funding formulas resulted in certain communities' never receiving equal levels of funding support. They also prevented equal access to quality educational resources comparable to those provided to children living in higher-income neighborhoods.

An "absolute must-have" is a new formula based on fairer and more equitable needs-based assessments, and allocation of quality educational resources tailored to the needs of each school.

The quality of educational resources in all schools is also an "absolute must-have." Educational resources, inside of new school buildings, will influence school performance outcomes. The most valuable education resource inside of every school is the teaching staff. They too should and will have a list of "absolute must-haves." However, on behalf of all school employees, particularly teachers, the most immediate "absolute must-have" for them is a substantial pay raise. Teacher salaries have languished for too many years. Not only are salary increases a must, but the cost-of-living gaps, which have widened each year while they waited years for contracts that never got ratified, have to be calculated into the pay increase. Health care cost-distribution formulas have shifted, requiring teachers to pay significantly more for coverage than in previous years; pay raises should be adjusted so new increases go well beyond the amount teachers will need to cover their increased share (while not really fair) of health care coverage fees.

Further, teachers won't ask parents to think about asking their teachers to fill out an inventory list of items they purchased for their class at the start of each new school year. Truthfully, most teachers working in poor communities never want to burden their students' families with having to purchase class materials that were not budgeted, yet mysteriously appear in classrooms, thanks to the unbelievable generosity of teachers who funded the new pens, pencils, notebooks, backpacks, rulers, and in some cases new books out of their own pockets. In a world where no one should ever have to apologize for being poor, teachers with incomes that require additional part-time jobs to help make ends meets—which suggests they too may have lives that hover barely above poverty income levels—are too dignified to ever even think of making parents aware of personal funds they provided to ensure their students had the necessary "absolute must-haves" every student has to be seen with so they can fit in and feel as economically well off as the students sitting right beside them. That's a feeling of equity that truly matters to students. But how much more gratifying is it when they enter a classroom with every desk top gifted with brand new school supplies, instead of a list of school supplies teachers know their students' families cannot afford. Those acts of kindness are a unique attribute of special teachers who perceive socially consequential gaps and take steps to close them.

Deserving veteran teachers ought to be entitled to pay raises and bonuses for exceptional acts representing genuine caring for others. After all, they invested years earning a distinguished record worthy of recognition and gratitude for their dedication, were committed to results-oriented teaching, and earned the respect of students who saw them as authentic when expressing concern for and caring about their well-being as individuals and students. Thus, the very first "absolute must-haves" for all school personnel working in America's public education system are substantial pay raises.

Among the "must-have" items on a teacher's list should be professional development to advance their teaching skills. The potential closing of achievement gaps absolutely must include teachers highly skilled in contemporary diverse instructional practices. Improvements in the quality and methods of delivering instruction will positively impact the quality of education and lead to higher performance outcomes.

Not that there is a need to, but let's further clarify the impact of the disproportionate allocation of funds detrimentally contributing to the failure of public schools in poor communities. Generally, it is easy to predict high school graduation rates of inner-city kids by the glaringly obvious performance outcomes on standardized tests. And standardized test results add to the mountain of predictable indicators of which populations of students are most likely to drop out of school, adding to the reduction of inner-city high school graduates.

But seriously, the failures unfairly attributed to students are the direct result of systemic education failures over many decades. Those failures created the current state of a poorly managed public education system with little meaningful oversight. Lack of oversight resulted in the hiring of sometimes-unqualified school district leaders, who were handpicked by even less educationally knowledgeable city, state, and federal officials freely running amok with no accountability. Their decisions to underfund schools while forcing school leaders to operate their school with diminishing resources reveal their true lack of commitment towards ensuring all students have access to quality education. The hardships of undervalued and extremely underpaid teachers, many of whom have been working without renewed contracts for years, is an egregious sign of disrespect for one of our nation's largest unions consisting of highly talented professionals. The fact that it is the largest and most predominantly female-based union does have many wondering if efforts to be dismissive of their members is indicative of gender bias.

In classrooms, test-performance outcomes are less a revelation about the true ability of students and more a reflection of the absence of high-quality standards due to shrinking investment in public schools across the country. What if those poor results are then used as an excuse to close schools in low-income communities? Where is the equity in a process that further disenfranchises predominantly poor and minority communities by underfunding education, annually decreasing public school budgets and triggering the further decline of academic performances, which then conveniently become the reason to close more public schools in black and brown neighborhoods?

School closures across many urban communities in our nation are very profitable to cities in need of attracting big corporations and other high-profile industries to bolster the city's profile. And coincidentally, property values across large areas of urban communities where poor citizens have dwelled for many, many years, are on the rise and in high demand. City officials are aligning themselves with corporations and wealthy residents demanding more charter schools. In some cities, leaders are planning a mass exodus of poor citizens who live in communities predominantly populated by minorities. These individuals are perceived as a strain on, and an economic drain of, public resources. Choosing wealth and capitalism over the needs of long-term residents is the new norm.

The current design of state assessments disqualifies many newcomers whose primary language is not English. If we want to promote equity and ensure genuine equal access to those who migrate to America from all over the world but who arrive without having been taught the English language, state exams should be translated into multiple languages.

Then there are those children who were born and raised and participated in the American education system, and yet they struggle with specific or all subjects throughout their elementary, middle, and high school years. For some students who continue to struggle in various courses, they too can feel like the information is elusive and always beyond their grasp. The experience can make them feel like the concepts are too foreign to them; foreign in a way that feels like they are trying, with little to no success, to learn a completely different language. Subjects that consistently or always academically challenge students before taking state assessments get magnified in the scoring process. So, teachers, students, and parents already know the results when they arrive at schools.

Any subject taught using a one-dimensional format, delivered to everyone at the same pace, overlooks some children's learning potential. Lessons need to be tailored to each student's individual learning profile. Modifying lessons and broadening the scope of instructional methods will maximize the learning potential of every student in every classroom. If we provide every student the opportunity to excel, we will finally make good on the promise to leave no child behind.

XI.
Appendix

How We Close Academic Achievement Gaps

Academic Achievement Plan
Mission • Purpose • Resources • Preparations • Process
Road Map to Attain Successful Closure of Academic Gaps
Resourceful Tools • Meetings • Tasks • Scheduling

Mission

- Ensure all students are provided high-quality instruction, education resources, and equitable instruction aligned with their current performance levels.

- Prepare an instructional plan to developmentally enable continued growth in learning skills at progressively higher levels that scaffold into cognitively challenging and more complex skills, designed to elevate competency in students' ability to maintain pace with increased and more rigorous assignments.

Advancing academic achievement requires:

Pedagogical policies that advance academic achievement and never allow any student to experience failure

Formation of a partnership with students

Pledging to work collaboratively

Pursuing academic excellence

The pursuit of academic excellence elevates expectations and makes clear:

Doing just enough to earn passing grades is not the goal, because it devalues each student's true potential, discourages maximal effort, and lays a foundation for becoming satisfied with marginal outcomes.

Purpose: To Advance Each Student along Their Academic Learning Continuum

- Help them recognize the value of rigorous learning
- Elevate them to perform at higher levels to achieve higher standards
- Encourage them to embrace challenges, not fear them
- Make them aware that the ability to perform at their highest potential is unknown and yet to be realized
- Explain that the purpose of your role in the partnership is to help them achieve at the highest academic standards
- Show them what they are truly capable of achieving

Resources

Teachers & Teaching Assistant

- Work in academic achievement collaboratives

Academic Achievement Leader

- Oversees and manages advancing the academic achievement plan
  - Leads teacher collaborative meetings
  - Assists the Collaborative Team in establishing academic, competency, and performance standards
  - Establishes standards-based rubrics—academic rubric, competency rubric, performance rubric
  - Gathers and shares academic achievement performance data for students falling behind
- Ensures the learning progress of all students schoolwide
  - Assesses what and how well students are learning in public schools
  - Consults with teachers about strategies for effective remediation
  - Identifies multiple forms of assessments (competency, academic, and other types of performance-based standards) that will capture a broader and more accurate portrait of what students are capable of achieving
  - Provides standards-based rubrics that capture measurable outcomes to ensure improved academic performance
  - Conducts professional development trainings to show *how* to create cultures of learning
  - Teaches teachers how to teach study habits to students
  - Conducts remediation

- Helps students self-assess their learning experience, including strengths and areas in need of improvement
- Identifies and implements adaptive technology to support access to content in classes

Instructional Leader

- Leads professional development
  - Provides direct instructional guidance to teachers
  - Supports teachers in gaining proficiency in diverse methods of instruction
  - Shares resource catalog containing multi-instructional methods

Preparations

Task 1: Research Learning Styles and Profiles

Familiarize teachers with how students learn, by assigning prerequisite professional development research

- Learning styles
  - Auditory (prefer audio books)
  - Visual (spatial)
  - Physical (kinesthetic/tactile)
  - Verbal (linguistic)
  - Logical
  - Social
  - Independent (solitary)
- Learning profiles
  - Cognitive Learning Theory
  - Behavioral Learning Theory
  - Constructive Learning Theory

Task 2: Research Proven Instructional Practices

- Multisensory instructional methods
- Integration of learning styles and learning profiles

Task 3: Build a Comprehensive Lesson Plan

Design a five-day instructional model for each content area and include the following elements:

- Diverse methods of instruction
- Integration of multisensory tasks
- All learning styles and profiles

Process

Phase I	Detect learning gaps
Phase II	Initiate Learning Gaps Assessment process
Phase III	Gather evidence—student work samples, standards-based rubric outcomes, tests
Phase IV	Analyze learning gaps detected
Phase V	Cross-reference and match pedagogical practices used with learning gaps detected
Phase VI	Proceed to remaining phases, if evidence reveals insufficient understanding of what was taught
Phase VII	Assess, objectively and without judgment, effectiveness of instructional methods, lesson plans, and student engagement strategies
Phase VIII	Share findings and analysis of Learning Gaps Assessment with Instructional Leader
Phase IX	Develop a remediation plan to target and close learning gaps
Phase X	Assess weekly the effectiveness of the Remediation Plan
Phase XI	Establish a method of accountability for ensuring long-term sustainable achievement as 100% evidence of successfully closing the learning gap

Road Map to Attain Successful Closure of Academic Gaps—Resource Tools and Key

Standards-Based Rubrics—makes expectations explicit in set written criteria with standards teachers will use to determine levels of achievement that students attain in meeting the criteria. This is a valuable assessment to identify academic strengths and areas needing improvement, and a means to capture evidence of learning gaps and enable teachers to tailor remedial instruction directly aligned with gaps detected.

Student Artifacts—samples of student work, tests results, class performance, and documentation of observations related to student participation.

Student Learning Profile Report—description of learning style; preferences, modality (auditory, visual, tactile, kinesthetic), length of sustaining focus, distractibility, reminders needed for redirecting attention to task, degree of cooperation in small group projects, and level of social distraction.

Student Performance Report—teacher's observations of student's participation; active or passive engagement, verbal and nonverbal responses to instruction and activities.

Student Learning Gaps Assessment Report—documented errors showing evidence of learning deficiencies or gaps, and determining level of understanding demonstrated in correct responses, the goal being to quantitatively assess measurable and consistent evidence of mastery at the highest performance standards on a consecutive number of tasks.

Contributing Factors Report—diagnosis of probable causes for learning gaps, including documented observations of what may be interfering with the student's ability to learn, including but not limited to social distraction (specifying what that looks like) or difficulty maintaining focus; also identifies any other extemporaneous factors that might impact learning, such as absences on days topic was taught, students consumed with concerns beyond school, and/or having one or a series of days experiencing difficulty with focusing, etc.

Instructional Remediation Plan—prescription of steps outlined to address specific learning gaps, including errors and enhancement of correct responses to ensure proficiency and mastery of skills performed at highest standards. Plans include but are not limited to researched sources of proven Best Practices.

Pre-Meeting Preparations

1. The grade-level Collaborative Team constructs *common* **Standards-Based Rubrics** for all content areas. Rubrics will be included with samples of student work and assessments.

2. Individual teachers follow guidelines for process of gathering and examining samples of **Student Artifacts**.

3. Teacher lists the name of course, class, and content area in which student is in danger of falling behind.

4. Teacher creates a **Student Learning Profile Report**.

5. Teacher lists **Student Artifacts** used to identify learning gaps.

6. Teacher lists learning gaps.

7. Teacher lists method(s) of instruction used.

8. Teacher prepares **Student Performance Report**.

9. Teacher documents preliminary data results in **Student Learning Gaps Assessment Report**.

10. Teacher attaches and submits the Student Learning Profile Report, **Student Artifacts, Student Performance Report, Contributing Factors Report,** and list of instructional methods with the Student Learning Gaps Assessment Report to Academic Achievement Leader prior to presenting student's case at Team Collaborative Meeting.

Meetings

1. Academic Achievement Leader shares Student Artifacts, Student Performance Report, and **Contributing Factors Report** with Collaborative Team members. Members examine evidence presented by teacher and discuss findings, including student's responses. These may include evidence of learning gaps, as well as types of learning gaps. For example, skill deficiency signals a need of further development; and even correct responses may still demonstrate a need of additional instruction to attain full mastery.

2. Academic Achievement Leader facilitates Collaborative Team discussions.

3. Collaborative Team members discuss findings of all reports, highlighting similarities and differences of opinions.

4. Academic Achievement Leader records team's overall assessment of learning gaps; then, guided by researched sources of Best Practices tailored to the Student's Learning Profile, the team proceeds with drafting an **Instructional Remediation Plan** to close learning gaps and improve proficiency for correct responses not yet mastered.

5. Academic Achievement Leader and Instructional Leader schedule in-classroom visits to observe implementation of remedial plan and meetings with teacher.

6. Teacher documents results of remedies applied.

7. Teacher reports results of remedies to Collaborative Team.

Assessing Effectiveness of Remediation Plan
(Tasks Performed by Affected Teacher[s])

1. Method(s) of instruction used.

2. Additional instruction time provided.

3. Student and family contributions to **Instructional Remediation Plan.**

4. Other accommodations and contributing factors.

5. Methods of quantitative and qualitative assessments used to determine levels of effectiveness for each accommodation.

Sustainable Achievement of Learning Gaps Closed
(Tasks Performed by Affected Teacher[s])

1. Ascertain what short-term and long-term standards will be used to show evidence that the **Instructional Remediation Plan** resulted in closing of learning gaps.

2. Share what steps will be taken to ensure closed learning gaps are sustainable.

3. Prepare Remediation Plan Results Report.

4. Establish evidence-based monitoring process to ensure gains made are sustained.

Scheduling

Achieving the steps required to identify learning gaps, provide instructional remedies, and assess outcomes of applied remedies will require weekly Collaborative Team support and daily remedial intervention.

Weekly Planning Time for Collaborative Team Achievement Gaps Meetings

1. Block time in daily schedule to thoroughly search through various artifacts of student work.

2. Identify and highlight concrete evidence of learning gaps.

3. Follow the steps outlined in pages 207 through 210.

Daily Planning Time to Detect and Apply Remedies to Achievement Gaps in Real Time

Immediate intervention of evident achievement gaps, during or at the conclusion of a lesson, is necessary to avoid potential widening of learning gaps. In the daily introduction of new concepts or tasks, a student's performance, as evidenced in their rubric and teacher observations, may demonstrate they have not acquired the specific skills, or they lack comprehension of instruction during a lesson. These matters must be addressed prior to the next lesson. To ignore learning gaps in real time and on a daily basis impedes a student's ability to progress along their learning continuum and keep pace with the class. Daily responsive remedial interventions for students experiencing academic learning challenges must be a part of a teacher's daily routine.

1. Each day, assess a student's performances on Standards-Based Rubrics for Academic, Competency, and Performance.

2. Based on student's rubric performances, construct **Instructional Remedial Plan** for the following day.

3. Consult with Instructional Leader to address learning gaps detected, method of instruction needed, specific tasks, and alternative or additional learning exercises to embed in following day(s) of lessons planned.

4. Focus daily assessments on immediate concerns, including whether gaps were related to lack of understanding content, task expectations not being clearly understood, special-needs-related issues, and/or general pattern of learning lapses that affect the ability to successfully participate and complete assignments.

5. Schedule one-to-one sessions with students, or additional time to meet with small remedial instruction cohorts of students, throughout the remainder of the week to apply instructional remedies.

Appendix B

Academic Achievement Partnership Plan with Students and Families

Agenda—Topics for Discussion

Open every meeting with a reminder about the purpose and mission of helping the student achieve a successful school year, and the process and resources that will be used to ensure a successful outcome. Place special emphasis on the Partnership Plan that will require the school to work in partnership with the student and their family throughout the year to achieve and maintain progress. Topics for discussion include:

- Student's Self-Assessment (encourage them to speak openly and truthfully; then just listen without judgment)

- Overall academic performance status (always start with student's strengths and areas of agreement with the student's self-assessment; it's how they and their families will know you listened and they were heard)

- Review performance expectations (from teacher, student, and parent; all prepare a list of their own expectations and academic aspirations of the student)

Documents Mailed to Families

Batch 1: Documents sent home with information about content. Invite parents in need of further explanation or clarification to bring the documents to meeting. The same documents will be among materials referenced and shown in upcoming meetings. They will be among the Student Artifacts shared with student and families at future meetings. Early dissemination of documents will give students and families time to become familiar with them, then eventually become seasoned experts of content.

- **Academic Rubric, Competency Rubric, Performance Rubric,** and description of Rating System

1ˢᵗ Meeting—Informational Session: Explain and Allow Time to Process Information

Batch 2: Documents shared and discussed at meetings

- Student Learning Profile Report and **Student Performance Report**
- **Student Artifacts**
- **Standards-Based Rubrics**
- Student Learning Gaps Assessment Report
- **Instructional Remediation Plan**

2ⁿᵈ Meeting Session—Orientation Session: How to Implement Home Remediation Plan

- Home Remediation Plan and Rubric for home use
- Orient student and family members in how to perform remedial tasks in Home Remediation Plan, and use the Rubric model designed for home

- Schools alone will not successfully help students develop study habits necessary for closing learning gaps; partnerships with students and families is essential

- Tasks should be tailored with student and family input

- Ask them what is practical and doable in their homes

- Buy-in from students and families may have to start with minimal steps to acclimate them to the process and enable them to experience success, which will lower intimidation

- Achieving favorable results will inspire students and families to stay with the process

- The initial priority for parents and students is to develop comfort with the process during the initial stage of launching the home version of the Home Remediation Plan

Timeline and Method of Communication—Co-Plan with Students and Families

- Proposed scheduling options for future Partnership Meetings

- Methods by which academic performance and learning gaps will be monitored

- Methods of assessment for home and school to measure impact of proposed remedies

Appendix C

Annual Student Learning Profile Report

Why should an Annual Student Learning Profile Report matter? It is a means of providing a more complete profile about how and what students learn and areas in need of additional support. Portraying a fuller and more detailed student performance profile is necessary to a new process intended to invest students and their families in the student's educational success. Teachers need a different process of engaging with parents and students to foster a healthier educational relationship, instead of operating in secrecy and then waiting until quarterly report cards reveal how well, or how poorly, students are performing. For those experiencing a downward trajectory that is without any meaningful recourse to reverse their academic plight, it makes grading periods a nightmare. It's also too late. Information that could have been revealed within the first few weeks of school, but was withheld, makes parents feel helpless about intervening on behalf of their son or daughter. They need a system that is equitable and fair and allows them greater access to a fuller educational profile of their child's performance in school. Closing academic achievement gaps will enhance learning and discontinue the practice of failing students. But closing academic achievement gaps is going to have to be the combined responsibility of students, parents, and teachers.

It's vital to rebuild the trust of students and parents who have routinely engaged with school staff members and leaders under some fairly contentious circumstances. Everyone needs to start with a clean slate. Launching any new initiative requires that everyone be willing to participate. Explain what's at stake and why participation by students and their families is vital to improve academic outcomes. Even if due to a lack of trust after experiencing so many years of divisiveness, resulting in families' being skeptical, that should not thwart efforts to encourage their participation. Schools invested in creating partnerships with apprehensive students and families must respectfully see their skepticism as justified—and then move along parallel tracks, conceding their right to feel skeptical, while proceeding forward with the process of developing a working partnership. For those continuing to show reticence, a respectful response to their concerns might be to state, *"We have waited a very long time to put an end to the barriers that kept certain populations in America from achieving in public schools. Yes, you have been deeply wounded and badly scarred by past and current practices, but we can influence better outcomes for future generations of kids if we take advantage of new and different pathways so many were previously denied the right to travel. To do nothing would then make us all complicit in the perpetuation of a cycle of inequitable policies and practices that denied too many, for too long, access to a quality public education."*

It is time to embrace a new process of educating students. Feelings about the past should not be denied or dismissed. They should serve as a motivation to call on everyone to actively participate in partnerships with schools to help current and future generations of kids achieve success.

Incentives can include examples of positive outcomes by similar teacher-student-family partnerships that have had success using a team approach. Teachers and schools have to make the welcoming overtures to families to enlist their participation. Building and maintaining the habit of full transparency about a student's learning profile and academic progress can be another recruiting tool in initiating a partnership. Report cards listing grades earned limit the broader scope of how students experience education. Creating and regularly sharing updated information about a

Student Learning Profile Report can be informative and increase the value of efforts students put forth in school. Much of their efforts are unknown to families because report cards are limited to revealing final outcomes without ever providing a more in-depth learning profile about what students have accomplished and skills still needing development. Regardless of the form in which information is shared, more of it is needed on a regular basis, especially if we want and need to find ways to engage students and families in helping educators close academic achievement gaps. Explaining the range of benefits directly linked to the successful closure of academic achievement gaps on closing future income, employment, and other opportunity gaps may help impress upon on students and families why closing academic achievement gaps in schools matters today.

- Submitted to receiving teachers, students, and parents at the start of every school year
- Report cards can be designed to include a summary of student's learning profile assets
  - Student Learning Profile Reports included with, but separate from, report cards to provide a broader portrait of each student's individual learning profile and learning style
  - Student Learning Profile Reports that include student's, family member's, and former teacher's input in a detailed assessment of a student's preferred style of learning and method of instruction would be a valuable source of information for the receiving teacher the following school year

Appendix D

Staff Position to Protect Students from Bullying: Conflict Resolution Counselor

Responsibilities and Scope of Work

- The Conflict Resolution Counselor position should be staffed by a caring and observant adult who is culturally sensitive to the needs of students represented across the spectrum of the school's culturally diverse population.

- The Conflict Resolution Counselor's role and responsibilities should be made public to all members of the school community, including students, staff, and families. The role and responsibility of ensuring the safety of all students should be made transparent.

- The Conflict Resolution Counselor should have a highly visible presence everywhere in the school.

- The Conflict Resolution Counselor's presence throughout the school will send a message to potential bullies that they are no longer free to hurt their peers.

- Schools should also create a system that allows any student experiencing any form of bullying (including physical, social, emotional, and cyber) to check in with the Conflict Resolution Counselor on a daily basis.

- Incidents can be anonymously reported by victims, witnesses, or bullies. However, to ensure an equitable and fair process on behalf of the person allegedly accused, anonymous reports have to follow a thorough and fair investigative process to first determine the validity of the alleged incident, or anonymous reporters will eventually have to reveal their identity. The person(s) reporting the incident must also have their identity protected until it is necessary to provide full transparency about what was done or seen and by whom. Rules about potential retaliation against reporters of incidents must be made clear; and if those rules are proven to have been violated, they will be immediately enforced.

- A first incident must be responded to immediately and taken seriously.

Steps for Addressing First Reported Bullying Incident

- Provide space and time for Bullying Incident Interventions among all parties involved in bullying incidents reported.

- Clearly state protocols for addressing any and all further bullying incidents that occur after the first intervention.

- Enforce compliance with the school's Anti-Bullying Policy and in accordance with the protocols outlined under the purview of the Conflict Resolution Counselor's role. The Conflict Resolution Counselor is the primary protector, but every adult employee is responsible for ensuring the safety of every student.

- As mediator of resolving reported incidents of bullying, the Conflict Resolution Counselor, in accordance with clearly stated school policies, is responsible for implementing a fair and equitable intervention process that holds all students accountable for violating anti-bullying policies at school or via social media.

Appendix E

The 9 *R*'s for Resolving Conflicts

Review: To effectively address any conflict or concern, it is necessary to look back on what occurred. During the review process, everyone has to be honest in their representation of what occurred.

Reflect: After sharing what occurred, please listen to a review of what you shared. After hearing back what you reported, you will be asked three critical questions:

- What precipitated the incident?

- Why did you respond in the manner you chose?

- Is there anything you had not shared that you would like to add, so we can be sure we have all facts related to the incident?

Redress: In your opinion, if you were in the other person's (or people's) position, how would you have chosen to respond to the situation? This is an opportunity for you to see the incident from the other person's (or people's) perspective. Please be honest.

Reconsider: Considering the other person's (or people's) perspective, can you think of a different and better way of communicating how you felt or what you needed?

Reconcile: What do you think it will take to end the conflict and help all people involved to reach an understanding about what occurred, and then return to a comfortable and safe place?

Recommend: What suggestions can you propose for achieving a fair and comfortable reconciliation for all people involved?

Renew: Do you feel ready to start over again?

Repair: Are you willing and prepared to participate in a discussion with the other person so you can hear their perspective and then share your point of view, followed by an exchange of recommendations for how to move forward and then ensure there will not be a recurrence of a similar incident?

Return: Upon completion of the Conflict Resolution Process, which, if warranted, should include an apology or exchange of apologies from all parties, the desired outcome is the following:

1. Assurances and mutual agreement by all persons involved that the matter has been resolved to everyone's satisfaction.

2. *{Here is what "resolved to everyone's satisfaction" means.}*
   Everyone can peacefully coexist.

3. All persons involved will conduct themselves in a manner that honors the commitment, by demonstrating a willingness to contribute to a peaceful coexistence.

4. Once everyone agrees, they will be permitted to return to their classes.

Final Thoughts

W HILE I FERVENTLY DISAGREE WITH EFFORTS TO PRIVATIZE public schools, I do understand the motivations behind those who are sincere in their advocacy for change so we can stop throwing money at a system that in some communities rarely nets favorable results. Like them, I am fed up with failing schools that are responsible for the underperformance of students. Like them, I feel compelled to change the educational landscape. But I do not agree with our broken public education system's being transferred into the hands of private corporate entities, who fund charter schools. The privatization of federal prisons and now efforts to do the same with our public school system narrows the already shrinking distance of the connected pipeline that exists between schools and prisons across many predominantly low-income minority communities.

While I do not want students to continue being condemned to a status quo system that has not produced well-educated students from low-income communities, I believe the central issue related to school failure is that America has never taken adequate measures to equitably address academic achievement gaps. We have spent decades participating in conferences, webinars, and other public forums where educational experts rolled out numerous models touting promising results for closing academic achievement gaps, yet in 2022 the problems still persist. Will my proposed ideas and detailed roadmaps achieve different results? Yes, they will. *America's Educational Crossroads* and the video, *A Collaborative High School Campus Model*, emerged from a desire to advance our public education system on behalf of students. The book and video reveal how we can reimagine our public education system from the perspective of how students can find genuine purpose in the pursuit of their education. Permitting students to experience education as a means of preparing them for achieving their future career and college aspirations is a departure from our current models.

The current models have unfairly tethered current and past generations of students to outdated ideas of what constituted a "good enough" education during an era of segregation; and the bar of academic standards was set very low. Those policies still resonate inside of old school facilities set adrift and forced to manage with the scraps of minimal shrinking educational resources, signaling a fading commitment of the promise to "leave no child behind." I believe it is time to resurrect and keep that promise. My decision to take an honest look under the proverbial hood at the problems evolved from a recognition that reconstructing our public education system must be done in ways that align students' aspirations with their education. I will admit to being compelled by the belief that a better education system, with new schools across our entire country, will propel every child's ability to achieve at the highest educational standards.

Restoring our trust and faith in a public education system has to start by insisting that promises made to our nation's children and families must be kept. Our collective efforts in adopting a new narrative that unequivocally affirms our belief that public schools are worth saving will be the nudge needed to initiate the seismic shift towards 21st century schools that will make our children educationally prosperous, which inevitably influences the level of prosperity they will obtain in future employment and economic endeavors. Their future quality of life will be determined by how well we educate them today.

Endnotes

1   Annie Murphy Paul, *Brilliant: The New Science of Smart* (New York, NY: Random House, 2017).

2   Social Security Administration, "Education and Lifetime Earnings" (Research, Statistics & Policy Analysis), https://www.ssa.gov/policy/docs/research-summaries/education-earnings.html.

3   Catherine Mobley et al., "The Influence of Career-Focused Education on Student Career Planning and Development: A Comparison of CTE and Non-CTE Students," *Career and Technical Education Research* 42, no. 1 (May 1, 2017): 57–75.

4   Lacy Reynolds, Dwalah Fisher, and J. Kenyatta Cavil, "Impact of Demographic Variables on African-American Student Athletes' Academic Performance," *Educational Foundations* 26, nos. 3–4 (2012): 93–111.

5   Bruce J. Biddle and David C. Berliner, "What Research Says about Unequal Funding for Schools in America. In Pursuit of Better Schools: What Research Says," Education Policy Studies Laboratory, College of Education, Educational Leadership & Policy Studies, Arizona State University, Tempe (2002), ERIC no. ED473409; and Diana Epstein, "Measuring Inequity in School Funding," *Center for American Progress* (August 2011), https://www.americanprogress.org/issues/education-k-12/reports/2011/08/03/10122/measuring-inequity-in-school-funding/.

6   Complete College America, "Remediation: Higher Education's Bridge to Nowhere" (April 2012), ERIC no. ED536825.

7   Lauren Dotson Davis, "Common Core and the Continued Socioeconomic Achievement Gap: How Can We Better Prepare Future Teachers?" *Journal of Education and Learning* 8, no. 6 (2019): 1–14.

8   "Employment Projections," US Bureau of Labor Statistics (n.d.). https://www.bls.gov/emp/; and John Raidt, "Capable Workforce," installment 4 in the 10-part report, "American Competitiveness—A National Assessment through the Eyes of Job Creators" (n.d.), US Chamber of Commerce Foundation, https://www.uschamber-foundation.org/capable-workforce.

9   J. C. Barnes and Ryan T. Motz, "Reducing Racial Inequalities in Adulthood Arrest by Reducing Inequalities in School Discipline: Evidence from the School-to-Prison Pipeline," *Developmental Psychology* 54, no. 12 (2018): 2328–40.

10 Christopher Ingraham, 2016. "The States that Spend More Money on Prisoners than College Students," *The Washington Post.* (2016), https://www.washingtonpost.com/news/wonk/wp/2016/07/07/the-states-that-spend-more-money-on-prisoners-than-college-students/.

11 "Education vs Prison Costs," US Census Data and Vera Institute of Justice, *CNN Money* (n.d.), https://money.cnn.com/infographic/economy/education-vs-prison-costs/.

12 John Nally et al., "An Evaluation of the Effect of Correctional Education Programs on Post-Release Recidivism and Employment: An Empirical Study in Indiana," *Journal of Correctional Education* 63, no. 1 (2012): 69–89.

13 Claude M. Steele, "A Threat in the Air: How Stereotypes Shape Intellectual Identity and Performance," *American Psychologist* 52, no. 6 (1997): 613–29.

14 Camille Jackson, "Treating All Students as Gifted Yields Impressive Results," *Duke Today* (March 24, 2011), https://today.duke.edu/2011/03/darity.html.

15 James J. Kemple and Jason C. Snipes, "Career Academies: Impacts on Students' Engagement and Performance in High School," Manpower Demonstration Research Corp. (March 2000), ERIC no. ED441075.

16 US Government Accountability Office, "K–12 Education: Discipline Disparities for Black Students, Boys, and Students with Disabilities." Report to Congressional Requesters. GAO-18-258 (March 22, 2018), https://www.gao.gov/products/gao-18-258.

17 Nancy A. Heitzeg, "Education or Incarceration: Zero Tolerance Policies and the School to Prison Pipeline," Forum on Public Policy (2009).

18 National Council on Disability, "Breaking the School-to-Prison Pipeline for Students with Disabilities" (June 18, 2015), https://ncd.gov/publications/2015/06182015; and National Council on Disability, "National Disability Policy: A Progress Report—October 2011," https://ncd.gov/publications/2015/06182015.

19 Richard D. Kahlenberg, "Bipartisan, but Unfounded: The Assault on Teachers' Unions," *American Educator* 35, no. 4 (January 1, 2012): 14–18.

20 Michael Mahoney, "Implementing Evidence-Based Practices within Multi-Tiered Systems of Support to Promote Inclusive Secondary Classroom Settings," *Journal of Special Education Apprenticeship* 9, no. 1 (2020).

21 Soyeon Kim et al., "Cyberbullying Victimization and Adolescent Mental Health: Evidence of Differential Effects by Sex and Mental Health Problem Type," *Journal of Youth and Adolescence* 47 (2018), 661–672.

22 Janis Carroll-Lind and Alison Kearney, "Bullying: What Do Students Say?" *Kairaranga* 5, no. 2 (2004): 19–24.

23 Andrew P. Huddleston, "Achievement at Whose Expense? A Literature Review of Test-Based Grade Retention Policies in U.S. Schools," *Education Policy Analysis Archives* 22, no. 18 (2014), DOI: 10.14507/epaa.v22n18.2014.

24 Samuel Rauschenberg, "How Consistent Are Course Grades? An Examination of Differential Grading," *Education Policy Analysis Archives* 22, no. 92 (2014), DOI: 10.14507/EPAA.V22N92.2014.

25 Thomas S. Dee, "Teachers, Race and Student Achievement in a Randomized Experiment," National Bureau of Economic Research, Working Paper 8432 (2001), DOI: 10.3386/w8432.

References

Barnes, J. C., and Ryan T. Motz. "Reducing Racial Inequalities in Adulthood Arrest by Reducing Inequalities in School Discipline: Evidence from the School-to-Prison Pipeline." *Development Psychology* 54, no. 12 (2018): 2328–40.

Biddle, Bruce J., and David C. Berliner. "What Research Says about Unequal Funding for Schools in America. In Pursuit of Better Schools: What Research Says." Education Policy Studies Laboratory, College of Education, Educational Leadership & Policy Studies, Arizona State University, Tempe. ERIC no. ED473409.

Carroll-Lind, Janis, and Alison Kearney. "Bullying: What Do Students Say?" *Kairaranga* 5, no. 2 (2004): 19–24.

Complete College America. "Remediation: Higher Education's Bridge to Nowhere" (April 2012). ERIC no. ED536825.

Davis, Lauren Dotson. "Common Core and the Continued Socioeconomic Achievement Gap: How Can We Better Prepare Future Teachers?" *Journal of Education and Learning* 8, no. 6 (2019): 1–14.

Dee, Thomas S. "Teachers, Race and Student Achievement in a Randomized Experiment." National Bureau of Economic Research, Working Paper 8432 (2001). DOI: 10.3386/w8432.

"Education vs. Prison Costs." US Census Data and Vera Institute of Justice. *CNN Money* (n.d.). https://money.cnn.com/infographic/economy/education-vs-prison-costs/.

"Employment Projections." US Bureau of Labor Statistics (n.d.). https://www.bls.gov/emp/.

Epstein, Diana. "Measuring Inequity in School Funding." *Center for American Progress* (August 2011). https://www.americanprogress.org/issues/education-k-12/reports/2011/08/03/10122/measuring-inequity-in-school-funding/.

Heitzeg, Nancy A. "Education or Incarceration: Zero Tolerance Policies and the School to Prison Pipeline." Forum on Public Policy (2009).

Huddleston, Andrew P. "Achievement at Whose Expense? A Literature Review of Test-Based Grade Retention Policies in U.S. Schools." *Education Policy Analysis Archives* 22, no. 18 (2014). DOI: 10.14507/epaa.v22n18.2014.

Ingraham, Christopher. "The States That Spend More Money on Prisoners than College Students." *The Washington Post* (July 7, 2016). https://www.washingtonpost.com/news/wonk/wp/2016/07/07/the-states-that-spend-more-money-on-prisoners-than-college-students/.

Jackson, Camille. "Treating All Students as Gifted Yields Impressive Results." *Duke Today* (March 24, 2011). https://today.duke.edu/2011/03/darity.html.

Kahlenberg, Richard D. "Bipartisan, but Unfounded: The Assault on Teachers' Unions." *American Educator* 35, no. 4 (January 1, 2012): 14–18.

Kemple, James J., and Jason C. Snipes. "Career Academies: Impacts on Students' Engagement and Performance in High School." Manpower Demonstration Research Corp. (March 2000). ERIC no. ED441075.

Kim, Soyeon, Scott R. Colwell, Anna Kata, Michael H. Boyle, and Katholicki Georgiades. "Cyberbullying Victimization and Adolescent Mental Health: Evidence of Differential Effects by Sex and Mental Health Problem Type." *Journal of Youth and Adolescence* 47 (2018): 661–672.

Mahoney, Michael. "Implementing Evidence-Based Practices within Multi-Tiered Systems of Support to Promote Inclusive Secondary Classroom Settings." *Journal of Special Education Apprenticeship* 9, no. 1 (2020).

Mobley, Catherine, Julia L. Sharp, Cathy Hammond, Cairen Withington, and Natalie Stipanovic. "The Influence of Career-Focused Education on Student Career Planning and Development: A Comparison of CTE and Non-CTE Students." *Career and Technical Education Research* 42, no. 1 (May 1, 2017): 57–75.

Nally, John, Susan Lockwood, Katie Knutson, and Taiping Ho. "An Evaluation of the Effect of Correctional Education Programs on Post-Release Recidivism and Employment: An Empirical Study in Indiana." *Journal of Correctional Education* 63, no. 1 (2012): 69–89.

National Council on Disability. "Breaking the School-to-Prison Pipeline for Students with Disabilities" (June 18, 2015). https://ncd.gov/publications/2015/06182015.

National Council on Disability. "National Disability Policy: A Progress Report—October 2011." https://ncd.gov/publications/2015/06182015.

Paul, Annie Murphy. *Brilliant: The New Science of Smart.* New York, NY: Random House, 2017.

Raidt, John. "Capable Workforce." Installment 4 in the 10-part report, "American Competitiveness—A National Assessment through the Eyes of Job Creators" (n.d.). US Chamber of Commerce Foundation. https://www.uschamberfoundation.org/capable-workforce.

Rauschenberg, Samuel. "How Consistent Are Course Grades? An Examination of Differential Grading." *Education Policy Analysis Archives* 22, no. 92 (2014). DOI: 10.14507/EPAA.V22N92.2014.

Reynolds, Lacey, Dwalah Fisher, and J. Kenyatta Cavil. "Impact of Demographic Variables on African-American Student Athletes' Academic Performance." *Education Foundations* 26, nos. 3–4 (2012): 93–111.

Social Security Administration. "Education and Lifetime Earnings." *Research, Statistics & Policy Analysis.* https://www.ssa.gov/policy/docs/research-summaries/education-earnings.html.

Steele, Claude M. "A Threat in the Air: How Stereotypes Shape Intellectual Identity and Performance." *American Psychologist* 52, no. 6 (1997): 613–29.

US Government Accountability Office. "K–12 Education: Discipline Disparities for Black Students, Boys, and Students with Disabilities." Report to Congressional Requesters. GAO-18-258 (March 22, 2018). https://www.gao.gov/products/gao-18-258.

Acknowledgments

WRITING HAS BEEN ONE OF MY FAVORITE PASTIMES FOR MANY years. *America's Educational Crossroads* is my first book. When presented with options for publishing the book either with an established publishing company or independently, the opportunity to finally be my own boss was too enticing to pass up. But what really propelled my decision to publish independently was my steadfast belief in my purpose for writing the book. I wanted to calmly sound an alarm about our need to save our public education system. Waiting for a publishing company to decide whether or not my manuscript was worthy of publication was simply unacceptable.

The contents of the book and writing were familiar terrain. Venturing into the world of independent publishing was an unfamiliar and novel experience. Despite the many unknowns, my decision to take on the responsibilities of independent publishing ensured I would have the opportunity to be in control of the fate of my book. I simply found it worthy of the public's attention and consideration of the ideas presented. Having made that decision, I began my journey. Fortunately, I did not have to make the journey alone.

First, I want to acknowledge and thank friends and colleagues who started this journey with me and never relinquished their support. I will be eternally grateful to Talya Marshall, one of the most extraordinary teachers I've had the pleasure to work with for several joyful years. Special thanks to Anshul Jain, my fellow traveler, who is one of the most exceptional *outside the box* thinkers I was fortunate to often cross paths with throughout our journey as educators. Over the span of many years, I have appreciated Anshul's wisdom and advice, his enormous contributions during my tenure as a school leader, and his consummate friendship. I was pleased when Anshul agreed to write the foreword for my book. I was profoundly moved by his eloquence and even more so when I discovered the level of admiration he holds for me, personally and professionally. And now I get to confess: the feeling is mutual.

I am enormously grateful for the many years I have known Kaileigh, a special friend, confidante, and amazing supporter. I often leave conversations with Kaileigh smarter and wiser. Engaging in such discussions about the book in the pre-writing phase fueled my motivation to open a document and start writing.

As luck would have it, I continued to meet and work with extraordinary people when I entered the independent publishing world. Some within my new publishing network extended their assistance, informing me about tasks I was not aware of. They became my valued "go to" people.

My initial contact with each of them was for their expertise. Along our journey I discovered they were extraordinary in other ways. In addition to possessing a wealth of knowledge in their respective fields, they were willing to school me about areas beyond their chosen field of expertise. What I valued most was their tireless guidance that helped make it possible to place this book into the hands of readers. I am so grateful for the generosity they extended to me. It was a privilege working with the following people:

Jeremy Goldenberg, Web Designer and Logo Creator, Pearl White Media

Christine-Marie Lauture, Attorney, Lauture IP

Elena Reznikova, Book Designer for Cover and Interior, DTPerfect

Lynette M. Smith, Copyeditor and Proofreader, All My Best

Ebonye Gussine Wilkins, Developmental Editor, Inclusive Media Solutions LLC

The collaboration I experienced while working with each of them was tremendously helpful to my induction as a new independent publisher and business owner. In many ways each felt as though I was participating in a master class for emerging independent publishers, as we teamed in editing my manuscript, preparing to transition the manuscript to a book, building each component for my very first website, and learning important details about intellectual property and copyright protection. All these activities were time consuming but beneficial.

Professionally, I would also like to thank the following individuals:

Juho Lee, co-creator and illustrator of the *Collaborative High School Campus Model*

Shana Murph, Revise and Rewrite Editorial, LLC, for her ongoing resourceful support with outreach and assistance. Shana's tutorials helped me understand how to access and navigate my way through the maze of talented people and organizations in the independent publishing industry.

Nia Norris, Freelance Research Assistant

Tia Ross, WordWiser Ink, who initially advised me about the list of must-haves for successfully launching my book into the public domain. I especially appreciate Tia for referring me to highly reputable people and organizations, such as Pearl White Media and DTPerfect.

Sabiraputul, Fiverr artist, for her exceptional creativity of the 9 *R*'s poster.

Cindy Severino, producer of the *Collaborative High School Campus Model* video

Finally, I wish to acknowledge and thank family members, colleagues, and friends who supported me along the way: Vernon C., Deborah C., Jim C., Naiema and Donald F., Randi H., the Fitch Family, the Marshall family, Nilsa R., Karen G., Carleton J., Joanne A. W., Munish R., Khadijah B., Sam C., Jerry B., Renee B., Megan W., Edith B., Tracy M. G., Ally J., the Canavan family, Pam K., the Gray family, Lionel R., Mec and Terry M., Gail D., Nalani D., Megan B., Alexis C., Nelson and Suely M., Flavio V., Warren M., Michele S., Brenda H. W., Humphrey M., Giscar C., Wayne G., Brianna B., Lindsay C., Rosann T., Eddie S., Candace W., Carina M., Laryssa G., Nicole S., Kaya K., Michael L., Edward P., Shawn B., Michele K., Gretchen O., Maureen L., Denise S., Domingo S., Juan S., Michael K. T., and the GEHS students I had the privilege of working with and who are the real inspiration for the Collaborative High School Model.

About the Author

JULIE COLES is currently an independent publisher of educational books. After retiring from the teaching profession where she held positions as a special education teacher, classroom consultant, vice principal, and headmaster, she made a seamless transition to becoming a writer. Having a fondness for thinking of and implementing innovative ideas to improve the quality of education, retirement afforded Julie the time to write about new ideas for rebuilding America's public education system.

As Julie progressed along her professional educational journey, many of her innovative ideas were recognized by various distinguished organizations.

Some of her many honors and awards include induction into Phi Delta Kappa; Massachusetts Teacher of the Year (MTY) Runner Up, and the City of Cambridge Mayor's Citation (in recognition of that distinction); Edward Calesa Foundation Terrific Teachers Award; and Boston Private Industries Council (PIC) Award. Julie was featured in the article, "Gains are Measurable in This Special Education Setting," published in the Teaching Tools–Learning section of the *Boston Globe Sunday Magazine*; and she served as a panelist on the Boston Foundation *Educators and Community Resources Televised Forum* for NECN TV. She was the keynote speaker for Harvard University Principals' Center, and she delivered the keynote address at her high school's convocation.

One of her most treasured honors occurred during a surprise encounter with Boston Public Schools Superintendent Dr. Carol Johnson and the Mayor at a museum, where Julie annually held scavenger hunts for history lessons for her summer school program. Upon introducing a recent graduate and summer school teaching assistant to the superintendent, Julie was deeply gratified to hear the superintendent say to her graduate, "Ms. Coles is a special school leader because she inspires others to aspire."

Besides teaching and leading a school, Julie provided educational consulting services to K–12 teachers and school principals, including professional development presentations for leaders and teachers at district conferences.

America's Educational Crossroads is Julie's first published book. As a companion to the book, Julie created a video of a state-of-the-art 21st century high school campus model *(ImagineAMorePromisingFuture.com/video)*. The book and video illustrate Julie's ability to reimagine ways to modernize our educational system to support all students in achieving their promising futures.

Future books planned for publication are *Cultivating Exceptional Classrooms: Unmasking Missing Links to Achieve Quality Education* and *Changing Misconceptions About the Principal's Office: A Lifeline for Teachers When the Cavalry of Support Doesn't Arrive.*

For more information about the author, visit
ImagineAMorePromisingFuture.com

CPSIA information can be obtained
at www.ICGtesting.com
Printed in the USA
LVHW080033120122
708313LV00012BA/202/J